CIVIL REPAI

For my grandchildren –
Emil, Agnes, and Josephine – and their future

CIVIL REPAIR

JEFFREY C. ALEXANDER

polity

The right of Jeffrey C. Alexander to be identified as Author of this Work has been asserted in accordance with the UK Copyright, Designs and Patents Act 1988.

First published in 2024 by Polity Press

Polity Press
65 Bridge Street
Cambridge CB2 1UR, UK

Polity Press
111 River Street
Hoboken, NJ 07030, USA

ISBN-13: 978-1-5095-0644-6 (hardback)
ISBN-13: 978-1-5095-0645-3 (paperback)

A catalogue record for this book is available from the British Library.

Library of Congress Control Number: 2024938128

Typeset in 10.5 on 12 pt Sabon LT Pro
by Cheshire Typesetting Ltd, Cuddington, Cheshire
Printed and bound by CPI Group (UK) Ltd, Croydon, CR0 4YY

The publisher has used its best endeavors to ensure that the URLs for external websites referred to in this book are correct and active at the time of going to press. However, the publisher has no responsibility for the websites and can make no guarantee that a site will remain live or that the content is or will remain appropriate.

Every effort has been made to trace all copyright holders, but if any have been overlooked the publisher will be pleased to include any necessary credits in any subsequent reprint or edition.

For further information on Polity, visit our website:
politybooks.com

CONTENTS

In the night of thick darkness enveloping the earliest antiquity, so remote from ourselves, there shines the eternal and never-failing light of a truth beyond all questions: that the world of civil society has certainly been made by men, and that its principles are therefore to be found within the modifications of our own human mind.

Giambattista Vico, *The New Science*[1]

PREFACE

Some of the essays collected here reach back more than two decades; others are pretty much hot off the press. They all are rooted in civil sphere theory, which made its appearance in book form in 2006, with the publication of *The Civil Sphere*, but was presented piecemeal in articles published earlier and elaborated later in other articles and books.

Yet, while anchored in a general social theory, each of these essays was triggered by events of the day. By explosive if short-lived utopian upheavals like the Arab Spring and Occupy Wall Street; by long-lived, still ongoing, world-transforming social movements like feminism; by dramatic leaps into racial reconstruction like the Civil Rights and Black Lives Matter movements; by surprisingly democratic denouements after vicious civil wars; by slow-boiling institutional dangers like the digital-induced crisis of journalism; and by shocking and portentous dangers, like the Trump presidency. I would like to think that this combination of the very abstract and the very concrete makes for a certain felicity; I am certain, at least, that the combination is unusual.

In our present historical circumstances, emphasizing civil repair might strike some readers as untimely, if not unlikely. Perhaps this is all the more reason to highlight its significance. "To be truly radical," Raymond Williams once wrote, "is to make hope possible, rather than despair convincing." *Civil Repair* lays out the grounds for hope. It will be followed by *Frontlash/Backlash*, a decidedly more worried, if still not despairing, companion volume that explores the dark forces that civil repairs ineluctably unleash.

I offer my gratitude to generations of doctoral students, visiting scholars, and colleagues at Yale's Center for Cultural Sociology; their insightful suggestions and criticisms have done much to shape the investigations undertaken here. I thank two persons in particular for their ingenuity and enduring support. In the preparation of this volume, I have been fortunate to have been able to rely, as so often in the past, on the assistance of Nadine Amalfi. I have also benefited, as often before, from the advice of John Thompson, who is not only my publisher but my friend.

The chapters have been revised, some in small, others in larger ways, since their original publication. The Introduction is new.

ACKNOWLEDGMENTS

Each of the chapters in this volume has been previously published, but they are revised here in minor and sometimes in significant ways. I am grateful to the following for permission to republish them here.

Sociological Theory for "The Long and Winding Road: Civil Repair of Intimate Injustice," 19(3): 371–400, November 2001.

Cultural Sociology for "Presidential versus Civil Power: Public Opinion, Second-Wave Feminism, and Party Politics in the USA" (with Willa Sachs). Special Issue: Civil Sphere Theory 17(1): 3–156, March 2023.

American Sociological Review for "The Societalization of Social Problems: Church Pedophilia, Phone Hacking, and the Financial Crisis," 83(6): 1049–1078, December 2018.

Polity Press for "Chapter 7: #MeToo," *What Makes a Social Crisis? The Societalization of Social Problems*, 2019; "Chapter 1: Seizing the Stage: Mao, MLK, and Black Lives Matter Today," *The Drama of Social Life*, 2017; "Chapter 7: Performing Counter-Power: The Civil Rights Movement," *Performance and Power*, 2011.

Philosophy and Social Criticism for "The Arc of Civil Liberation: Obama–Tahrir–Occupy," 39(4–5): 341–347, 2013.

International Journal of Politics, Culture, and Society for "Civil Sphere and Transitions to Peace: Cultural Trauma and Civil Repair," 35: 85–93, 2022.

Cambridge University Press for "Introduction: Journalism, Democratic Culture, and Creative Reconstruction," in *The Crisis of Journalism Reconsidered: Democratic Culture, Professional Codes, Digital Future* (with Elizabeth Butler Breeze and Maria Luengo), 2016.

INTRODUCTION
CIVIL REPAIR AND SOCIAL THEORY

The essays in this book develop a democratic theory of social reconstruction, not in a normative manner – the history of Western thought is replete with good intentions – but in a manner that is resolutely empirical and realistic. I advance a *sociological* theory of how democratic reconstruction works and deploy it to illuminate striking cases of civil repair in real social life.

Which is not to say that normative aspirations have no place. The theory being developed here is inspired by normative aspirations for democracy; it is not simply social reconstruction but *civil* reconstruction that is the topic of this book. What is crucial, however, is not whether theory has a normative dimension, but whether moral aspirations can be institutionalized inside actually existing societies. To the degree they are, a civil sphere exists, a relatively independent social world structured by a critical utopian discourse about the good society. While such a civil–normative discourse is highly generalized, it is continuously applied to the exigencies of time and space by communicative institutions – journalism, literature, voluntary associations, social movements, and polling. The result is public opinion, the continuous stream of judgments about whether individuals and groups, power holders, institutions, and events are civil or anti-civil, and to what degree. If they are deemed to endanger the civil-sacred, they trigger indignation about injustice, and from such outrage there emerge powerful social sentiments about "what is to be done" – today, in the here and now – to make society a more just, more democratic place.

At the core of civil reconstruction is extending and deepening feelings of social solidarity. Only if we feel connected to another will we be concerned about one another's dignity, about the restrictions that inhibit others' actions, about what we can do to help others become

1

more free. The Bible's golden rule and Kant's categorical imperative mandate us to treat others as we wish to be treated ourselves. The social contract is a more mundane *deux ex machina*, calling us to respect the putative promises that allowed humankind to move from the state of nature to the protections of an orderly civil life. John Rawls suggested that justice will be achieved only if we can return to the "original position"; only if we don a "veil of ignorance" that prevents us from knowing our own social position will we be able to think fairly about just social policies, for we ourselves may be among the least privileged. These deeply humanitarian injunctions are morally instructive thought experiments, but they say little about how to get from here to there. One can do so only by developing a *sociological* understanding of how solidarity can be deepened, amid the stresses and strains, the inequalities and the repressions, the imagined fears and hoped-for possibilities, of actually existing social life.

Showing us how to get from here to there is exactly what social theory has too often failed to provide. The great social theories that have entranced the modern imagination have been unremittingly critical. Mired in despair about the modern condition, they offer scant hope for social reconstruction. They fail to illuminate the discursive pathways, the symbolic and institutional inventions, the creativity and persistence that are sustained even by the deeply compromised civil spheres of actually existing democracies.

While Marx sat in the reading room of the British Museum theorizing a capitalist order of ruling-class domination and unadulterated exploitation, the British civil sphere, for all its fissures and faults, made it possible for workers to fight for their rights, organize trade unions, shorten the working day, make alliances with middle-class reformers, elect members to parliament, and eventually put Fabian and Socialist parties into positions of state power. Weber likened modernity to a cold and hard cage of steel, theorizing the vertical powers of bureaucracy rather than the horizontal solidarities of democracy. Imagining a thoroughgoing process of cultural rationalization, Weber's modernity banished not only utopian hopes for justice but also the very possibility of a meaningful and ethical collective life. Even as Durkheim put solidarity at the center of his thought, he was convinced that the core conditions of contemporary modernity – industrialization, secularization, and institutional differentiation – allowed egoism and anomie to prevail. Foucault built upon these pathways of despairing critique, subordinating truth to disciplinary power, obliterating autonomy by translating selfhood into subject position, and replacing self-government with governmentality. Bourdieu theorized society as a ruthless struggle for field position, mocking the very possibility of a moral universalism that might sustain a democratic life. Bauman equated modernity with alienation, homogenization, and powerlessness; his master binary of modern/postmodern obliterated the difference between democratic and anti-democratic modern forms; his late postmodernism decried a liquification that renders social actors supine.

There are good empirical and normative reasons to investigate the demonic dark sides of modernity (Alexander 2013) and to worry, if not despair, about escaping their awful effects – war and colonialism; orientalism and genocide; patriarchy; racial, ethnic, and religious hatred. But modernity is not only darkness. The one-sidedness of critical social theory is a product of the narrowness of its theoretical imagination, not keen observation of social reality. Too often it has failed to recognize the democratic thread in modern life, to give space and power to the emancipatory and participatory ideas that, while hardly triumphant, have pulsated persistently throughout the 2,500-year history of Western social life.[1]

If it was Weber who established the framework for a meaning-oriented historical sociology, it is to Weber we must look for the democracy gap in modern social science. In his study of Western history, Weber focused on religion and economics. He measured cultural power in terms of developments inside the Judeo-Christian tradition, ignoring the extraordinary force of "secular" civic-republicanism. Where is the Greek polis in Weber's writing, with its genial republican thinkers and its revolutionary democratic institutions? Where are the extraordinarily influential, if also deeply compromised, Roman institutions of Senate and law, and their flawed but inspiring imperial efforts at extending cosmopolitan citizenship? Where are medieval parliaments? Weber is silent about the social and cultural achievements of the great Renaissance city states, inspired by humanism, outward looking and significantly democratic (Skinner 1978a; Pocock 1975). It is rather to the Reformation that Weber gives historical pride of place, fascinated by how its dour, self-lacerating asceticism energized modern capitalism. Blinkered by his focus on religion and economy, this foundational sociological theorist had almost nothing to say about the cultural and institutional foundations of Western democracy, whether republican or liberal.[2] The seventeenth-century democratic revolution in England, the American and French revolutions a century later, the Age of Democracy in the century after that – these world historical movements that shaped modern civil spheres so powerfully merit scarcely a mention.[3]

3

It is true that the doyens of Western political theorizing were not sociologists but elite philosophers, whose writing is much more normative then empirical. But, as Quentin Skinner and colleagues have shown to great effect, republican ideals, and theorizing about how to institutionalize them, sank deep into the grassroots of late medieval and early modern societies (Skinner 1978a; Pocock 1975; Pettit 1999). By the end of the first millennium, republicanism was not only an intellectual idea but a social force capable of producing significant civil power, one that was deeply interlarded with Axial religious convictions about the critical leverage exerted by divine judgment. Martin Luther was able to reform the Church because he was immersed in the ideals of the republican tradition (Skinner 1978b). The founding figures of American democracy were cosmopolitan Christians and the masses fighting the American Revolution were God-fearing men and women, but the political ideas that inspired them and the Constitution they created were organized along democratic, republican-cum-liberal lines (Bailyn 1967; Wood 1969).

The civil sphere is much more than the extension of republican tradition. It is, in the first place, a thickly elaborated semiotic discourse, which defines the motives, relations, and institutions that inform not only the civil-sacred but also the anti-civil-profane. Social reconstruction is motivated by the need for purification; it is an effort to transform what has come to be experienced as evil and dirty into new social relationships, new motives, and new institutions, which can be experienced as sacred and good. Civil repair is triggered when feminists can persuasively pollute traditional male behavior as patriarchal and anti-democratic; when Black civil rights activists succeed in polluting whiteness as racial domination; when Dalit protestors can convince other Indians that casteism represents not Hindu purity but anti-civil filthy domination. Social activists' harshly critical judgments can inspire successful social and cultural movements when they are broadcast sympathetically by the civil sphere's communicative institutions; articulated and dispersed by journalists, filmmakers, and novelists; and taken up as causes by democratically minded associations and pressure groups. Via such communicative processes, critical judgments that were once iconoclastic become the new shape of progressive public opinion; polls register growing "public" antagonism to the status quo; and a zealously reformist civil power becomes central to the attention space in the social scene.

Whether this newly shaped, and shaping, civil power can be translated into state power depends on the civil sphere's regulative institutions, which mediate the relationship between the "subjective" evaluations of communicative institutions and the "objective" powers of the state. The most straightforward of these mediations is voting, for it is elections that place representatives of civil judgments into state positions that command the bully pulpit and pull the levers of coercive control. Yet, if law is not as immediately responsive to shifts in civil power as elections, it constitutes another critical regulative institution, stipulating generalized norms about civil actions and generating even-handed procedures for identifying anti-civil deviations, whether in contractual relations about property, intimate relations about love, or religious relations about faith. Central to the civil functioning of both elections and law is the institution of office. When power is constrained by office obligation, undergirded by professional ethics and sworn oath, power holders are legally and morally bound to act, not in their own self-interest but on behalf of the wider civil sphere. When office obligations are violated, power is corrupted, and neither elections nor legal procedures can fairly regulate the state on behalf of civil power. Political parties are the most democratically labile of the civil sphere's regulative institutions. They mediate civil and state power by mobilizing enough votes to carry their candidates into state office. Condensing and elaborating ideological oppositions, party rhetoric polarizes and, in the heat of fiercely fought electoral campaigns, the binding claims to a broader, civil solidarity often seem implausible. The ritual of gracious losers conceding defeat reaffirms the extra-political rules that bind party conflict and revivifies the civil solidarity that underlies democratic life (Alexander 2023).

Civil repair responds to the disappointing, frustrating, and sometimes horrifying compromise formations that diminish actually existing civil spheres. A fully civil solidarity is a utopian aspiration that must continuously contend with institutional differentiation and value plurality, conditions that, even as they inhibit civil solidarity, are intrinsic to the very meaning of a modern democratic life (Berlin 1998).

Real civil spheres are permeated by contradictions. They are created in particular times and places, by founding groups with particular primordial qualities, of race, religion, ethnicity, gender, and class. The operational meaning of "civil" is particularized, the qualities of the civil-sacred restricted to arbitrary primordial qualities. The founders of America's civil sphere were white, male, heterosexual Anglo-Saxon, and Protestant. If those who arrived later did not possess such primordial qualities, they were deemed less capable of exhibiting the civil qualities that were necessary to sustain American democracy. Women were not founding mothers; Catholics, Jews, Muslims, and Hindus were not Protestant; people of "color" were not white; Indigenous Peoples, who possessed none of the above, were out of luck, strangers in what had once been their own land.

Civil spheres are surrounded by non-civil spheres, institutional worlds whose operating procedures and ideas of justice differ markedly from their own. Market-bound companies, faith-bound churches, loyalty-bound families, love-bound couples, bureaucratically bound government – each of these spheres has its own, non-civil values and operating procedures, which work according to imperatives of market, faith, loyalty, love, and efficiency. The boundary relations between civil and non-civil institutions are often tense. Members of the civil sphere come to experience an adjoining institution, not simply as *non*-civil but as *anti*-civil; its values and procedures appear dangerously intrusive, threatening the cherished values, institutions, and procedures of the civil sphere itself. Companies are attacked as greedy and selfish, churches as fanatically faithful, governments as soulless machines. Strains between spheres that once seemed routine are experienced as intolerable contradictions; radical ideas for restructuring values and institutions explode; social and cultural movements form. It is during such heightened and pressured conditions that civil repairs can be made.

Civil repair undermines vested ideal and material interests, challenging the legitimacy of long-established practices and beliefs. Civil repair is democratically progressive but sociologically it creates losses alongside gains. Those on the losing side of "progress" sometimes feel as if they have been in a car crash, and whiplash is often the result. Civil repair is a "frontlash" movement that leaves broken hearts in its wake. It generates backlash movements whose character varies from the civil conservative to the anti-civil extreme.

We have come back full circle to the one-sided misunderstandings of modernity that so often distort critical social theory. The dark sides of modernity are not the expression of some rotten, alienated, oppressive, and dehumanizing essence. They are a response, paradoxically, to some of democratic modernity's most idealistic achievements, efforts to put roadblocks along the long and winding road of seemingly inexorable and relentless repair. The Klu Klux Klan and Jim Crow emerged in violent response to the progress of post-Civil War "Reconstruction," which forced white civil spheres in Southern states to allow entry to Black Americans. The murderous repression and primordial rancor of Nazism responded to the fledgling cosmopolitan democracy of Weimar and to the decades of mobility and achievement that had been made by German Jewry. Today's right-wing

6

populism responds to fears that immigration is triggering a "great replacement," that "this isn't our country anymore." Trumpism is an angry and defensive backlash against the frontlash shocks of feminist success and multicultural incorporation.

It is when faced with the destabilizing seesaw of civil repair and the reactions against it that civil spheres must prove their mettle. Provoking civil repair while tolerating conservative reaction, civil solidarity becomes frayed and polarized, but the ties that bind may not break. Whether they are brittle or supple is of vital concern, socially and theoretically, and it is the topic of a companion volume, *Frontlash/Backlash*. In the chapters that follow, we concern ourselves with the complex manner in which world-historical changes have successfully been achieved, and how actually existing civil spheres have been wedged open (Stack 2019), persuaded, and compelled to come more closely to resemble the utopian promises of which they are made.

THE LONG AND WINDING ROAD
CIVIL REPAIR OF INTIMATE INJUSTICE

The contradictory institutionalization of the civil sphere is triggered not only by the inevitable gap between normativity and facticity but by the dualistic, fundamentally ambiguous nature of the discourse at the core of the civil sphere itself. What democratic theorists have tended to ignore – from Marx and Durkheim to Habermas, Rawls, and Parsons – is that civil discourse, not merely from its first modern institutionalization in the seventeenth century but from its first appearance in ancient Greece 2,000 years before, has included not only classifications for inclusion but categories for exclusion. If the former justifies inclusion, the latter mandates repression.

The reasons for the binary structure of civil discourse are complex. In part, it follows from the processes of classificatory splitting discovered by structuralism, cognitive psychology, and psychoanalysis. But there is also a paradoxically normative reason. In order to establish a self-governing, anti-hierarchical community, those with whom one interacts must be assumed to be trusting, open, honest, independent and rational, honest and calm, cooperative, and able to manage self-control. If the members of a community are believed to be suspicious and distrustful, secretive and dishonest, dependent and irrational, unable to control their emotionality, or fundamentally aggressive, it becomes difficult to conceive of them as able to sustain a self-governing, democratic community; to the contrary, it would seem as if a community composed of such actors would be compelled to depend upon various forms of hierarchy and external control.

The qualities that are necessary to form a democratic self-governing community, and those that would make it impossible, form a binary code such that, in semiotic terms, the meaning of one side cannot be understood without the other.

The Binary Discourse of Civil Society

Motives

Civil Motives	Anti-civil Motives
Active	Passive
Autonomous	Dependent
Rational	Irrational
Reasonable	Hysterical
Calm	Excitable
Self-controlled	Wild-passionate
Realistic	Distorted
Sane	Mad

Relations

Civil Relations	Anti-civil Relations
Open	Secretive
Trusting	Suspicious
Critical	Deferential
Honorable	Self-interested
Altruistic	Greedy
Truthful	Deceitful
Straightforward	Calculating
Deliberative	Conspiratorial
Friendly	Antagonistic

Institutions

Civil Institutions	Anti-civil Institutions
Rule-regulated	Arbitrary
Law	Power
Equality	Hierarchy
Inclusive	Exclusive
Impersonal	Personal
Contracts	Bonds of loyalty
Groups	Factions
Office	Personality

The sociological problem is this: What are the social referents of these cultural categories? This has been a matter for history to decide, and, from a normative perspective, it has never been decided in a consistently beneficent way. From the beginning of its institutionalization in ancient Greece, large categories of persons who would have putative membership in civil society have been excluded from it. Their otherness has been constructed in terms of civil incompetence, their

9

exclusion essentialized as a matter of democratic self-protection. It is no wonder that dominated groups have struggled not only for power but for cultural reclassification.

In a plural and differentiated society, there will always be multiple and fundamentally different spheres of culture and practice (Berlin 1998; Walzer 1984; Boltanski and Thevenot 1990) – market economies; private families; scientific institutions; minority sexual, racial, and ethnic communities. Still, as long as a social system contains a putatively civil sphere – an imminently utopian social sphere whose culture and institutions are proclaimed to be civil and democratic – the question can always be posed: What is the relation between the idealizing requisites and demands of the civil sphere and the non-civil spheres that surround it?

Such "boundary relations" between civil and non-civil spheres have assumed three ideal-typical forms. The activities of non-civil spheres can be seen as providing "facilitating inputs" to the civil sphere or as presenting "destructive intrusions" into it. In the former case, the existing boundary relations between civil and non-civil spheres will be left intact. In the latter case, by contrast, the norms and practices of the non-civil sphere will be criticized on the grounds that they endanger the integrity of the civil sphere. The third possible boundary relation is the actively reconstructive route of civil repair. Through communicative and organizational intervention, the offending practices, whether sexism, racism, or economic exploitation, are symbolically polluted and reconstructed to one degree or another. The process of civil repair is never linear; it always involves mixed cases and compromise formations.

Justifying Gender Domination:
Relations Between the Intimate and Civil Spheres

It is illuminating of the contradictory nature of the civil sphere, and of the infernal, often maddening, suppleness that marks its binary symbolic code, that when the egalitarian codes of democracy were first institutionalized on a national scale in seventeenth-century Europe, women could be conceived as having absolutely no place. As Blackstone, the first great codifier of democratic law, put it, once women were married they ceased to have any civil existence at all: "Husband and wife are one person in law, that is, the very being or legal existence of the woman is suspended during the marriage, or at least is incorporated and consolidated into that of the husband; under

10

whose wing, protection, and *cover*, she performs everything; and is therefore called ... a *feme covert* [*sic*]" (in *The Law of Domestic Relations* 1995; original italics). The fictive social contracts – which allowed democratic societies to move from the state of nature into the public world of civil society – were represented as having been written by men. With women relegated to the private, invisible sphere of family life, first protected by fathers, later by husbands, what Carole Pateman called the "sexual contract" always accompanied the democratic one.

> In a world presented as conventional, contractual and universal, women's civil position is ascriptive, defined by the natural particularity of being women; patriarchal subordination is socially and legally upheld throughout civil life, in production and citizenship as well as in the family. Thus, to explore the subjection of women is also to explore the fraternity of men. (Pateman 1988: 121)

The Republican traditions that inspired the first great democratic revolutions were irredeemably masculinist. As Joan Landes (1998: 2–3) pointed out, the very conception of public derived from the Latin *publicus*, meaning "under the influence of *pubes*, in the sense of 'adult men,' [the] 'male population.'" In describing the early American Republic, Mary Ryan explained how female motives were constructed as antithetical to civil ones. "Republican ideology," she writes (1992: 266; italics added), "held that the female sex embodied those uncurbed human passions that inevitably subverted the *self-control* and *rationality* required of citizens." Under this semantic but also very political distortion, civil wisdom is contrasted with domestic love, and female exclusion is represented as being compelled by the necessity to protect against enslavement. These associations are manifest, for example, in an after-dinner "toast to the ladies" that one (male) wit offered at a civic occasion in New Orleans, circa 1825: "The fair sex – excluded by necessity from participation in our labors: we profess *equality*, [but] the presence of woman would make us *slaves*, and convert the temple of wisdom into that of love" (Ryan 1992: 266).

Despite its strangeness and even repugnance to contemporary sensibilities, however, there is not an "objective contradiction" between the promises of a democratic society and the subordination and exclusion of women from its civil sphere. It is not something that, in and of itself, manifestly defies the norms of a plural and differentiated society. To believe so betrays the naturalistic approach to contradiction so well displayed in the later, though not the earlier, Marx.

11

Between the belief that there are irredeemable differences between men and women, and the conviction that such differences *unfairly* disqualify women from participating in the civil sphere, there is no more of a "factual" contradiction than between capitalist market relations and the democratic promises of civil society. As the French say, "*ça depend.*" What it depends on is context.

Women's Difference as Facilitating Input

Throughout the nineteenth century, a period of dramatic advances in the institutionalization of civil society in such domains as class and, to a much lesser but still real degree, as race, female subordination in the family sphere seemed perfectly compatible with the sphere of civil equality. Indeed, it was conceived as a fundamentally important facilitating input to it.

This understanding of boundary relations, not only accepted but actively promoted by women as well as by men, was crystallized by what feminist historians have called the "ideology of separate spheres." As the historian Jeanne Boydston (1995: 144) has put it, "the doctrine of gender spheres expressed a worldview in which both the orderliness of daily social relations and the larger organization of society derived from and depended on the preservation of an all-encompassing gender division of labor." In terms of the present argument, separate sphere ideology legitimated the anti-democratic exclusion of women by constructing them in terms of the negative categories of civil discourse. In 1825, a widely read periodical, *Ladies Museum*, applied this binary code to the men and women of its day.

> Man is strong – woman is beautiful. Man is daring and confident – woman is diffident and unassuming. Man is great in action – woman in suffering. Man shines abroad – woman at home. Man talks to convince – woman to persuade and please. Man has a rugged heart – woman a soft and tender one. Man prevents misery – woman relieves it. Man has science – woman taste. Man has judgment – woman sensibility. Man is a being of justice – woman of mercy.   (quoted in ibid.)

This binary rhetoric specifies the more general categories of civil discourse to gender. It genders civil discourse, providing a pragmatically available *parole* to the more structural *langue*. The very same feminine qualities that were conceived as allowing women to manage the intimate sphere – which were vital because they allowed not the reproduction of labor power but the reproduction of democratic virtue – were the very same characteristics that disqualified women

12

from participating in the body politic. John Keane has explained how women's non-civil qualities were understood as resulting from her centrality in the intimate sphere.

> Within this [intimate] sphere, women's functions of child-bearing, child-rearing and maintaining the household are deemed to correspond to their *unreason*, *disorderliness*, and "closeness" to nature. Women and the domestic sphere [were] viewed as inferior to the male-dominated "public" world of civil society and its culture, property, social power, *reason* and *freedom*.
>
> (Keane 1988a: 21; italics added)

Women's Difference as Destructive Intrusion

Despite this prevailing, anti-inclusive model of facilitating input, the first wave of democratic revolutions had the effect of drawing women, along with men, into its effervescent wake. The result was a growing suspicion, among some parties, that women might actually not be so different from men after all. In America, as Linda Kerber (1991: 89) has observed, "the experience of war had given words like independence and self-reliance personal as well as political overtones."

As the song played at Yorktown had it, the world could turn upside down: the rich could quickly become poor, wives might suddenly have to manage the family economy, women might even shoulder a gun. Revolutionary experience taught that it was useful to be prepared for a wide range of unusual possibilities; political theory taught that republics rested on the virtue and intelligence of their citizens (ibid.).

The American Revolution had markedly increased the authority and attraction of the liberating side of civil discourse, with the result that efforts to institutionalize it further intensified. For many women, their subordination in the separate sphere of the family began to seem an abomination, a destructive intrusion into the normative and institutional core of the newly democratic nation. In one early post-Revolutionary proclamation, Judith Sargent Murray decried the idea that girls should be trained in fashion, flirtation, and charm, with the aim of procuring a successful marriage. She insisted, instead, on the socialization of girls to civil, not specifically feminine, values: "*Independence* should be placed within their grasp [and] the Sex should be taught to depend on their own efforts, for the procurement of an establishment in life" (quoted in ibid.: 89; italics added).

If female difference were criticized, then male superiority would be reframed as a potential threat to the civil sphere. The argument that began to emerge was not that men were unloving or uncaring – such criticisms would have evoked not civil standards but the values of the non-civil family sphere. Rather, the criticism launched by post-Revolutionary American women drew directly upon the constructions of anti-democratic repression against which Americans had fought the Revolutionary War. When Abigail Adams, wife of the second president, suggested that women ought to have the right to participate in the new system of government, she offered as the reason that "all men would be tyrants if they could" (quoted in ibid.). In the late twentieth century, feminist criticism would employ the term "patriarchy," but the civil reference of the category was much the same: The dependent and authoritarian relations that might well prevail between men and women inside the family should not be allowed to intrude upon the relations among men and women in the civil sphere. Now viewed as a "destructive intrusion" rather than facilitating input, such relations were deemed not only to be non-civil but anti-civil, a characterization that implied, perhaps, that they should no longer be allowed even within the intimate sphere itself. When nineteenth-century temperance activists pilloried men for drunkenness and licentiousness, and for violence against their children and wives, it was just such civil criteria that were being critically deployed.

At the conclusion of history's first national women's congress, the Seneca Falls Women's Rights Convention in 1848, 100 persons signed a document entitled *Declaration of Sentiments* attacking the threat to civil ideals posed by the ideology and practice of separate spheres and by the underlying principle of innate female difference. Asserting that "all men and women are created equal," the document insisted, in a less metaphorical than literal extension of the *Declaration of Independence*, that both sexes were "invested by their creator with the same capabilities." By violating such a civil stipulation, the traditional relations between men and women were condemned as undemocratic, and the polluting language of civil society was everywhere employed.

> The history of mankind is a history of repeated injuries and *usurpations* on the part of man toward woman, having in direct object the establishment of an *absolute tyranny* over her ... He has *compelled* her to *submit* to laws. He has oppressed her on all sides ... He has made her ... civilly dead. He has taken from her all right in property ... He has made her, morally, an *irresponsible* being [and] she is *compelled* to promise *obedience* ... He has created a false public sentiment by giving to the world a different code of morals for men and women, by which moral delinquencies which exclude women from society, are not only

14

tolerated, but [encouraged] to make her willing to lead a dependent and abject life.

(*Declaration of Sentiments* [1848] 1995: 568; italics added)

"We are a nation and not a mere confederacy," as one suffragist put the matter in 1880. "The theory of a masculine head to rule the family, the church, or the State is contrary to republican principles and the fruitful source of rebellion" (quoted in Edwards 1997: 11).

Gender Universalism and Civil Repair

If male superiority and tyranny in the domestic sphere were considered a destructive intrusion into the civil one, it followed that there must be a project of civil repair. In the course of the Second Great Awakening, women had achieved unprecedented equality in the religious sphere, and they also played powerful roles in the growing Abolitionist movement. As the nineteenth century progressed, there were, in fact, increasing demands that women be given a civil status appropriate to their equal capacities. These took the form of demands for equal education, equality before the law, and, eventually, the right to vote. Activists viewed these policies as steps to deepen the institutionalization of the liberating discourse of civil society. At the "Women's Centennial Agenda," the counterconvention to the American Centennial in 1876, the feminist declaration *avant la lettre* charged that "women's degraded, helpless position is the weak point in our institutions today" (Anthony 1995 [1876]: 225).

To avoid any suggestion of American exceptionalism, and to highlight the systemic nature of the processes I am describing here, it seems important to note that the other great revolutionary effort to institutionalize civil principles, the French Revolution, initially produced the same movement from separate sphere arguments to universalistic demands for women's rights. In the land of the Enlightenment, it is hardly surprising that the argument over women's civil capacity, which centered on difference versus universality, would focus more attention on the possession of reason. In his essay "On the Admission of Women to the Rights of Citizenship," the influential liberal physiocrat, the Marquis de Condorcet, emphatically made the link between reason and civic participation central to his famous argument for the inclusion of women.

Now the rights of men result simply from the fact that they are sentient beings, capable of acquiring moral ideas and of reasoning concerning those ideas. Women, *having these same qualities*, must necessarily

15

possess equal rights. Either no individual of the human species has any true rights, or all have the same. And he or she who votes against the rights of another, of whatever religion, color, or sex, has thereby abjured his own.

(quoted in Landes 1998 [1790]: 114; italics added)

Rather than viewing female-specific social activities as indicating fundamental difference, and, thus, as constituting grounds for confinement to a separate sphere, Condorcet dismissed "motherhood and 'other passing indispositions'" as indicating nothing at all about women's civil capacities (quoted in ibid.: 115).

Stimulated by the effervescence of the Revolution, the most influential and radical feminists emphasized human universality and the shared capacities that men and women possessed. "The nature of reason must be the same in all," Mary Wollstonecraft declared in her pathbreaking book *A Vindication of the Rights of Woman*. It was on this basis that Wollstonecraft declared traditional female subordination a threat to the civil values of the Revolution. Addressing herself to the all-male Constituent Assembly, she asked "whether, when men contend for their freedom, and to be allowed to judge for themselves respecting their own happiness, it be not inconsistent and unjust to subjugate women, even though you firmly believe that you are acting in the manner best calculated to promote their happiness?" Such paternalism, she argued, must be criticized as a destructive intrusion into the realm of revolutionary democracy – as long as it was agreed that the intellectual and moral capacities of women are equally constructed in a civil way. "Who made man the exclusive judge," Wollstonecraft demands, "if woman partake with him the gift of reason?" (quoted in ibid.: 127).

Assuming that civil, not separate sphere, standards must apply to male–female relations, protofeminists attacked male paternalism as uncivil, warning that it presented a destructive intrusion into democratic life. As Wollstonecraft observed:

> If women are to be excluded without having a voice, from a participation of the natural rights of mankind, prove first, to ward off the charge of injustice and inconsistency, that they want reason – else this flaw in your NEW CONSTITUTION [*sic*] will ever shew [*sic*] that man must, in some shape, act like a *tyrant*, and tyranny, *in whatever part of society it rears its brazen front*, will ever undermine morality.
>
> (quoted in ibid.; italics added)

In 1790, Etta Palm, another leading revolutionary activist, similarly asserted that civil values must reconstruct the intimate sphere. In

16

a scathing speech, she told her male revolutionary confreres, "We are your *companions* and not your *slaves*" (quoted in ibid.: 119; italics added). Once again, traditional forms of maleness were being reframed as the signifieds of anti-civil signifiers – as indicating the failure not only of women but of men themselves to exercise rationality, self-control, and honesty. In Wollstonecraft's words, "men are certainly more under the influence of their appetites than women; and their appetites are depraved by unbridled indulgence and the fastidious contrivances of satiety" (quoted in ibid.: 131).

The Compromise Formation of Public M/Otherhood[1]

It was such confrontations as these that laid the basis for the "feminist" movement to displace the "woman" movement in the early years of the twentieth century (Cott 1987: 1–10). That it would take more than 100 years for such an assertive female movement to build upon the earliest expressions of gender universalism demonstrates that, in the early phases of the institutionalization of civil society, most men, and women, were not persuaded by representations that female subordination constituted a destructive intrusion to democracy, much less by policy recommendations for its civil repair. Abstract models of boundary relations are one thing; the messy reality of actual processes is another. In concrete historical terms, civil repair is never a linear process in any domain. It cannot be deduced from the ideal-typical concepts of a theoretical model. Feminist historians, social scientists, and philosophers have reluctantly come to grips with this fact, though in thinking about what to make of it they have sometimes fundamentally disagreed.

As Kerber attests, the postrevolutionary efforts to apply civil democratic codes to women often met fierce resistance. "To accept an openly acknowledged role for women in the public sector," she writes (1995: 92), "was to invite extraordinary hostility and ridicule." The ideology of natural difference and the practice of separate spheres were simply too deeply entrenched. Arguments about female intellectual power and political autonomy were analogically linked to masculine manners. Typical of such responses was a newspaper letter written by a Marylander calling himself "Philanthropos," in 1790, that warned against any overly literal interpretations of the phrase "All mankind are born equal." Philanthropos was concerned with the separation of spheres. If equality were "taken in too extensive a sense," he argued, "it might tend to destroy those degrees of subordination which nature

17

seems to point out," most particularly the subordination of women to men. Philanthropos suggested an alternative that proved prophetic, pointing the way to a compromise between maintaining separate spheres and furthering civil repair. "However flattering the path of glory and ambition may be," he declared, "a woman will have more commendation in being the mother of heroes, than in setting up, Amazon-like, for a heroine herself" (quoted in Kerber chapter in Kerber and de Hart 1995: 92).

What quickly became apparent, in the face of the concerted opposition to gender universalization, was that women would be allowed to enter the public realm only if they remained tethered to their subordinate status and separate sphere. Protected by the ideology of what Kerber called "the Republican Mother," men and women alike justified partial participation in public life on the basis that women would become better – more virtuous and more democratic – mothers to their male children and provide more soothing emollients to their already civilly virtuous husbands. Making use of what we would today call gender essentialism, they claimed control over a special expertise that allowed them to influence certain domains of public affairs. But the very mothering qualities that legitimated some degree of female public participation confirmed their fundamental difference from men. Republican motherhood was, in fact, merely another kind of "otherhood." Public m/otherhood simply put a positive spin on the very anti-civil qualities that excluded women from full participation in civil society.

The new role of Republican M/otherhood can be seen as what Bellah (1970a) once referred to, following Freud, as a "compromise formation," one that responded to a classic situation of role strain. On the one hand, the increasingly strained boundary relations between familial and civil spheres could not be resolved by civic repair; on the other hand, women were unwilling to return entirely to the confines of their traditionally assigned place. The result was the creation of a new role, whose compromise character was revealed by the manner in which it persistently combined "not only" with "but also."

> The concept [of Republican Mother] defended education for women not only for their autonomy and self-realization but also so that they could be better wives and better mothers for the next generation of virtuous republican citizens – especially sons.   (Kerber and de Hart 1995: 93)

According to its advocates, the role of Republican M/other would provide sorely needed facilitating inputs to the American civil sphere. As one (male) newspaper editor put it in 1844, the family is "the

18

foundation of public morality and intelligence" (quoted in Ryan 1992: 273). Another wrote, "if all is right in the private domain, we need not be concerned for the public" (ibid.). Ironically, but very functionally, the authority for this civil contribution came from the very emphasis on inherent difference that excluded women from more assertive, and genuinely civil, participation. Public m/otherhood allowed some female activity to be viewed as a facilitating input to civil society, but it stalemated women's efforts to gain actual incorporation into it.

The sorry story of a Madam Ranke, who addressed a meeting of unemployed men camped in New York City's Thompkins Square in 1857, records this stalemated attempt to desegregate the male public. When Madam Ranke took the public podium, she was greeted by cries like, "Don't listen to a woman," or alternatively, "Damn it, don't interrupt a woman." The female voice was neither easily blended nor distinctly heard in the embattled sectors of the male public sphere, and Madam Ranke was escorted from the square under a protective escort of women (ibid.: 270).

Kerber salutes the Republican Mother as a "revolutionary invention," yet she points, equally emphatically, to its "deeply ambivalent" status. While sanctioning participation, the new role ensured the continuity of women's uncivil status.

> Republican Motherhood legitimized only a minimum of political sophistication and interest . . . Women were expected to be content to perform their narrow political role permanently and were not expected to wish for fuller participation. Just as planters claimed that democracy in the antebellum South rested on the economic base of slavery, so egalitarian society was said to rest on the moral basis of deference among a class of people – women – who would devote their efforts to service by raising sons and disciplining husbands. (ibid.: 95)

In France as well, the social and cultural barriers to the civil repair of gender relations generated what Landes (1998: 2) calls a "paradoxical" compromise. Even Mary Wollstonecraft found it "difficult to deny the central presumption of her age, that women possess natures different from men" (ibid.: 13). Despite her insistence on the principle of women's rationality, the great protofeminist believed that most women actually were less rational in practice. Without the semantic anchor in civil discourse that had been provided by women's putatative rationality, it became difficult for Wollstonecraft to enthusiastically recommend the full civil inclusion of women.

> Novels, music, poetry, and gallantry, all tend to make women the creatures of Sensation . . . This overstretched sensibility naturally relaxes the other

19

powers of the mind, and prevents intellect from attaining that sovereignty that it ought to attain to render a rational creature useful to others, and content with its own station: for the exercise of the understanding, as life advanced, is the only method pointed out by nature to calm the passions.

(quoted in ibid.: 132)

If female activists were themselves so uncertain about the civil qualities of women, French men were much more so. Such widespread lack of confidence allowed free rein, in France as well as in America, to the compromise formation of Republican M/otherhood. Women did indeed play active, and at times vitally significant, public roles during the early Revolutionary period. The legendary march of women to Versailles in October 1789, for example, represented a strategically significant moment of women's public participation. Yet, even in this great march, Landes (ibid.: 109; italics added) is careful to inform us, the Parisian women only "asserted their right *as women* to participate in public affairs," not as potential citizens. Their aim was to call upon the self-exiled king and to bring him back to Paris.

> They desired to see the king [back] at Paris, where he would find wise women to give him good counsel. They referred to him as "poor man," "dear man," "good papa." The marchers appealed to the king in a paternalist discourse, yet they cried out for "bread and arms."
>
> (ibid.: 109–110)

As a contemporary feminist, Landes is pointed in her criticism of the new kind of otherhood role: "[It] functioned to preserve difference and hence guarantee sexual inequality," despite its connection "to a universalist, egalitarian protest" (ibid.: 123).

> As citizens, women would be educated beyond their limited horizons and wholly self-oriented concerns in order to embrace the larger polity, but ultimately in a passive not an active manner. The potential for providing women with a route into the public sphere by way of republican motherhood was undermined by the claims of nature ... If women's service to the community was viewed as a function of her mothering role, the most likely consequence was to offer women political representation in a *mediated* fashion.   (ibid.: 138; original italics)

In the hothouse atmosphere of revolutionary France, this compromise formation proved much less viable, and ultimately less productive, than it proved to be in the immensely more stable, and less radical, American scene. By 1791, the Committee of General Security recommended that women's rights to active public participation be entirely eliminated. The cultural framing for this recommendation emphasized the uncivil qualities of public behavior that were held to be the inevitable product of women's difference. Because their "moral education is almost nil" and because they are "less enlightened concerning principles," the committee's representative told the convention, "women's associations seem dangerous."

> Their presence in popular societies, therefore, would give an active role in government to people more exposed to error and seduction. Let us add that women are disposed by their organization to an over-excitation, which would be deadly in public affairs, and that interests of state would soon be sacrificed to everything which ardor in passions can generate. Delivered over to the heat of public debate, they would teach their children not love of country but hatred and suspicions.
>
> (quoted in ibid.: 144)

In the United States, the contradictory effects of the compromise formation were far less dramatic, but they were equally fateful and far-reaching. In fact, as feminist historians have long noted, by framing a limited degree of female participation as a facilitating input to the public sphere, Republican M/otherhood provided legitimation for women to make their sphere less hermetically separate than ever before. Yet, as many contemporary feminists have insisted on also pointing out, the nineteenth-century American women who moved into the public sphere justified their participation, not by proclaiming their equal civil competence, but by utilizing notions of innate "difference" and the ideology of separate spheres. In the 1870s, for example, women made use of what Ryan calls "an arsenal of weapons and an array of avenues through which to influence public policy." But Ryan immediately adds the following qualification:

> In keeping with the Victorian moral code, [these] female sex reformers used the stereotype of pure womanhood as a point of personal privilege in the matter of prostitution legislation . . . The politics of prostitution, like female moral reform, was but one rather prickly way to generate gender identity. It placed the woman citizen in a defensive position and identified her by her sexual and reproductive biology. To contemporary feminists, this is an invitation to essentialism and a narrow base on which to mount gender politics. (Ryan 1992: 281)

In fact, it is possible to argue that the creation of the new role of public "m/otherhood" established a paradigm that allowed every subsequent phase of female participation to be justified, and narrated, in an anti-civil way. The editors of a leading anthology of contemporary feminist history make the following observation.

> At an ever-accelerating pace between 1820 and 1880 women expanded [the] role [of Republican Motherhood] into what might be called

"Reformist Motherhood." Instead of influencing the public domain indirectly through the lives of their sons, women began to extend their role as nurturer and teacher of morals from the domestic sphere into the public sphere through church, missionary, and moral reform groups. Women sought to make the world conform more strictly to values taught in the home – sexual responsibility and restraint for men as well as women, self-discipline for those who used strong drink. [Then,] between 1880 and 1920 a new role developed that might be called "Political Motherhood." The "womanhood" identified with "mothering" was becoming less a biological fact – giving birth to children – and more a political role with new ideological dimensions.

(Kerber and de Hart 1995: 229–230)

During the industrial revolution of the late nineteenth century, another historian has recently observed (Edwards 1997: 3), Americans "were fascinated by the power and complexity of machines," and "in political debate they used machines as a metaphor for both the electoral system and for parities." Yet the ideology of separate spheres remained alive and well. Its metaphors could be readily adapted to the new technological situation.

Party structures found their ideal opposite in the gentle domesticity attributed to women. Like their English Victorian counterparts, leaders of American opinion hailed the home as "woman's sphere," a place where wives and mothers conserved family bonds and religious devotion. Both men and women of the era described women as "angels of the home." To many, women's selflessness and purity were the very qualities that unfitted them for politics. Politics, however, could not function without the virtues women represented. The institutions of political life might resemble machines, but each party fought for deeply held values. At a fundamental level, elections were disputes about faith and family order . . . In 1886, New York politician John Boyle O'Reilly expressed his abhorrence at the idea of woman suffrage. "It would be no more deplorable," he declared in a public letter, "to see an angel harnessed to a machine than to see a woman voting politically." (Edwards 1997: 3–4)

In sharp relief to such observations, Rabinovitch (2001) suggests that the ethic of m/otherhood should, to the contrary, be viewed as the beginning of an argument for the "universal," democratic status of women. The difficulty in doing so is revealed by the fact that, in the process, he actually provides ample evidence for exactly the opposite position. Despite itself, his discussion reveals that the m/otherhood umbrella for women's nineteenth-century public interventions had the illocutionary force – the semantic effect – of affirming, rather than denying, women's second-class, uncivil status.

22

Women's public demands for "shelter and protection for women," Rabinovitch acknowledges, rested on claims "about the denial for the victimized women of the possibility to live up to the ideal of true womanhood." In "keeping with the submissive nature of women," such demands affirmed the notion that women were "helpless." Citing Ryan's own investigations into how activist women used such tactics as public prayer, weeping, and silent presence to compel men to alter their behavior, Rabinovitch writes that "it seemed [as] if women could not directly speak unto men with discursive authority." He notes, for example, how one leading temperance activist, Francis Willard, hailed what she called the "omnipotent-weakness which is the incommunicable characteristic of womanhood" in order to justify women's rights to publicly preach. Rabinovitch allows that "Republican mothers . . . went to great lengths to reject any association with civil independence or autonomy, even as they demanded greater respect and recognition in civic politics," and he himself recognizes that reformers repeatedly associated their own intentions with "sympathy, sentiment, and passion at the expense of autonomy and civic independence."

Public Stage and Civil Sphere

How could this be? How could a clearly particularistic and anti-civil understanding of women also function, at the same time, as the basis for launching their public careers? How could unprecedented female public activism have the effect of underscoring, rather than undermining, the second-class position of women? How could this new intervention of women into public affairs, which powerfully blocked the civic repair of female subordination, be hailed by some interpreters as the key transition to democratizing gender relations?[2]

This paradox faithfully reflects the contradictory social and cultural structures of nineteenth-century society. It is the failure to recognize these contradictions that must now concern us here. We will see later that this failure has become a central bone of ideological contention within feminist scholarship, the trigger, indeed, for a new kind of "warring" of the schools (Cott 1995: 363). This contemporary debate pits "difference" feminism against "universalist" feminism, a so-called cultural feminism emphasizing an "ethics of care" against a so-called political feminism upholding a more citizenship-oriented standard (cf. Hirsch and Keller 1990; Scott 1990). As we will see below, one of the problematic results of this contemporary philosophical, historical, and ideological dispute is its blurring of the vast

23

disparity between contemporary multiculturalism, which emphasizes difference, and the pre-feminist, woman-centered "m/otherhood" ideologies of the nineteenth century.[3]

Before entering into these controversies, however, I want to suggest that the failure to recognize the contradictory nature of nineteenth-century women's history stems, in the first place, from problems of a more theoretic-sociological sort. These have to do with contemporary approaches to public sphere and public participation. Misunderstandings about these terms go all the way back to Arendt's pathbreaking efforts to reinsert the public, as a sphere of radical democracy, into political and social theory. More recently, however, the difficulties can be traced to the vague and diffuse manner in which the term "public" is deployed by Jürgen Habermas. The problem is the false equation of the mere fact of "publicness" with participation in the "civil sphere," that is, the conflation of public with democratic. For publicness, both theoretically and in ordinary language, actually has many different meanings. It can suggest the simple fact of visibility. It can refer to governmental or official status. And it can indicate, in a more democratic manner, a connection to the diffusively and invisibly expressed, yet normatively very restrictive, opinion of the demos, that is, to public opinion. In the Habermassian tradition, which interweaves normative, empirical, and theoretical claims, these meanings are typically blurred.[4]

The position I want to gesture toward here – which I will develop more elaborately in Chapter 4 – is more strictly sociological, and more specifically culture-theoretic. It is the dramaturgical notion of the public as stage, a virtual forum that exists in symbolic space.[5] Upon this public stage, performances are delivered for, and projected to, the presumed audience of citizens. These performances are diverse, dramatizing a kaleidoscope of ethical positions and political programs. Racists, misogynists, homophobes, and militarists make their cases. So do movements and ideologies of a more expansive and inclusive sort.

The moral superiority of any public movement will, first and foremost, be dramatized in its own terms – as the validity of what Walzer (1984) calls a particular "sphere of justice" and what Boltanski and Thevenot (1990) call a *régime de grandeur*. It will also be legitimated by linking it to the rhetorics of other particularistic movements and other non-civil spheres. It is highly revealing, in this regard, that during the nineteenth century public m/otherhood was often employed to legitimate other, equally particularistic but much less palatable ideological claims.

24

On this reordered plane of late-nineteenth-century public life, women continued to locate and exploit the political possibilities for their sex. In many ways women's public presence remained veiled and distorted by the manipulation of gender symbolism dating from antebellum political culture, which was now used to garnish the increasingly stark racial and class partitions of the public. During the [civil] war women were an honored presence, and female symbols were prolifically displayed amid the pageantry of sectional solidarity. When white dominance was reported in the South, it was portrayed as an act of public purification, a defense of the honor of the ladies. Meanwhile, antiwar Democrats in the North raised cheers to white ladies. Both labor and capital draped their interests in female symbols. The parades of the Workingmen's Party of California mounted wives and daughters in carriages ... in support of their demand for a family wage, and as a countersymbol to Chinese immigration, which they pictured as a flood of bachelors and prostitutes. The upper-class opponents of the Tweed Ring in New York characterized the rapacious city politicians as simian-featured Irishmen preying on a demure Miss Liberty.   (Ryan 1992: 278)

When Union victory brought Black freedom, Democrats around the United States reacted with a race-based appeal for white women's protection, warning of the sexual threat allegedly posed by Black freedmen. From the secession movement of the 1850s to the disfranchisement campaigns of the 1890s, Southern Democrats drew a strong connection between expansions of federal authority and the sexual violation of white women. Both were encroachments on the patriarchal home; rape and seduction served as consistent metaphors for the perils of excessive government force (Edwards 1997: 6).

To the degree that a society is democratic, however, publicly projected claims and demands must do something more than dramatize their own particularism, and they must go beyond making use of it to legitimate other ethics of an equally non-civil kind. They must also make their public case *vis-à-vis* the overarching binary discourse of civil society. In a democratic society, public success cannot be finally assured unless a narrative is also found to interpolate particularist ethics with the universalizing discourse of civil society. For this reason, it is sociologically very probable, even if normatively very undesirable, for positions, arguments, rhetorics, and movements practicing anti-democratic politics and asserting anti-universal principles to achieve great popularity on the public stage. Via this public popularity, the discourse and institutions of the independent civil sphere can be employed, and often have been, to gain organizational

25

power in a democratic state. Being publicly popular – ably displaying and dramatizing one's wares on the public stage – does not ensure the democratic nature of one's claims; nor does it mean that the bearer of these claims either promotes or will be successful in attaining incorporation into the civil sphere.

Yet this is exactly what Rabinovitch's argument does assume, as do other accounts that emphasize the civil and democratic contributions of nineteenth and twentieth-century m/otherhood movements. They equate women's simple presence on the public stage, even when it functions to dramatize an essentialist and restrictive equation of women and m/otherhood, with the incorporation of women into the civil sphere. Because the movements inspired by Republican M/otherhood represented "examples of voluntary public agency," Rabinovitch suggests that they should be seen as "democratic modes of expression." In fact, of course, there are many different kinds of voluntary public associations. While their mode of expression – uncoerced communication – may be democratic, the content of their message, and the kind of society they envision, may very well not be. Nor does the fact that they are allowed, or compelled, to dramatize their message publicly mean that they have gained empirically, or even should gain normatively, political, or cultural inclusion. According to Rabinovitch, because "women were able to translate the strong popular emphasis on the importance of motherhood onto the national stage," they were able to gain significant "incorporation." Yet, while such civil translation is indeed vital, it does not represent an expression of, or even a commitment to, incorporation within the civil sphere that marks democracy. This mediation is a necessary, but far from a sufficient, requirement for the successful expansion of civil solidarity.

While Rabinovitch enthuses that "a marginalized public [gained] integration into the general public sphere and did so without any loss of its own particularized identity," it is precisely such particularized identities that must be symbolically purified, and thus fundamentally transformed, if a movement actually is to increase democracy and expand civil incorporation. It is by no means an indication of their democratic success that, as Rabinovitch suggests, "the 'primordial' qualities of woman were left largely intact" by the m/otherhood movements of the nineteenth century. This was an indication, rather, of their inability to step more confidently into the universal categories of civil society. Instead, limited by their hypothesized difference and their separate sphere, they could provide only facilitating inputs to it. That women could enter the public sphere, but only as "woman," is not the fulfillment of the civil promise but a paradox that reflects a debilitating social and cultural contradiction. The all-important difference between civil and public was deftly articulated by Mrs. J. B. Gilfillan, president of the Minnesota Association Opposed to Woman Suffrage. Representing the powerful if ultimately unsuccessful "Anti" movement, Gilfillan dramatized "difference" as the basis for opposing women's right to vote, and she did so by embracing for women a very public role.

> Anti-suffragists are opposed to women in political life, opposed to women in politics. This is often interpreted to mean opposition to women in public life, which is a profound mistake. We believe in women in all the usual phases of public life, except political life. Wherever woman's influence, counsel or work is needed by the community, there you will find her, so far with little thought of political beliefs. The pedestals they are said to stand upon move them into all the demands of the community. (quoted in Thurner 1993: 40)

Only by theoretically distinguishing between public and democratic, in fact, can we recognize the hegemonic and regulatory role played by civil discourse *vis-à-vis* women's movements of every kind. Women's movements in the public sphere, no matter what their ideologies, felt compelled to legitimate themselves by translating their interests and rhetorics into the broader and more encompassing categories of the civil sphere. This was as true for those who rode into the public sphere wearing the hat of m/otherhood as for those who had aspirations for a more independent and equal role. In the preceding discussion, we have already seen how such a reference informed both sides of nineteenth-century women's history. It also informed the early years of the twentieth century.

It is perhaps not so surprising that, in the struggle over women's right to vote, supporters of female suffrage, themselves carriers of the more universalist position, would pollute their female opponents, the well-organized "Antis," as incompetent interlocutors in civil terms. Nonetheless, to document that they did so serves to highlight the regulating role that the discourse of civil society played *vis-à-vis* the conflicting currents of the women's movement. Anna Howard Shaw, president of the National American Woman Suffrage Association from 1904 to 1915, contemptuously compared the Antis to "vultures looking for carrion," who "revel in the dark and seamy side of human nature" and "are always emphasizing the small and mean in women" (quoted in ibid.: 34). Questioning their sincerity and autonomy, Shaw described the Antis as dependent, as mere puppets of powerful male forces, human shields for "liquor interests, food-dopers, child-labor exploiters, white slavers and political bosses." According to her, it was because the Antis were selfish, cynical, and irrational, and thus incapable of honest civil behavior – not because of their sincere loyalty to the values of motherhood – that they emphasized the inherent difference of women and opposed the voting right.

Its members were mainly well-to-do, carefully protected, and entertained the feeling of distrust of the people usual in their economic class. Their speeches indicated, at times, an anxious disturbance of the mind lest the privileges they enjoyed might be lost in the rights to be gained. Their uniform arguments were that the majority of women did not want to have the vote, therefore, none should have it; that "woman's place was in the home," and that women were incompetent to vote (quoted in ibid.: 34).

What is perhaps even more revealing is that leaders of the "Anti" side also felt compelled to justify their exclusionary and essentialist arguments vis-à-vis the civil discourse. When Mrs. Henry Preston (Sarah C.) White addressed the Judiciary Committee of the U.S. House of Representatives in 1914, she defended the Antis, not as faithful mothers and loyal wives, but as "disinterested, public-spirited citizens who give their time and service to questions of public service without the hope of political reward or preference" (quoted in ibid.: 38). In fact, alongside their well-publicized commitments to husband, hearth, and home, the Antis consistently framed their opposition to voting rights, as Manuela Thurner has so insightfully shown, as a way of keeping female partisanship at bay. Women would remain more impartial and universalistic, the argument went, if they could stand "apart from and beyond party politics" (quoted in ibid.: 41). Another prominent anti-suffragist, Mrs. Barclay Hazard, provided a similar frame in her address to the New York State Federation of Women's Clubs in 1907:

> We must accept partisanship, political trickery and office-seeking as necessary evils inseparable from modern conditions, and the question arises what can be done to palliate the situation. To our minds, the solution has been found by the entrance of women into public life. Standing in an absolutely independent position, freed from all party affiliations, untrammeled by any political obligations, the intelligent, self-sacrificing women of to-day are serving the State (though many of them hardly realize it) as a third party whose disinterestedness none can doubt.
> (quoted in ibid.: 48)

Universalism Versus Difference:
Feminist Fortunes in the Twentieth Century

In her pathbreaking synthetic work, *The Grounding of Modern Feminism*, Nancy Cott recounts the state of affairs for American women at the beginning of the twentieth century. The woman's movement of the preceding century had, indeed, brought women into the inlets, nooks, and crannies of public life. However, because these movements had been conducted under the framework of m/otherhood, "the effort to find release from the 'family claim,' which Jane Addams had eloquently described in the 1880s, was being painfully repeated decade after decade" (Cott 1987: 40).

> Despite the economic changes that had brought women into the paid labor force, despite the improving rates of women's entry into higher education and the professions, and despite the collective and political strengths women had shown through voluntary organizations, the vast majority of the population understood women not as existential subjects, but as dutiful daughters, wives, and mothers.   (ibid.)

By the second decade of the twentieth century, girls and women "swarmed" into what had once safely been male-only arenas – "the street, the factory, store, office, even the barber shop." Yet the interpretive understanding of these places continued to be framed according to the ideology of separate spheres: They remained "terrain culturally understood as male" (ibid.: 7). The boundary relations between the intimate and civil spheres, in other words, were still conceptualized in terms of "facilitating input," even as the behavioral walls separating these spheres were being challenged on the ground. Changing boundary relations required breaking from an image of complementarity. Male–female relations in the intimate sphere would have to be seen as destructive intrusions into the ideal of civil solidarity, a reconceptualization that would usher in the project of civil repair.

The time was ripe for a new ideology, one that would cast women's public participation in an entirely different frame. This new perspective was feminism, the ideology of gender's civil repair. Steering sharply away from the shoals of difference and otherhood, "feminists offered," according to Cott (ibid.: 8), "no sure definition of who woman was." What they sought, rather, was "to end the classification woman" as such. The first explicitly "feminist" mass meetings took place in New York City in February 1914, at the People's Institute of the Cooper Union. The handbill publicizing the meetings

29

made the following announcement: "Subject: BREAKING INTO THE HUMAN RACE" (ibid.: 12, original caps).

With feminism in full gear, and the suffrage amendment passed in 1920, this universalizing ethic led to a fight for an Equal Rights Amendment, the first ERA. Feminists viewed the ERA as a "civic innovation" (Cott 1995: 356) that would give legal teeth to gender repair. Building on the Nineteenth Amendment and an emerging consciousness of women's equality with men, an amendment mandating equality in every aspect of women's lives would have the potential to restructure non-civil spheres in a dramatic way. The non-civil sphere of particular concern was the economic. "By the 1910s," Cott writes (ibid.), "suffragists linked political and economic rights, and connected the vote with economic leverage." Reformers "emphasized that women, as human individuals no less than men, had the right and need to use their talents to serve society and themselves and to gain fair compensation" (ibid.). As members of the civil sphere, women workers shared a common human status with male workers, and it was this common humanity that would provide leverage for repairing gender-triggered economic inequality.

While this effort at civic repair certainly had significantly ameliorating effects in the long run, it not only failed miserably in the political arena but had the cultural effect of igniting an "intra-feminist controversy" (Cott 1995: 362) that polarized publicly active women and created a fateful backlash against feminism. As Cott sees it, the demand for an ERA pitted the traditional arguments for women's difference against the more radical argument for gender universalism "as never before." After the success of suffragism and the advent of the category feminism, the compromise formation of public m/otherhood could no longer camouflage the contradictions between civil and intimate spheres. More accurately: The sense that there actually *was* a contradiction, not a complementarity, became much more widely believed. Difference and equality "were seen as competing, even mutually exclusive, alternatives." The result was that "the ERA battle of the 1920s seared into memory the fact of warring outlooks among women" (ibid.).

The ERA's purpose was to allow women to have the same opportunities and situations as men. It was triggered by the conviction that women could not continue to emphasize their differences without the adverse consequence, usually unintended and often unwished for, of reinforcing civil inequality. The problem was that, while antidifference arguments were becoming widely accepted among America's cultural and political avant-garde, they remained "extraordinarily iconoclastic" among America's mainstream (Cott 1987: 179). Difference entered the ERA debate in the pivotal argument over the wisdom of abolishing sex-based protective legislation. Opponents of ERA became outspoken advocates of such protection, "echo[ing] customary public opinion in proposing that motherhood and wage earning should be mutually exclusive" (Cott 1995: 362). The outcry showed the vast distance between arguments for public m/otherhood and arguments for genuine civil equality.

Opponents of the ERA believed that sex-based legislation was necessary because of women's biological and social roles as mothers. They claimed that "the inherent differences are permanent. Women will always need many laws different from those needed by men"; "women as such, whether or not they are mothers present or prospective, will always need protective legislation"; "the working mother is handicapped by her own nature." Their approach stressed maternal nature and inclination as well as conditioning, and implied that the sexual division of labor was eternal (ibid.: 361).

Despite their deep resonance with the traditional values of the intimate sphere, such particularistic arguments for maintaining separate spheres could be fully justified only if they were also vouchsafed in civil-discursive terms. ERA activists were polluted as civil incompetents, as "pernicious" women who "discard[ed] all ethics and fair play," as an "insane crowd" who espoused "a kind of hysterical feminism with a slogan for a program" (quoted in ibid.). The effect of this equation of feminism with anti-civil was fateful. As the ERA went down to crushing defeat in the 1920s, the victorious difference discourse had the effect of making feminism a dirty word for decades to come. Without the universalizing ideology of feminism, it remained impossible to conceive of how women could be fully incorporated into the civil sphere. Even during World War II, when the most dire objective exigencies propelled women into the very public world of factory production, their participation was framed as a facilitating input that preserved difference, not as civil incorporation. This, of course, was one of Ruth Milkman's core findings in her revisionist study "Gender at Work."

Accompanying the characterization of women's work as "light" was an emphasis on cleanliness. "Women can satisfactorily fill all or most jobs performed by men, subject only to the limitations of strength and physical requirements," a meeting of the National Association of Manufacturers concluded in March 1942. "However ... jobs of a particularly 'dirty' character, jobs that subject women to heat process or are of a 'wet' nature should not be filled by women ... despite the

31

fact that women could, if required, perform them" (Milkman 1995: 448). In fact, this framework was but another version of public m/ otherhood, the compromise formation that had the effect of preserving the gender contradictions between civil and non-civil spheres, not of repairing them.

There was a contradiction in the management literature on women's war work. It simultaneously stressed the fact that "women are being trained in skills that were considered exclusively in man's domain" and their special suitability for "delicate war jobs." These two seemingly conflicting kinds of statements were reconciled through analogies between "women's work" at home and in the war plants. "Note the similarity between squeezing orange juice and the operation of a small drill press," the Sperry Gyroscope company urged in a recruitment pamphlet. "Anyone can peel potatoes," it went on. "Burring and filing are almost as easy" (ibid.: 449).

Even in the 1950s, amid the boasting about modernity and the theorizing about modernization, the equation of feminist demands for universalism with anti-civil pollution remained widely accepted. "Most women as well as men," Jane Sherron de Hart (1995: 540) writes, "still accepted as one of the few unchanging facts of life the conviction that woman's primary duty was to be 'helpmate, housewife, and mother.'"

Feminism could not be revived, nor could the civic repair of gender relations become a realistic political possibility, until universalist arguments about gender relations were much more widely accepted. This happened with the creation of feminism's "second wave," which was stimulated by the effervescence of demands for equalizing the status of African Americans, another group whose inequality had been legitimated by the construction of an essentializing difference. Betty Friedan, whose enormously influential writings earned her the title of "mother" to this second wave, equated arguments for difference with the "feminine mystique." Her argument should be taken less as an empirical description of women's status in the 1950s – which had, of course, already been partially reconstructed by modern feminism – than as a culturally sensitive polemic against the degree to which difference arguments had managed, nonetheless, to sustain their mainstream viability.

> The suburban housewife – she was the dream image of the young American women and the envy, it was said, of women all over the world . . . She was healthy, beautiful, educated, concerned only about her husband, her children, her home. She had found true feminine fulfillment. As a housewife and mother, she was respected as a full and

equal partner to man in his world. She was free to choose automobiles, clothes, appliances, supermarkets; she had everything that women ever dreamed of. The words written for women, and the words women used when they talked to each other, while their husbands sat on the other side of the room and talked shop or politics or septic tanks, were about problems with their children, or how to keep their husbands happy, or improve their children's school, or cook chicken or make slipcovers. Nobody argued whether women were inferior or superior to men; they were simply different. Words like "emancipation" and "career" sounded strange and embarrassing; no one had used them for years.

(Friedan 1995: 515)

The women's liberation movement rejected the mystique of difference and demanded the civil repair of gender relations on the basis of universality. "The first step toward becoming feminists," de Hart (1995: 545) writes, "demanded a clear statement of women's position in society, one that called attention to the gap between the egalitarian ideal and the actual position of women in American culture." In 1966, on the basis of such sentiments, the National Organization for Women was formed. NOW's statement of purpose, signed by 300 men and women, reached back to the universalizing attack on separate spheres ideology that marked the long-ago meeting in Seneca Falls. On behalf of women, it demanded "full participation in the mainstream of American society NOW, exercising all the privileges and responsibilities thereof in truly equal partnership with men" (quoted in ibid.: 548).

What finally destroyed difference ideology was the persuasive feminist insistence, which became hegemonic in the course of the 1970s and 1980s, that gender was a social construct, not a natural condition. This contextualization allowed male domination to be labeled as a "sexist" condition that marked a destructive intrusion into civil equality, one that demanded energetic civil repair. "Given the pervasiveness of sexism," de Hart noted, "many feminists saw no possibility for real equality short of transformation not only of individuals but also of social institutions and culture values" (quoted in ibid.: 552). As with every effort to further institutionalize the idealizing codes of civil society, deepening incorporation and reforming "the system" required deep shifts in boundary relations and fundamental institutional repairs. Thus, "what seemed to be a matter of obtaining equal rights within the existing system, in reality demanded changes that transform the system" (ibid.: 552). Instead of feminine difference, women would be constructed in terms of civic competence. According to one programmatic statement, published in 1979, feminist transformation involved nothing less than a re-evaluation of

33

women as workers, of women as mothers, of mothers as workers, of work as suitable for one gender and not for the other. The demand implies equal opportunity and thus equal responsibilities. It implies a childhood in which girls are rewarded for competence, risk taking, achievement, competitiveness and independence-just like boys.

(quoted in ibid.: 552)

The Ethical Limits of "Care"

The ERA may once again have been defeated, but this new belief in gender equality has, nonetheless, increasingly permeated the culture and institutions of contemporary life. Certainly, it has been far more widely accepted than at any other time in human history. It is precisely within this context of a less gender-distorting institutionalization of the promises of civil society that we must understand the growing popularity over the last three decades of the movements, within feminism, for emphasizing the separating particularities of "women's culture" and the possible superiority of a woman-generated ethics of care. These must, in other words, be viewed as developments that have emerged from within feminism itself. They have unfolded, not as an alternative to civil discourse, but within the very rubric of an underlying belief in the equal civil competence of women and men. It is exactly the same for those movements that have restored the vitality of the idiocultures of ethnicity, race, sexuality, religion, region, and those relating to different physical abilities. Contra such identity advocates as Iris Marion Young (1990), justice has not become simply a matter of accepting the politics of difference. Different cultures have not become entirely distanced from one another, allowing their particularity to be recognized and separation and self-governance to be fostered. Difference can be recognized, in a positive manner, only if the particular is viewed as a concrete manifestation of the universal. This is possible only if civil solidarity is expanded to include subaltern communities, an expansion that de-essentializes and cleanses once-polluted identities, recognizing differences as legitimate by constructing them as variations on the theme of a common humanity (cf. Calhoun 1995; Benhabib 1986: 341).

It should not be surprising that many of the radical advocates of "women's culture" themselves fail to recognize, much less to appreciate, that its growing legitimacy actually depends on an expanding civil frame. As civil ideals become more deeply institutionalized, they become more transparent, less visibly taking on a primordial hue. Feminists themselves have often worried about the failure of difference

34

theorists to recognize the continuing reach of civil universalism. Twenty years ago, Ellen DuBois warned that any single-minded focus on "women's culture" risked ignoring "the larger social and historical developments of which it was a part" and thus failed to "address the limitations of the values of women's culture" itself (quoted in Kerber 1986: 308). It was precisely on such grounds that, in the mid 1980s, a furious debate erupted inside the feminist community over Carol Gilligan's arguments for a distinctively different female morality in her controversial book *In a Different Voice* (1982). This debate, one part of the broader argument about difference and universalism in the postmodern civil sphere, has not died down to this day.

Against Lawrence Kohlberg's studies of moral development, Gilligan argues that boys have "a self defined through separation," whereas girls have "a self delineated through connection." Women thus feel "a responsibility to discern and alleviate the 'real and recognizable troubles' of this world," while, by contrast, men's imperative "appears rather as an injunction to respect the rights of others" (ibid.: 100). Feminist critics of these claims attacked Gilligan for drawing her data exclusively from women's decision-making processes – primarily from decisions about abortion – and for failing to study parallel processes that might be involved in male decision making. If Gilligan had done so, her critics argued, she might have found that, beyond the differences she discovers, there is an underlying human universality.

> Do not men also in some circumstances find themselves similarly stretched on the rack between selfishness and responsibility? Were we to listen to men during their process of decision on, say, draft resistance, might we note also their similarly anguished contemplation of their responsibility to their families, to the needs of those who depend on them for care? (Kerber 1986: 305)

> Gilligan has been attacking a straw man [*sic*] . . . In childhood and adolescence, there is no trend whatever for males to score at higher levels than females on Kohlberg's scales . . . There is no indication whatever that the two sexes take different developmental paths with respect to moral thought about abstract, hypothetical issues.
> (Greeno and Maccoby 1986: 312)

What disturbed Gilligan's feminist critics was the possibility that her argument for difference – despite her own heated denials (e.g., Gilligan 1986) that it was essentializing, or even gendered – might obscure the difference between then and now, between the days of public m/otherhood and the contemporary period of relatively universalist morality. Linda Kerber (1986: 306) wrote that "this historian, at least, is haunted by the sense that we have had this argument before, vested in different language [about] the ascription of reason to men and feeling to women." The psychologist Zella Luria (1986: 320) asked, "Do we truly gain by returning to a modern cult of true womanhood?"

> Modern women will need *not* to be always caring and interrelated, if indeed they ever were constantly so. And they are also in situations where being abstract and rights oriented is a necessity. My purpose as a feminist is to train women to choose their actions sensibly and flexibly depending on the situation they confront.   (ibid.; original italics)

Such concerns point to broader moral issues. The argument for the desirability of a new ethics of care is not simply sociological and empirical. It is also normative and philosophical. Rooted in the anti-Kantian, Aristotelian tradition (e.g., Tronto 1993), the care argument inserts itself into the highly charged dichotomy between what John Rawls famously called "justice as fairness," an ethic involving rights and rules, and the denial, by more communitarian thinkers as Michael Walzer and Michael Sandel, that justice can ever be anything other than context bound, that it must always remain particularist in its essential part. Whether or not an "ethics of care" were tied to the social condition of gender subordination – and, in principle at least, it certainly need not be – this broader philosophical question remains.

Can an ethic of care sustain the kinds of commitments to impartiality, fairness, self-criticism, and inclusion that must sustain the civil sphere in a truly democratic society? One influential feminist philosopher, Susan James, has criticized the notion that "the activities typically undertaken by women can be described, without strain, as partial, personal or particular." What she fears is that, if "the affections and concerns that go into them are usually directed to particular people and set within specific relationships such as those of mother to child, nurse to patient, secretary to boss, wife to husband," then women may be portrayed as if they "think and behave in ways that are antithetical to the norm of impartiality" that is so essential in constructing a tolerant and democratic world (James 1992: 55). She points out that, if an ethics of care bases itself on ties of love, there is no theoretical role for rules, "for one another's well-being is enough to ensure that differences are resolved and that feelings of resentment, frustration or anger are contained" (ibid.: 58). Such an ethic is well and good for the intimate sphere, but can it actually be extended to the civil one?

> To extend these practices (or something like them) beyond the private sphere would be to extend them into a territory where people are not bound by emotional ties and may perceive themselves as having little more in common than the fact they happen to be living under the same political jurisdiction.   (ibid.)

Another feminist philosopher, Mary Dietz, wonders whether the motives that bind mother and child, the ties that sustain friendship, and such quintessentially care-giving institutions as families actually provide the appropriate normative standards. Should they be used as models for the kinds of motives, relationships, and institutions that must inform a democratic society? She suggests, to the contrary, that such relationships and institutions might, at least in certain fundamental respects, be anti-civil in form.

> Who would not argue that the growth and preservation of children are vital social imperatives, or that the protection of vulnerable human life is important. But surely a movement or a political consciousness committed simply to caring ... offers no standards ... when it comes to judging between political alternatives ... The mother and the child are in radically different positions in terms of power and control. The child is subordinate to the mother ... In other words, the special and distinctive aspects of mothering emerge out of a decidedly unequal relationship, even if benign or loving ... This is an intimate, exclusive, and particular activity. [Because] democratic citizenship, on the other hand, is collective, inclusive, and generalized, [b]ecause it is a condition [in] which individuals aim at being equal, the mother child relationship is a particularly inappropriate model ... Furthermore, the bond among citizens is not like the love between a mother and child, for citizens are, not intimately, but politically involved with each other. Citizens do not, because they cannot, relate to one another as brother does to brother, or mother does to child ... Intimacy, love, and attentiveness are precious things in part because they are exclusive and so cannot be experienced just anywhere or by just anyone with just any other. That is why love and intimacy ... must not be made the basis of political action and discourse.   (Dietz 1998: 57–58)

Even when she first began to develop her arguments for the superiority of an ethics of care, Joan Tronto, one of the most influential thinkers in this philosophical movement, acknowledged that "we do not care for everyone equally," indeed, that "we care more for those who are emotionally, physically, and even culturally closer to us." Not only are the particularism and exclusiveness of such a standard plain to see, but Tronto also admits that the ethics of care has an implicitly conservative quality, for "in focusing on the preservation of existing relationships," there is "little basis for critical reflection on whether these relationships are good, healthy, or worthy of preservation" (1987: 659–660). In her most ambitious statement of this position, *Moral Boundaries: A Political Argument for an Ethic of Care*, Tronto writes that, while paternalism and parochialism are unwelcome, they are inevitable "dangers of care" (1993: 170), going so far as to identify "particularity" as the ethic's central "moral dilemma" (ibid.: 141). By way of solution, Tronto recommends that the care ethic be "connected to a theory of justice" (ibid.: 171), which would provide a "transformed context" (ibid.: 158) for its application. Yet Tronto originally presented the ethics of care as an alternative to just such universalizing theories of justice.

The discourse of civil society is not concerned only with individualism; nor does it represent an instrumental and strategic colonization by instrumental and abstract rationality. It codes altruism and trust, emphasizes honor and truthfulness over selfishness and deception, demands friendliness and openness, and suggests that social relations should be inclusive, egalitarian, and cooperative. Yet, however positive and socially oriented, these qualities do not suggest love, and for this reason they do not denote the lifeworld centered "ethics of care." The question is not whether love, care, emotional feeling, loyalty, and a relativizing contextualism are good things in themselves. Certainly, they are. Plural societies need ethics that are informed by these qualities. Nor is the question whether women's culture, as distinct from men's, is important to preserve and sustain, often in a separated place. Certainly it is. The question, rather, is whether such qualities can define the sphere of civil justice, indeed, whether identifying moral ethics by such qualities would make it possible to mark out a relatively autonomous civil sphere at all.

Sexuality, Difference, and Civil Society

Keeping these considerations about plurality and the openness of the civil sphere in mind, I would like to return, in conclusion, to sexuality. From a Foucauldian perspective (Meeks 2001), to emphasize incorporation into civil society is to embrace normalization, which connotes conservative social conformity. So the growing acceptance of LGBTQ+ merely reinforces essentialism.

To think about recent developments in sexuality is to think about the relation, once again, between civil and non-civil spheres. During modernity, sexuality was tightly bound to the family, part of the

38

package of reproduction, socialization, love and marriage, and sharply delimited age sequencing that made the intimate sphere a world of strict asceticism and the repression of pleasure. All sorts of "differences" were bundled into this straitjacketed modern package – between men and women, youth and age, work and pleasure, and hetero- and homosexuality. Each difference was entered into the binary discursive grid of civil society, and in this way various behaviors were sequestered and various possibilities cast aside. Among these, homosexuality received perhaps the most strongly polluting stain, for it threatened the asceticizing package in all sorts of ways. Homosexuality was conceived as the consummately anti-civil activity, emphasizing pleasure over control, perversion over honesty, secrecy over openness, domination over cooperation, irrationality over common sense.

In the course of the twentieth century (Seidman 1991), the tightly bound package that defined the intimate sphere began to come apart. Marriage became separated from sexuality; sexuality from love; procreation from marriage, love, and sexuality; and socialization from all of the above. One result was the creation of the free-floating "erotic complex" that has so roiled the intimate relationships of postmodern societies (Bauman 1998). It has now become possible, indeed even normative, to value sexuality for its own sake. With this postmodern sexual turn, the choice of sexual objects opened up as well. It was pleasure that mattered, and pleasure had come to be viewed as a medium that should be available to all. Indeed, each of the once disreputable "differences" once bundled and sequestered in the privacy of the intimate sphere was now brought into the light of day. To one degree or another, they were purified of their most polluting anti-civil traits. Divorce, single parenting, unmarried motherhood and out-of-wedlock births, singlehood, female sexuality, and public eroticism – each of these has, subject to the usual sociological variations, been rendered in the liberating discourse of civil society. Insofar as they were so rendered, they became "respectable."

In terms of sexuality, "identity politics" can be understood as referring to the social movements that have succeeded in translating these polluted differences into civil terms, thereby, giving their proponents power and space. According to this perspective, identity politics has not, in other words, fortified and essentialized differences, nor has it had the effect of keeping them bundled together. Rather, by allowing once polluted, and still precarious, identities the free air of the newly multicultural civil sphere, so-called identity politics has actually undermined the fusion of intimate roles.

39

It was the closet, not the civil sphere, that made homosexuality the all-defining, all consuming identity of an individual's life (Seidman 2001). In contemporary society, homosexuality is less significant and less all-consuming, though it is valorized all the same, for it is conceived as a choice and a construction, not as an essence and a necessity. Choosing to be homosexual, and choosing also to leave the closet, are increasingly constructed as ultimately civil acts. They suggest courage, independence, openness, and honesty. Men and women, whether teenagers or adults, who exhibit such qualities are "allowed" to assume other, equally civil roles, such as teacher, rabbi, parent, movie star, athletic star, and role model. Yes, homosexuality has been normalized, but in the civil and democratic sense, not in the Foucauldian one. It is increasingly accepted as a form of civil behavior, one governed, like other sorts of relationships, by what Seidman (1999) has called, following Habermas, a "communicative ethic." With these changes in the social construction of homosexuality and other intimate behaviors, postmodern civil society has been expanded to include what Meeks (2001) has called "sexual citizenship."

The categorical divisions of the civil sphere have been stable for centuries, but the signifieds of these civil and anti-civil signifiers certainly have not. At different historical times, differences of gender, class, race, religion, and sexuality are condemned as deviant vis-à-vis the "natural," so-called primordial qualities of the groups that organize and represent the civil core. At other historical times, however, the earlier embodiments of these qualities are seen as having been merely "constructed." What was the transgressive, forbidden fruit of one period can become the meat and potatoes of another. This has affected class and race, gender and homosexuality. Shifts in signification will continue to occur as "modern" societies continue to develop. Such civil semiosis must be continuous if democracy is to survive. Reflexivity is not about changing the categories that define the civil sphere, it is about learning how they can be applied in new ways.[6] What seems natural today will surely be constructed tomorrow.

— 2 —

FEMINISM, PUBLIC OPINION, AND PRESIDENTIAL POWER

(with Willa Sachs)

Americans characterize historical periods with the names of presidents – The Age of Jackson, the Eisenhower Era, the Reagan Years, Bush I and II, the Clinton Decade, the Obama Era. Inside this civil religion of presidential power, citizens are swept up into ferocious, frenzied electoral campaigns, certain that the election of their heroes will transform society and make America whole again (Alexander 2010). Electing the opponent is a disaster too terrible even to contemplate. Every four years, the fate of the world seems at stake (Alexander and Jaworsky 2014).

The focus on who assumes executive power seems merely a matter of common sense in historical terms and a matter of sophistication in theoretical ones. After all, one of the singular accomplishments of modern societies is enormously powerful states, nation-wide bureaucracies headed by charismatic leaders that monopolize violence, control taxation, raise armies, and decide ultimate questions of war and peace (Weber 1978a,b). It is hardly surprising, then, that generations of sociologists and social movement scholars have focused on how power can be wrested from antagonistic states.

In this chapter, we develop a contrary position. We argue that the effective functioning of presidential power depends on support from power of a different kind, a "civil power" (Alexander 2006) whose roots are located in collective meanings and whose generation occurs outside the state. Movements exercise civil power, we argue, by not only transforming public opinion but by serving as vehicles for public concerns, giving expression to the desires of "the public" imagined as a putative whole – to which presidents are then beholden. While sociologists have long neglected the relationship between policy outcomes, social movements, and public opinion, we

41

argue that these interlinkages are key agents of American democratic life.

Presidents have often been important targets of movement efforts for social change. Yet sociologists have had little to say about presidential administrations, and presidential studies scholars, in turn, have seldom analyzed social movements (Milkis and Tichenor 2019; Martin 2003). The fact that literatures on the executive office and American social reform efforts rarely intersect is particularly curious given their parallel historical development. As a wide swath of organized interests expanded in the first half of the twentieth century, Progressive-era reforms expanded the scope and power of the executive office, paving the way for the so-called "modern" presidency (ibid; Mast 2012). The modern presidency solidified the expectation that the president, not party elites or congressmen, would "[give] expression and effect to the nation's aspirations for economic and social improvement" (Milkis and Tichenor 2019: 34). In the U.S., the president is the only figure in whom "the state" achieves a national collective representation. It is through the election and support of the president that members of the civil sphere articulate their sense of what the laws should be and become (Mast 2012).

The empirical material through which we will demonstrate these claims is the second-wave feminist movement and the countermovements that arose against it in the mid 1970s. We trace the intersection of (anti-)feminism and presidential politics in what we view as three particularly illustrative cases: the presidencies of Richard Nixon, Jimmy Carter, and Ronald Reagan. Our analytical focus is the liberal, "mainstream" movement, for it was this branch of the wider movement that most often had the explicit goal of influencing presidential administrations and the national political agenda (Hartmann 2012: 150).

Public Opinion, Society, and State

Social theorists in the late nineteenth through early twentieth centuries, from de Tarde to Durkheim to Dewey, recognized the centrality and independent power of public opinion as a social force (Alexander 2006: 69–106). Tocqueville, for instance, described public opinion as "the dominant power" in a democracy. Because public opinion asserts "itself through elections and decrees," Tocqueville observed that, in "exercising executive power, the president of the United

States is subject to constant and jealous scrutiny" (de Tocqueville 2004 [1835]: 40).

As the twentieth century unfolded, however, social theory became decidedly more skeptical about the independent power of public opinion in capitalist societies and, correspondingly, about the possibility of democracy itself (e.g., Lippmann 1925). Habermas ([1963] 1989) argued, for example, that twentieth-century capitalism, via its culture industry, had destroyed the public sphere and commodified public opinion. Mills (1956), like Habermas, acknowledged that an independent public sphere had once existed, but claimed it had been buried by industrial capitalism and that, ever since, public opinion was an ideology manufactured and controlled by the power elite. This theoretical logic also informed the arguments of Bourdieu, whose assertion that "public opinion does not exist" (Bourdieu 1980) became an infamously dismissive marker of such a position. Critical theory's demolition job on public opinion found crucial support in Weber, whose work on the "social" as independent from the political – sustained by religion, prebendary power, and the horizontal associations of urban life – was mostly about the premodern. As rationalization proceeded, Weber insisted, social life was no longer bottom-up, but top-down. Bureaucracy, political parties, and state power became the names of the modern game. Such powerful sites of social hegemony and political domination rendered the existence and influence of an autonomous public sphere a theoretical impossibility.

As Weber's work became metabolized, it served as a central influence on the intellectual reorientation of sociology – and political sociology in particular – in the mid to late twentieth century, after which the study of public opinion and its central role in democratic politics "virtually disappeared" from the subfield (Manza and Brooks 2012: 89; Weakliem 2020). As Manza and Brooks recount, Millsian skepticism over survey research and a newfound emphasis on the macrostructural drove political sociologists away from anything that smacked of "cultural values," the latter seemingly fatally yoked to Parsonian functionalism. The causal role of "generalized attitudes or political cultures" (Tilly 2002: 205) in processes of political change was dismissed in favor of structural sources of power, including the features of states and political institutions (Skocpol 1979; Weir, Orloff, and Skocpol 1988), the organizational capacities and resources of social classes (Esping-Andersen 1990), concentrations of economic and political capital (Mann 1993), and alliances among the power elite (Domhoff 2006). Many came to consider the state as an autonomous site of power unmoored by the "elusive" (Tilly 2002:

205) realm of civil society (e.g., Evans, Rueschemeyer, and Skocpol 1985; Tilly 1995; Skocpol 1979; Mann 1993), even as political sociology grappled with social forces in a more structural sense.

Recent efforts to move away from state to "polity" centered models (Skocpol 1992) have refined rather than uprooted this reductive Weberian tradition. For example, in their ambitious volume *The Many Hands of the State*, Morgan and Orloff (2017) draw attention to work that disaggregates and culturalizes "state functions." Yet, they continue to equate "states' unique characteristics" with "the distillation and concentration of power," defining the central question as "how states induce, or force, people to obey" (2017: 12) and asserting that such "sinews of power" make states into "the distinctively powerful governing structures of our time" (13). Whereas Morgan and Orloff describe the aim of their work as demonstrating how "states profoundly shape the normative order" (10), our ambition is to show how profoundly the normative order shapes states – via shifts in public opinion that are crystallized by social movements in the civil sphere (cf. Berezin et al. 2020).

It would seem that such inattention to the role of public opinion in democratic life would surely be corrected by social movement theory, which examines how social activists challenge laws, policies, and dominant cultural beliefs. Yet this field has long neglected public opinion as well (Burstein 1998; 2020). Social movement theorists seldom assess how protests shape public opinion and vice versa (Banaszak and Ondercin 2016). To the extent that public opinion is analyzed, it is often treated as an "alternative" variable that competes with the direct efforts of movements to affect policymaking rather than as something meaningfully related to the efforts of movements themselves (e.g., Costain and Majstorovic 1994; Soule and King 2006; Amenta et al. 2010; cf McAdam and Su 2002; Giugni 2004; Agnone 2007).[1]

Political process theory (PPT), the dominant theoretical paradigm in social movement studies (Almeida 2019: 44), is particularly concerned with the direct impact of movements. PPT theorists argue that challenging state policy hinges on movements' ability to exploit openings in political "opportunity structures," or chinks in states' powerful "repressive, material, and regulatory capacities" (Bessinger 2015: 2), such as ruptures in political alignments. It is the disruptive capacity of movements – their ability to threaten organized interests – that allows them to wrest power from states (McAdam 1982; Tarrow 1998; Tilly 1992; see also Morris 1984; Piven and Cloward 1977; Gamson 1975). Even when public opinion is explicitly brought into play, what is decisive is not its "ideational content" (McAdam 1996: 348) but, rather, the ability of the protests that sensitize it to create a "breakdown in public order" (ibid: 353; McAdam 1982; Koopmans 1993; Kriesi 2004). Indeed, as critics have long charged (Armstrong and Bernstein 2008; Taylor et al. 2009), in such conceptualizations, cultural tactics, goals, or movement impacts are relegated to the epiphenomenal, understood as orthogonal to real processes of political change (e.g., Tilly 1995; Kriesi 2004; Jenkins 1983; Rucht 1988).[2] Our argument here is just the opposite. We see public opinion not as a disruptive tool, but as a system of meaning that is continuously constructed and reconstructed against the symbolic metalanguage of the civil sphere. It is to this idea that we now turn.

Civil Sphere, Public Opinion, and Social Movements

The alternative approach we propose is grounded in civil sphere theory (Alexander 2006, 2018). Societies possess a "civil sphere," an institutional and cultural domain that is analytically and, to some degree, empirically differentiated from such non-civil institutions as state, market, family, and religion. The civil sphere is grounded in a network of shared understandings drawn from a highly generalized symbolic system predicated on the binary classification of social groups, relations, and institutions as "civil" or "uncivil," defined according to ascriptive homologies that define motives, relations, and institutions, such as rational/irrational; open/secretive; inclusive/exclusive; autonomous/dependent; deliberative/conspiratorial; and egalitarian/hierarchical. "Public opinion" does not refer to the aggregation of individual opinions, but rather to the civil and anti-civil evaluations that members of society hold about one another, their social relationships, representative figures, and institutions. The normative reference of the "public" is constructed via the discourse of civil society.

Civil spheres have a utopian reference, pointing to a solidary community that intertwines individual autonomy and collective obligation, in which every person is treated with equal respect and accorded equal rights. In real as compared to ideal civil societies, however, these normative aspirations – that every individual is attributed such "civil" qualities as rationality, altruism, trust, and truthfulness – are never more than partially institutionalized. They are contradicted by non- and often anti-civil hierarchies in other social spheres and polluted in relation to the primordial qualities of race, sex, religion, ethnicity, gender, and region that mark a given national civil sphere's founding group. "Actually existing" civil spheres are deeply contradictory, generating strains that trigger collective efforts at "civil repair," demands that core groups live up to their democratic ideals by redefining excluded groups in terms that legitimate their civil incorporation (Alexander, Stack, and Khosrokhavar 2019c).

In order to gain influence, actors must speak in language that makes the democratic public into a normatively compelling idea, translating particularistic demands into more universalizing form. Frontlash and backlash movements (Alexander 2019a) refract public opinion (see also Gamson 2004). When frontlash movements expand civil incorporation, they trigger backlash movements that seek to narrow the civil sphere (Alexander, Kivisto, and Sciortino 2021). Activists on the left and right both claim to represent the wider public, addressing "society" on behalf of a particular interest and laying out a broader vision of how particular concerns pose problems to society at large.

Frontlash and backlash movements crystallize existing strands of public opinion, naming and legitimizing a pre-existing set of as-yet-unarticulated, collectively shared concerns, and/or they transform public opinion itself by orienting themselves toward the communicative institutions of the civil sphere. Communicative institutions, including the mass media, public opinion polls, and civil organizations, create messages that translate the civil sphere's normatively binding codes into situationally specific evaluations and descriptions (Mast 2012; Alexander and Jaworsky 2014). Social movements shift public opinion by reaching out to constituencies directly through media outlets such as newsletters and by garnering attention in the mainstream media for their protest efforts. Issue-oriented organizations and social movement groups, such as the NAACP or the National Organization for Women, not only shape national debate and opinion but also harness poll data that crystallizes the opinions they have strenuously worked to shape, with the aim of translating civil concern into political pressure. By wielding public opinion as an instrument of political control, movement activists exercise *civil power*.

Social movements also exercise civil power via the civil sphere's regulative institutions, including the electoral process and political parties (Alexander 2006). Many professionalized civil associations are closely linked to political parties, which allows social movements to channel public concerns into political campaigns and party platforms. Regulatory institutions have been defined as simple manifestations of social hegemony or state power, but their effective functioning depends on their ability to represent the interests of the civil sphere (Alexander 2006). By engaging in voter education campaigns and by mobilizing data on voting patterns – like the "gender gap"– movements can threaten electoral retaliation, transforming public opinion into a potentially regulative force that can constrain the range of actions the president and state actors can reasonably take. Civil associations also work to get "insider activists" appointed to government positions (Banaszak 2010), extending civil power deeply inside the organs of state.[3] When newly elected politicians take office, as president or as members of Congress, they move from civil sphere to the state. Yet, as we demonstrate in the following section, even as they wield the levers of power, presidents and their administrations remain face-to-face with the civil sphere.

Feminist and Anti-Feminist Movements, Public Opinion, and the Presidency

Feminism and Richard Nixon

If Nixon "could have it his way," reported Jack Anderson in 1971, "American women would confine their activities to homemaking and forget all this talk of 'liberation'." Indeed, President Nixon's initial response to the women's movement was somewhere between "patronizing neglect" (Freeman 1975: 205) and open hostility. After four decades of "abeyance" (Taylor 1989), the movement had re-emerged with a vengeance only a few years earlier, during John F. Kennedy's presidential tenure. In a half-hearted bid to placate female voters, Kennedy had created a presidential commission committed to women's legal equity (Harrison 1980), and in so doing, unwittingly helped birth the second-wave feminist movement by drawing together women activists from across the country in state-level commissions (Freeman 1975). The National Commission's major report, Betty Friedan's bombshell bestseller, *The Feminine Mystique*, and the formation of the National Organization for Women (NOW) three years later crystallized a silently swelling current of public opinion by giving name to the "problem that has no name" (Friedan in Rosen 2000). This new wave aimed to undo the anti-civil construction of female traits – "piety, purity, submissiveness, and domesticity" – which for centuries had warranted women's "civil death" (National Commission on the Observance of the IWY 1976: 3, 9).

By the time of Nixon's presidency, feminism had transformed into a mass movement, and media-oriented protests from liberal and radical feminist groups alike – such as the Women's Strike for Equality in 1970 – would continue to generate profound shifts in public opinion (Klein 1984: 25; Huddy, Neely, and Lafay 2000: 322; Banaszak and Ondercin 2016).[4] Nixon managed to evade major feminist concerns during his first year in office, yet his avowed anti-feminism would soon prove no match against the rising feminist tide.

One of the first indications that a change was in the offing was the reaction to a question that a feminist journalist named Vera Glaser posed to the President at his second televised press conference: Why had only three out of over 200 presidential appointments gone to women? "Can we expect some more equitable recognition of women's abilities," she asked Nixon, "Or are we going to remain the lost sex?" (Voss 2009). Feminist activists channeled Glaser's demand by picketing the White House in a series of widely publicized protests (Shelton 1969; *The Fort Meyers News-Press* 1969). Arguing that "a white male club is not a democracy" (*The Hartford Courant* 1972), they polluted Nixon's administration as exclusive and uncivil, triggering a national furor among women.

Women's organizations pushed Nixon to create an independent agency to bolster women's rights and opportunities. The idea was initially proposed by "insider activist" Rep. Florence Dwyer, who argued in a letter to Nixon that women's economic, social, and legal subordination "continued[d] to weaken our social structure and distort our system of moral principles" (Glaser 1969). Nixon chose at first to ignore the letter (Stout 2012), but its circulation in news outlets generated increasing feminist outrage. Women's discrimination was now widely constructed as a destructive civil intrusion, and the feminist movement channeled the newfound "public" commitment into political pressure. As Elizabeth Boyer of the Women's Equity Action League (WEAL) wrote to Nixon, "if I assess [societal] attitudes correctly, a groundswell of feeling is developing, on a highly responsible level, which will not brook very much delay or circumlocution. The burgeoning membership in our organization, which has expanded into nearly twenty states by word of mouth alone, certainly testifies to this" (in Martin 2003: 128).

After prodding from Glaser, Dwyer, and various women's organizations, Nixon finally budged, creating a President's Task Force on Women's Rights and Responsibilities, on which Glaser was asked to serve (Stout 2012: 21). The Task Force issued a report calling for the President's support on several women's rights initiatives. Nixon was reluctant to publish the report, dragging his feet for months (Shelton 1970), even as several of his own advisors urged him to release it. As the Special Counsel to the President wrote, "This is a bit like the school desegregation issue. It's beginning to build up a real head of steam. I would like to see us leading the parade rather than jumping on the band wagon after it is already well down the road" (Stout 2012: 44). Indeed, the civil sphere had its own agenda, and Nixon had no choice but to "take creative political leadership" on the matter, as his Chief of Urban affairs advised him in a memo (Skrentny 2014: 34). "OK," Nixon wrote in the margins (Stout 2012: 23).

The matter of releasing the report became moot when Glaser leaked it to the press in April 1970, further placing Nixon under the watchful eye of the civil sphere. Civil pressure from the feminist movement ultimately compelled Nixon to endorse nearly all the report's recommendations, and nineteen out of the twenty became law (Voss 2009). In fact, Nixon eventually appointed more than one hundred women to high-level administrative positions (Stout 2012: 84) and supported a host of anti-discrimination initiatives. He signed the Higher Education Amendments of 1972, which prohibited sex-based discrimination in federally funded educational institutions (Title IX); renewed and revised Lyndon Johnson's Executive Order 11375, directing federally contracted employers to submit timelines for promoting and hiring women; and gave the United States Commission on Civil Rights authority to investigate sex-based discrimination (Kotlowski 2001: 233).

As the women's movement caught fire, the ninety-second Congress (1971–72) passed more women's rights bills than all previous legislative sessions combined, and Nixon signed them (Freeman 1975). By building a favorable public opinion environment, the feminist movement had paved the way for the whirlwind of legislative and judicial victories in the early to mid 1970s (Klein 1984: 22). One key achievement was the congressional passage of the Equal Rights Amendment (ERA). The ERA campaign was a key vehicle through which feminists disseminated their demand for the civil repair of gender relations; arguing from a universalist position, they contended that gender and women's "difference" from men was a social construct rather than a natural condition. This contextualization allowed male domination to be labeled as a "sexist" intrusion into the democratic promise of civil equality (Alexander 2006: 258). Though introduced into Congress every year since 1923, male legislators had allowed the ERA to "gather dust" for over forty years, and women activists generated civil outrage by challenging the civility of their motives, accusing them of keeping the ERA under a "cloak of secrecy" (Moe 1969) and thereby impeding their fuller equality.

Nixon was personally lukewarm and politically evasive about the ERA. Yet activists, radical and liberal alike, channeled widespread public support into pressure on Nixon via protests and lobbying (see Shelton 1970; P. Shelton, 1970). With an eye toward his bid for re-election, Nixon finally endorsed it (Shelton 1972), and in 1972 the ERA passed in Congress with overwhelming majorities. The battle would now commence in the states, three-fourths of which would have to ratify for the ERA to take effect (Soule and King 2006).

It was during that same year, as Nixon launched his re-election campaign, that the women's movement managed, for the first time, to significantly affect the political platforms of the two parties – signaling a pivot toward what would soon become a close fusion between the movement and electoral politics (Young 2000: 32). In 1971, leading feminists, such as Betty Friedan, Gloria Steinem, Bella Abzug, and Shirley Chisholm, formed the National Women's Political Caucus (NWPC), a bi-partisan organization with the goal of electing women to office and influencing party platforms (Wolbrecht 2000: 35). Even as Nixon privately mocked the newly formed caucus in conversations with his top advisors, the NWPC warned, "Mr. Nixon is going to find out in 1972 that women will no longer let themselves be consigned . . . to the sidelines of political power" (Thomas 1971), reminding the President that they spoke on behalf of "the majority" (Shelton 1971). Publicly, Nixon did not want to be seen as taking feminism lightly. Republican Party strategists were keenly aware that feminism represented a "powerful source of change in the U.S. electorate" (Young 2000: 88), and such groups as the NWPC served as envoys for this shifting public consciousness. While both party platforms had been virtually silent on women's issues in 1968, by 1972 each featured lengthy sections on women's equity, thanks in no small part to the efforts of the NWPC (ibid: 92).

It was just after Nixon's landslide re-election that the Supreme Court gave every woman the legal right to abortion. In 1971, Nixon had actually ordered military hospitals to rescind their liberal abortion policies and backed the repeal of a liberal New York abortion law, hoping to woo Catholic voters (Kotlowski 2001: 251). Translating his backpedaling on abortion into the discourse of the civil sphere, feminists declared that Nixon was engaged in an anti-civil, "diabolical plot" to "keep women at home" (*The Hartford Courant* 1971; see also Shelton 1972). Armed with poll data on public support for abortion, which NOW activists insisted was "obviously" (*The Hartford Courant* 1971) what the public wanted – including, in fact, most Catholics (O'Brian 2020: 1042) – feminists exerted massive civil pressure on Nixon to change his position. In the middle of his re-election campaign, the President swiftly changed course. Nixon returned to his earlier position that it was a matter for the states to decide; he instructed his aids to "keep out" of the matter (Kotlowski 2001: 252) and made no efforts to restrict *Roe*'s scope after its passage (O'Connor and Epstein 1985: 219).

Nixon was no feminist (Skrentny 2014). There are certainly instances where he evaded feminist demands – most notably, by vetoing the Comprehensive Childcare Bill of 1971 (Kotlowski 2001), which would have offered universal childcare. Still, it was during Nixon's presidency, and with his grudging cooperation, that the women's movement truly became "a powerful force to reckon with" (Martin 2003: 166) *vis-à-vis* state power. This was made plain by *Newsweek* in 1972, which declared, "The person in Washington who has done the most for the women's movement may be Richard Nixon."

Anti-Feminist Backlash:
STOP-ERA Shifts the Tides of Public Opinion

Just when feminism's momentum seemed ineluctable, the cultural efflorescence and institutional codification of feminist ideals triggered a sharply anti-feminist counter-movement. Backlash against the front-lash movements of the 1960s had begun as early as Barry Goldwater's 1964 presidential campaign (McVicar 2016) and gained further traction under Nixon, who made explicit appeals to the "silent majority" of Americans disturbed by the onslaught of cultural and social change, including racial desegregation (Skrentny 2014: 16). During Gerald Ford's presidential tenure – during which all three branches of government were highly receptive to the mainstream feminist movement (Spruill 2018: 41) – the GOP viewed the antifeminist sentiments of a nascent "Religious Right" as antediluvian, representing a fringe segment of public opinion (Spruill 2017). It was not until Jimmy Carter's presidential bid in 1976 that the force of a newly ascendant religious and cultural conservatism would begin to more forcefully shape the contours of presidential politics (McVicar 2016: 1).

A focal point of mobilization for the counter-movement against feminism was the ERA, which fueled such resentment among conservative religious women that they created a series of organizations to defeat it, including Beverly LaHaye's Concerned Women for America and, most notably, Phyllis Schlafly's Eagle Forum (Schreiber 2017). Tapping into this simmering cultural resentment about feminism,

Schlafly connected with social conservatives across the nation through her newsletter, *The Phyllis Schlafly Report*, and televised debates with celebrity feminist figures (Critchlow and Stacheki 2008). The anti-ERA movement "spread like wildfire among traditional women," including fundamentalist Christians, evangelical Protestants, Roman Catholics, and Mormons, many of whom were previously uninvolved in the political arena (ibid: 165–8).

The anti-ERA movement dovetailed with the pro-life movement, each rooted in disdain for the "excesses" of liberalism and assailing the putatively arbitrary exercise of power by a bloated federal government using tax-payer dollars to pander to the demands of a narrow coterie of self-aggrandizing feminists (Wolbrecht 2000: 40;168; Klatch 1987). In this view, social engineering schemes to improve women's status (Flippen 2011: 242) represented anti-civil intrusions into the social lifeworld. By hitching the ERA to fears of government overreach, Schlafly's STOP-ERA campaign also garnered support from economic conservatives opposed to activist courts, "big government," and federal social welfare spending (Critchlow and Stacheki 2008: 168–169; Schreiber 2017: 9), contributing to an already-growing attenuation of public support for New Deal liberalism (Critchlow 2005: 302).

STOP-ERA advocates organized at the community and state level in key battleground states to transform public opinion against the ERA (Mansbridge 1986). Schlafly's success hinged on her ability to portray "women's libbers" as "intemperate" extremists (Schlafly in Critchlow 2005: 227), on the one hand, and anti-ERA activists as rational and altruistic on the other. She "exploited [NOW's] public image of radicalism" (Critchlow 2005: 229), which often flouted conventional political tactics in favor of more disruptive forms of public protest, equating such feminists with anti-civil incompetence. Schlafly also emphasized the "radical" consequences of the ERA, including such supposed civil intrusions as gender-neutral bathrooms and the inclusion of women in the military draft – which the majority of Americans disfavored (Mansbridge 1986: 164) – and the putative link between the ERA, abortion, and gay rights. Although contentious, many feminists had come to see these latter two issues as closely tied to women's rights (Mattingly 2015: 546).

Anti-ERA leaders, then, crystallized existing strands of public opinion by legitimizing concerns about cultural changes, further swaying public opinion by emphasizing a host of undesirable consequences the ERA could bring. Although their public campaign was implicitly centered on the religious conviction that women's primary role was in the domestic sphere, they did not present themselves as opposing the nation's central civil codes. They were careful, for example, always to emphasize that women had the right to choose whether to be homemakers *or* to pursue careers, while insisting that the majority of women chose the former, which they construed as "the most basic and precious legal right ... [of all]" (Schlafly in Schreiber 2017: 8). In other words, while feminists argued that patriarchal family relations undermined women's autonomy and served as a source of oppression, anti-feminist crusaders used the same civil metalanguage to argue that the ERA imposed an unwanted burden on women (see Klatch 1987). The movement, thus, gained traction by couching its public claims in universalizing rather than particularistic terms, making an appeal to the civil community at large. It was in this polarized public opinion environment that Carter entered office.

Carter and the Two Women's Movements

The ERA battle came to a head at the "International Women's Year" conference in Houston in November 1977, Carter's first year in office. Carter had pledged his full support of the ERA in his presidential campaign the previous year, assuring feminists that he "wanted to be known as the President who achieved equal rights for women" (Mattingly 2015: 538). Yet just a few months into his first term, upon observing the bitter tension and polarization the ERA produced, the President sought to distance himself from the IWY, declining an invitation to attend (Flippen 2011).

Carter warily kept tabs on the conference proceedings from the sidelines. Thousands of feminists attended, as well as a group of socially conservative delegates wearing yellow ribbons that said "majority" – iconizing their representation of the "mainstream." Meanwhile, Schlafly and the anti-ERA, anti-abortion, and anti-gay rights troops hosted a counter-conference the same day, the "Pro-Family Rally." Both conferences attracted significant media coverage, which further propelled the rapidly escalating "culture wars" into a national, mass-mediated social drama. While the IWY Conference was a powerful point of mobilization for feminists, the newly dubbed "pro-family" movement ultimately won the public relations battle (Flippen 2011: 147–149). Indeed, following the IWY, public support for the ERA in key non-ratifying states declined. By 1978, for example, a steep overall drop in ERA support was recorded among women in non-ratifying states, falling below 40% (Critchlow and Stacheki 2008: 158–163).

Throughout the ERA battle, STOP-ERA activists went head-to-head with feminists, portraying themselves as the true voice of women's interests and polluting feminists as an anti-democratic "well-financed and vocal minority," as the Alabama STOP-ERA chapter insisted in a letter to state legislators (Critchlow 2005: 225). Beverley LaHaye likewise asserted, "Feminists do not represent all women of America. It is the height of absurdity to suggest that all women are in lockstep march led by Betty Friedan and Gloria Steinem" (Rohlinger and Claxton 2017: 1). Anti-ERA activists were a constant lobbying presence in state legislatures, and ultimately convinced many that they spoke on behalf of "the public" as a whole, despite the fact that by 1980, 60 percent of women and 54 percent of men actually supported the ERA (Klein 1984: 159). In light of the ERA's increasing failure to gain traction at the state-level, Carter further distanced himself from the issue, loath to expend political capital on what by 1978 seemed certain to "be a losing cause" (Walker 2012: 364).

If a central factor in the STOP-ERA activists' success was their ability to transform anti-ERA strands of public opinion into a regulative force, failing to similarly translate pro-ERA strands of opinion was key to the failure of the feminist campaign. Because organizations like NOW and ERAmerica were primarily top-down and dedicated little time to grassroots lobbying, they failed in their efforts to turn "generalized public sympathy for reforms that benefit women into political pressure on specific legislators" (Mansbridge 1986: 4; Critchlow and Stacheki 2008: 165, 171). Unable to transform civil into state power at the grassroots, national women's groups and insider activists tried pressuring Carter directly to lobby more vigorously for the ERA, but to no avail. Despite feminists' privileged access to the state (Mattingly 2015) and greater financial and organizational strength than the counter-movement (Critchlow 2005), the civil power of the anti-ERA activists proved decisive. With the pro-family movement in the lead for the battle of public opinion in the state-level ratification process, the President felt backed into a corner. Failing to pick a side on the ERA, he angered both its supporters and its opponents.

The same equivocation marked the President's stance on abortion. A "born again" Christian, Carter assured his Southern religious constituencies that he supported an amendment to ban federal funding for abortion (the Hyde Amendment), while promising his Northern liberal constituencies that he was not in favor of outlawing abortion completely (McVicar 2016). Federal funding for abortion was a key plank in the IWY's "National Plan of Action," which also

54

included a call for government-sponsored childcare, shelters for "battered women," increased aid for people on welfare, and the elimination of legal discrimination against gay people (Flippen 2011: 150). These concerns reflected the radicalization of the mainstream liberal feminist movement in the late 1970s; feminist concerns had moved beyond equal legal rights, which reflected its white, middle-class bias, and toward more fundamental institutional change that would benefit minority and working-class women (Hartmann 1998: 228–229). Writings of feminist women of color in the 1970s and 1980s, including Audre Lorde, bell hooks, Toni Bambara, Frances Beale, and countless others, would change "the outlook of an entire political generation" (Whittier 1995: 98; Rosen 2000), inflecting, expanding, and unsettling the dominant liberal understanding of "universal rights."

The IWY's "Plan" had the potential to become a blueprint for presidential action, a direct translation of civil to state power. However, frontlash feminists were seeking to expand the very definition and scope of liberalism at the very moment when backlash movements were eroding public support for liberalism itself. Feeling constrained by "the increasingly conservative mood of the [White] electorate writ large" (Osgood and White 2014a: 7), President Carter implemented little of the Plan (Mattingly 2015). His acrimonious relationship with feminists was further strained when he demoted his aide Midge Costanza in mid 1978 for publicly speaking out against his stance on federally funded abortions, and fired Bella Abzug as co-chair of the IWY "National Advisory Committee" the following year for lambasting his failure to give the Plan adequate attention (Hartmann 1998: 227–228). "You're going to regret this," Abzug warned, and she was right: NOW and other women's organizations refused to endorse Carter for re-election (Walker 2012: 354). Caught between the fault lines of a civil sphere increasingly polarized between frontlash and backlash, Carter was unable to become a "collective representation" of America. Failing to align political with civil power, he increasingly appeared only a weakly civil figure and was forced out of office.

The culture wars over feminism paved the way for the consolidation of a powerful network of religious and political organizations midway through Carter's presidency. A revived conservative movement (the New Right) and a religious grassroots social movement (the Religious Right) both reflected and contributed to the increasingly conservative character of public opinion in the American electorate. GOP political operatives worked in tandem with such religious organizations as the Moral Majority and the Religious Roundtable to further meld the cultural politics of anti-feminism with larger conservative causes, including small government and free market economics (Spruill 2018: 47–52; McVicar 2016). In so doing, they crystallized existing strands of public opinion, naturalizing issue connections that many social conservatives already held (see Flippen 2011: 185, 242; Schreiber 2017: 9; cf. O'Brian 2020). This would set the stage for the "Reagan Revolution."

Reagan, Feminism, and the Religious Right

As the 1970s drew to a close, the boundaries between the civil sphere culture wars and party politics grew more and more porous, solidifying across party lines by 1980. Recognizing the electoral potential of groups like Eagle Forum and the Moral Majority, which now had half a million members (Coste 2016), Reagan forged what would become an enduring connection between the GOP, the pro-family movement, and the Religious Right (Milkis, Tichenor, and Blessing 2013; McVicar 2016). These groups' concerns were channeled directly into the 1980 GOP presidential platform, which included support for a "human life" amendment to federally prohibit abortion and, for the first time since 1940, failed to endorse the ERA (Freeman 2008).

Throughout his presidency, Reagan used the "bully pulpit" to advance anti-feminist policies consistent with the social conservative agenda, including restricting abortion access and funding; appointing outspoken opponents of *Roe* to the Supreme Court (Walker 2012: 388–414); cutting social programs that benefited single mothers and poor, minority women (Eisenstein 1987); and defunding federal agencies designed to support women and minorities, including the Women's Bureau (Sapiro 1986: 130). Adding insult to injury, by 1982, the ERA had officially failed, falling three states short of ratification (Soule and King 2006: 1872).

The setbacks feminists suffered under Reagan evince the workings of a powerful strain of religious and cultural conservatism that spoke on behalf of "majority" demands and excoriated the "minority of treacherous individuals" bent on destroying the country with their "godless, liberal philosophies" (Falwell in Spruill 2018: 60). Yet what is just as remarkable as these open pathways between backlash civil power and presidential power is how frontlash strands of feminist public opinion – whose roots continued to course deeply throughout the U.S. civil sphere – exerted significant checks on the presidency.

Indeed, the "overall rise in conservative political attitudes that characterized the eighties failed to carry over to public opinion toward women" (Costain 1992: 118). While many social conservatives associated longstanding conservative causes with the anti-feminist crusade, not all of those who championed conservative issues (e.g., laissez-faire conservatives) disfavored women's equality (see Klatch 1987). As Eisenstein observed, "Even though liberalism when defined as the social welfare state is rejected by many, the (liberal) notion of women's (legal and economic) equality is accepted by a majority of the public" (1987: 256). Although feminists faced a hostile White House, "feminist ideas had burrowed too deeply into our culture for any resistance or politics to root them out" (Rosen 2000: xv).

Social movement scholars have described the Reagan administration as a closed "political opportunity structure" that forced the organized women's movement into retreat (see reviews in Sawyers and Meyer 1999; Banaszak 2010). Blind to the cultural power of public opinion rooted in a civil sphere that sits outside the state, such a perspective fails to capture how feminist public consciousness was organized to curtail Reagan's political agenda. By the early 1980s, the mainstream women's movement had "institutionalized." In some part, this represented a natural progression as the movement achieved success (Ferree and Hess 1995: 130). In another part, however, this was due to a strategic push to lock in the gains that the Reagan administration threatened to roll back (Costain and Costain 1992). As various feminist sub-movements united under a common threat, the organized movement played defense (Whittier 1995; Spalter-Roth and Schreiber 1995; Ferree and Hess 1995).

While feminists had little direct control over the day-to-day actions of the White House, they knew they could "build on changes in public consciousness that were beyond the control of [the] presidential administration" (Bashevkin 1994: 692). Underscoring the threats the Reagan administration posed for women everywhere, feminists triggered a public outcry that transformed Reagan's antifeminist agenda into a political asset (Costain and Costain 1992). The membership and budgets of national women's groups, such as WEAL, NOW, and the NWPC, skyrocketed after the 1980 election (Sapiro 1986), and a host of new women's organizations emerged, such as EMILY's List and the National Political Congress of Black Women (Young 2000: 39), further enhancing the movement's visibility and political clout (Whittier 1995: 195). As one abortion rights activist recalls: "The irony is that during the Reagan/Bush years, we had money falling out of the skies. People genuinely believed reproductive rights were deeply in danger" (Bashevkin 1994: 693).

A key way in which feminists politicized the Reagan threat was giving name to, and generating public awareness of, a newly emergent "gender gap" in public opinion. Analyzing the 1980 election, pollsters identified a gendered discrepancy in voting patterns, in which more men than women voted for Reagan – 54 percent versus 46 percent (Bonk 1988: 85). Feminists jumped on this data, commissioning public opinion polls and publishing survey data regularly in the mass media, in NOW's monthly "Gender Gap Report," at the Democratic National Convention, and in books (Bonk 1988; Wolbrecht 2000). Most studies indicate that the gap actually did not result from explicitly feminist issues such as abortion and the ERA but, instead, from Reagan's social welfare policies and his defense and foreign policy agenda (Sapiro 1986: 134). Empirical facts are one thing, cultural constructions of reality another. Women activists tied the gender gap to a host of feminist concerns, building a feminized construction of public opinion and, in turn, harnessing it as a political tool.

The gender gap served as a vehicle through which feminists could speak "as" half of the members of the public "to" the public and its legislators. The politicization of the gender gap successfully demonstrated to politicians on both sides of the political divide the electoral consequences of antifeminism, and Reagan was no exception. The President had especially low approval ratings among women in both parties in the early years of his presidency (Mueller 1988a: 31) and took measures to close the gender gap prior to his 1984 bid for reelection. In order to address the so-called "woman problem," he created various policy boards and task forces centered on women's legal equity (Walker 2012) and made highly visible female appointments to his cabinet, including such Republican moderates as Elizabeth Dole and Margaret Heckler (Bonk 1988). More notably, to the great ire of social conservatives, the avowedly anti-affirmative action Reagan made good on his campaign promise to appoint the Supreme Court's first woman, Sandra Day O'Connor, who had previously voiced support for *Roe* (O'Connor and Epstein 1985). Despite the vitriol of the Religious Right and the apprehensiveness of Reagan's staffers, the President even got personally involved in the push for the Senate to confirm his nomination: "Clearly, American society was ready for a female Supreme Court Justice, and Ronald Reagan had felt this and had been ready to take a real risk to make it happen" (Coste 2016: 9).

Hoping to appeal to young working women, Reagan also promoted legislation centered on child support payments, increases in childcare tax credits for working mothers, tax code changes reducing the "marriage penalty" for households with two wage-earners, and pension reform (Mueller 1988a; Bonk 1988; Sanbonmatsu 2002). Feminists attributed these achievements to their gender gap strategy; indeed, as Ann Smith, director of the Congressional Caucus for Women's Issues, proclaimed, the gender gap represented "the basic mechanism that powers the whole thing" (in Sanbonmatsu 2002: 205).

In the 1984 GOP platform, Reagan retained his anti-abortion and "family values" commitments. At the same time, women's issues occupied a more significant part of the GOP platform than ever before, Reagan strategists having worked to ensure that nearly half of the delegates at the Republican National Convention were women (Freeman 2008: 108). His advisors had recognized that "it would probably be political suicide to make oneself an obstacle on the path of women" (Coste 2016: 10). Reagan won the election, winning 56 percent of the (primarily White) women's vote, having narrowed the gender gap by two percent (Mueller 1988a: 34).

Although Reagan's second term backsliding on "social" issues can be overstated, there is no doubt that feminist public opinion and organizational pressure was one of the principal reasons he turned his attention more to matters of foreign policy concerns and defense (see Milkis, Tichenor, and Blessing 2013: 661–2; Eisenstein 1987: 257; Costain 1992: 113). As one columnist observed, it was "striking how much loyalty Ronald Reagan won from [the Religious Right] without delivering much to them at all . . . There was no school-prayer amendment, no anti-abortion amendment, no [religious] school-choice program" (in Martin 2003: 309–310). Indeed, Reagan's commitment to outlawing abortion ultimately remained largely symbolic (O'Connor and Epstein 1985; Walker 2012; Sapiro 1986). Public opinion polls consistently indicated that only about twenty percent of all Americans supported a complete ban on abortion (Walker 2012: 387; Ferree and Hess 1995: 165), and feminists leveraged this opinion data in protest events and lobbying efforts (see Bashevkin 1994: 693). The President's advisors feared that a strong commitment to banning abortion would alienate millions of voters, and, thus, urged him to "[give] the lead" to Congress (Coste 2016: 8) and to the states. As a result of pressure from a deeply "feminized" civil sphere, Reagan shied away from the issue.

In this chapter, we have documented, historical case after historical case, how presidential power has been checked and sometimes checkmated, energized, and sometimes rocket-fueled, by cultural currents in the civil sphere and the feminist movement that crystallized them.

We have charted a cultural sociology of feminism that interprets the long sweep of women's struggles in the framework of a sociological theory that connects social movements with presidential power and examines public opinion as the crucial hinge in-between. This hinge can swing both ways, pulled open by progressive frontlash, pushed shut by conservative backlash. Yet, whichever direction it swings, movements work to represent themselves as the voice of the opinions that represent the normative aspirations of the civil sphere.

— 3 —

#METOO AS SOCIETALIZATION

How do endemic, ongoing institutional strains suddenly burst their sphere-specific boundaries and become explosive scandals in society at large? *Intra*-institutional authorities typically "handle" even severe institutional strains. This has the effect of making such strains relatively invisible and untroubling to those on the outside. Problems become crises only when they move outside their own spheres and appear to endanger society at large. This broader movement can be understood as a process of societalization (Alexander 2018, 2019b). It is triggered only when the discourses and material resources of the civil sphere are brought into play. When sphere-specific problems become societalized, routine strains become sharply scrutinized, once lauded institutions are ferociously criticized, elites are threatened and punished, and far-reaching institutional reforms are launched and sometimes achieved.

What is Societalization?

The civil sphere is a real social force, but it is also an idealized community, one that is imagined as being composed of individuals who are autonomous yet mutually obligated, who experience solidarity even as they respect each other's independence (Alexander 2006; Kivisto and Sciortino 2015; Alexander and Tognato 2018; Alexander, Lund, and Voyer 2019a; Alexander, Stack, and Khosrokhavar 2019c; Alexander 2021). In cultural terms, the civil sphere is organized around a discourse that sacralizes the motives, relations, and institutions necessary to sustain democratic forms of self-regulation and social solidarity. This includes qualities such as honesty, rationality, open-ness, independence, cooperation, participation, and equality (Jacobs 1996a, 2000; Mast 2006, 2012; Smith 1991, 2005). The discourse of civil society is binary; it identifies and pollutes qualities that endanger democracy, such as deceit, hysteria, dependence, secrecy, aggression, hierarchy, and inequality. The civil sphere, moreover, is not only discursive. It possesses powerful materiality, via factual and fictional communicative institutions and powerful regulative institutions backed by state coercion.

Vis-à-vis other, *non*-civil institutional-cum-cultural fields, the civil sphere is at once oppositional and aspirational. That is why nothing about the location and traction of civil boundaries is certain; they cannot be ascertained in the abstract (Ku 1998). What is deemed civil? What is deemed not to be? These questions have been answered in remarkably disparate ways over the course of historical time. Is gender hierarchy a family affair, handled by the domestic sphere's patriarchal elite, or is it experienced as violating broader, more civil norms (Alexander 2001; Luengo 2018)? Does what goes on inside a church stay within its walls, a matter between believers and their god, or is the dispensation of God's grace subject to civil scrutiny? Is an exploitative capitalist economy left alone to work its markets for better and for worse, or do more civil considerations have the right to intervene (Thumala Olave 2018; Lee 2019; Ngai and Ng 2019; Alexander 2019b: 39–54)? Civil spheres have continually legitimated what later came to be seen as egregiously anti-civil practices. Civil spheres are restless. Even as their ideals are compromised, their utopian promises continuously trigger radical criticism, social movement struggles, social crises, and institutional reform.

In this chapter, I conceptualize the relative, labile, and shifting status of social problems, not in historical or interactional terms, but analytically, as a systemic process. One might imagine, at T_1, a hypothetical "steady state" of boundary relations between civil and non-civil spheres, in which, from a bird's-eye view, there *appears* to be social stability and there is *imagined* to be reciprocity between spheres.[1] In such a putatively steady state, most civil sphere members do not experience the operations of other spheres as destructive intrusions; they do not feel compelled to shred existing institutional boundaries to mount antagonistic efforts to repair another sphere's insides.

In real time, every social sphere experiences continuous, often severe strain. In the economy, there are selfish economic decisions and irresponsible losses, bankruptcies and thefts, destructive inflations and recessions. The religious world experiences continual financial corruption, wrenching disciplinary and recruiting failures, and polarizing theological disputes. In the world of mass communication, the boundaries between privacy and publicity are repeatedly violated, professional norms are cast aside, plagiarism is frequent, and media elites often conflate financial self-interest with professional responsibility. In the familial sphere, patriarchal power has generated a long string of abuses, from the verbal abuse of women's capacity for autonomy to the violent suppression of it.

In conditions of steady state, however, such strains are institutionally insulated; because they remain intra-sphere, they do not generate much attention outside. Indeed, subject to intra-institutional logics (Friedland and Alford 1991), strains often bolster rather than challenge organizational authority. Rather than appearing to degrade civil sphere ideals, such strain-in-steady-state may seem to affirm democratic pluralism.

Steady state breaks down with societalization. A practice that once aroused little interest outside a particular institution now appears threatening to society itself. Matter out of place (Douglas 1966), it becomes something morally polluting, and strenuous efforts at purification are made (Alexander 1988a; Cottle 2004).

Societalization begins when a semiotic code is triggered (T_2), moving public attention space (Hilgartner and Bosk 1988) from institutional part to civil whole. Critical and emancipatory narratives now arise, and vast material resources can be brought into play. When ordinary occurrences become events (Mast 2006, 2012; Sewell 1996; Wagner-Pacifici 2017), confidence and trust give way to fear and alarm. Harsh regulatory interventions may follow (T_3), for the civil sphere's communicative and regulatory institutions intertwine. In response to critical cultural and regulatory interventions, however, backlash builds up (T_4). Institutional elites targeted by the civil sphere strike back, and where to draw the line between spheres becomes a matter of bitter struggle. Standoff, not problem-solving, marks the pathway back to steady state (T_5).

When the moral and institutional foundations of society seem endangered, anxieties frequently focus on the institution of office, a key regulative institution of the civil sphere (Alexander 2006: 132–50; Alexander 2023). At the heart of every democratic society is the fervent belief that power can be exercised for the public good, that powerful office not only should but also can be occupied by good-willed human beings.[2] For civil spheres to have teeth, those who possess power must be bound by a vocation, an ethics of office (Weber 1927 [1904–5]). Office translates abstract discourse about civil morality into the institutional demand that leaders act on behalf of others, eschewing nepotism and self-dealing. When semiotic shift defines a strain as endangering the civil center (Shils 1975a), institutional authorities are accused of failing their office obligations, triggering strenuous efforts to remove them.

Why Does Societalization Happen?

How is it possible that a temporal sequence can unfold in response to critical interpretations of strains, such that steady states are undermined, crises mushroom, and civil repairs become possible, before backlashes emerge and boundaries between spheres rebuild?

At the most general level, the reason is social differentiation, which not only separates the culture and organization of institutional spheres but, contrary to functionalist lore, makes their spheres of justice (Walzer 1984) often seem incompatible. Beyond the fact of agonistic spheres, a relatively autonomous civil sphere is the "mechanism" (Gross 2009; Norton 2014a) at the heart of the machine.

But who actually carries the water? Who evokes the discourse? Whose institutional prerogatives feel raw and bristled? Who and what are the civil sphere's elites? There are *agents* of societalization. Societalization is not only about systems, spheres, and institutions. It is also about social actors whose identities and roles compel them to societalize, and whose material status is vastly enhanced if they succeed.[3] Journalists and prosecutors have an interest in ferreting out what they see as civil violations, which they call "holy shit stories" (Havill 1993: 68) and "red hot cases" (Samuelsohn 2017).

At the micro-level, societalization can be conceptualized as a series of performances and counter-performances (Alexander 2011; Alexander et al. 2006; Mast 2016; Norton 2014b; Reed 2013). Investigative journalists scan the social horizon for big stories, hoping to lob incriminating constructions to citizen-audiences who will fuse with their indignant narrations, sharing their rage. Editors place what they judge to be seriously egregious reports about civil calumny on the front page, at the top of the hour, at the beginning of the digital news feed. Publishers supply critical resources for such endeavors and then watch their behinds. Prosecutors circle like hungry birds of prey, scanning with hawk eyes, itching to come in for the kill. Special investigators search for examples of malfeasance, issue arrest warrants, organize evidence and precedent, sequester grand juries, issue damning reports, and demand harsh penalties. If civil agents succeed, they gain not only a deep sense of personal vindication, but social glory – fame, stardom, prizes, wealth, and higher office await.[4]

Audiences are primed to be receptive to such civil performances by virtue of their belief that civil discourse is sacred, that its ideals must be protected from harm. Such background belief is necessary, but it is not sufficient. Only if these general codes have been organized into established "scandal genres" will reports of civil crimes be credible, and moral and emotional significance assigned. If pedophilia has already been powerfully scandalized, if yellow journalism has long been criticized and feared, if male chauvinism has frequently been harshly criticized, then the symbolic structures and memories of scandal provide background representations against which contemporary performances of civil indignation can arouse indignation (cf. Hunt, Benford, and Snow 1994). But at T_1, scandal genres lay latent; only if these background representations are triggered by skilled performers, via code-switching scripts (T_2) and intrusive regulation (T_3), will civil repair proceed – until backlash (T_4) intervenes.

When performances of civil indignation succeed, journalists and prosecutors are hailed as heroes of the civil sphere, larger than life figures whose daring deeds are held to exemplify truth, justice, and "the American way" (Bradlee 1995: 384). For the members of their occupations, they become sacred icons of exemplary professional practice (Bradlee 1995: 369; Revers 2017). Hagiographic biographies recount their glory, spinning tales of civil crusades (Stone 1963) and David versus Goliath (Havill 1993: 72). Often derided as selfish and strategic by the non-civil elites they target, civil agents see themselves as inspired by a sense of "mission" (Graham 1997: 434), by a "noble calling" (Hallock 2010: xvi) that holds "the keys to the gates of justice" (Dees 2011: 348). They are motivated, not by money, but by a "yearning to make a difference" (Bradlee 1995: 94; Friend 2015: 30).

Civil agents present themselves as vessels of transcendental morality, as arbiters of truth and standard bearers of openness and reason, describing the non-civil elites who oppose them as deceptive, secretive, and irrational (Ben-Veniste 2009; Bradlee 1991; Bradlee Jr. 2002; Friend 2015; Graham 1997: 457).[5] The powerful rich pray upon virtuous citizens; civil heroes attack hierarchy and defend independence (Beeson 2015; Ben-Veniste 2009; Comey 2013; Darrow 1961; Dees 2011; Henderson 2016; Morgenstern 2015; Russell 1933; Scott 2015).

Privately, civil agents often seethe with spluttering outrage and distemper, engage in fantasies of murderous revenge, and are motivated by boundless self-regard and ambition (Allen 2007; Friend 2015; Guthrie 2014; Meacham 2011; Roberts 2017). Those who mythologize them as civil heroes see them as altruistic, almost saintly figures who sacrifice for the common good (Havill 1993; Hofstadter 1955; Scott 2015)

Why Does Societalization Not Happen?

When prosecutors brandish evidence of fraud and bribery, they cannot always make it stick, and when tenacious reporters and editors publish outraged exposés, they do not always inflame. Scandal is performed, but audiences do not exclaim (Bradlee 1995: 409). This points to the existence of limit conditions to the societalization process.

Fully enunciated sequences of societalization are more exception than rule. Significant institutional strains usually do not trigger critical journalism. Code switching from intra-institutional to civil criteria fails to fuse with citizen-audiences. When societalization is triggered, it often stalls. When it does not stall, societalization can lead to spiraling conflicts that undermine the civil sphere rather than repairing it.

Marginalization

Societalization is blocked or stalled to the degree that those subject to institutional strain and dysfunction are subaltern groups (Fraser 1992). When stigmatized populations are hived off into segregated institutions and communities, the strains they are subjected to, and their agentic adaptations to them, are invisible to, or ignored by, those whose perceptions are mediated by the communicative institutions of the dominant civil sphere and whose actions are regulated thereby.[6]

This was certainly the case for the predations suffered by manual workers in early industrial capitalism (Marshall 1965); for Jews in medieval and early modern European societies (Trachtenberg 1961); for colonized peoples under imperialism (Said 1978); for South African Blacks under Apartheid rule (Frederickson 1981); for African Americans subject to slavery, Jim Crow, and Northern ghettoization (Frederickson 1971); for Irish Catholics in Northern Ireland after the end of the civil war and before the Good Friday agreements (Kane 2019, 2022); for women in patriarchal societies (Pateman 1988) and for gay men and lesbians in heteronormative ones (Seidman 1992).

It was unlikely that the strains and impositions to which such marginalized groups were subject would be reported in mainstream media; when such reports did appear, they would rarely generate code switching (Jacobs 2000). Core groups imagine such peripheral persons as less than fully human, as lacking civil capacity (Landes 1998). Indeed, to protect themselves from pollution by these putatively dangerous others, central groups engage in hostile aggression rather than empathic societalization, withdrawing to privileged enclaves rather than reaching out to under-privileged communities (Massey and Denton 1993).

In the face of such deeply rooted blockages to societalization, other kinds of responses to strain may arise, responses that can provide less direct pathways to amelioration. Social movements can emerge, some moderate, others more radical, confronting rigid hierarchies and projecting felicitous performances of injustice (Eyerman 2006; Eyerman and Jamison 1991; Kane 2019, 2022; Ostertag 2019). Intellectuals can make scathing critiques, and social scientists can launch far-reaching investigations; white papers can be published, and religious jeremiads made (Smith and Howe 2015).

Such social-cum-cultural reactions to blocked societalization appeal to an idealized civil sphere free from the destructive compromises that have legitimated marginalization in the actually existing civil spheres of the day. If such protests gain traction (Snow and Benford 1988: 205), they affect the collective representations against which subaltern institutional strains are viewed and excused. Indignant, counter-hegemonic narratives arise about abusive, anti-civil domination. These leave traces in the collective conscience, memories that dig the grooves along which future episodes of societalization can run, widening the reach of existing scandal genres and creating new ones as well. There is a gradual accretion of melodramatic stories about the pathos of sexual abuse, pedophilia, financial corruption, and reckless and irresponsible journalism. Such narratives project new civil heroes, recounting individuals and movements that courageously resisted anti-civil forces and institutions and triumphed in the end (Branch 1988; Cott 1987; Pfohl 1977). If such a reservoir of sacred and profane is not a sufficient condition for successful societalization, it is certainly a necessary one. Priestly pedophilia was a long-standing underground narrative in Western societies (Jenkins 1996). Only after pedophilia came under broad and increasing scrutiny in the last three decades of the twentieth century (Pfohl 1977), however, did a scandal genre emerge that eventually allowed the societalization of churchly practices.

Polarization

If societies are sharply divided against themselves, even such growing recognition of anti-civil abuse is not enough. Social indignation can become refracted in a manner that fails to engage the full horizon of common concern. The paradoxical result is that, rather than expanding solidarity, societalization may actually intensify division, a deepening polarization that can lead to the weakening, and sometimes even destruction, of the civil sphere, rather than to its strengthening and repair.

Consider the enslavement of African Americans in the antebellum United States. Abolition movements created increasing sensitivity to slavery and eventually massive indignation. However, the outrage was experienced primarily among Northern, not Southern, whites. The former began to experience code switch, but Northern media projections failed to fuse with broad audiences in the white South. Over time, those who promoted the societalization of slavery and those who blocked it came to see one another as irredeemably anti-civil, as enemies who must be physically destroyed if their respective Northern and Southern civil spheres were to be preserved. After decades of communicative and regulatory failure, force seemed the only way. Only after military victory were Northern civil institutions able to intrude into the Southern civil sphere and begin efforts to repair it, a "Reconstruction" that was itself eventually rolled back (Foner 1988).

Or consider the societalization of antisemitism in nineteenth and early twentieth-century Europe (Alexander and Adams 2023). Over the course of these decades, Western European societies introduced civil repairs, some dramatic, some incremental. These changes began to allow Jewish incorporation, providing once excluded Jewish people with political, economic, and cultural citizenship. Such a societalizing dynamic, however, began to fuel extraordinary blowback, with deepening chasms opening up between more cosmopolitan and more primordial cultural and political forces and their elites. In France, after Jewish incorporation had proceeded apace throughout much of the nineteenth century, the Dreyfus Affair exploded in the 1890s. Public expression of antisemitic sentiment dramatically increased, deepening political and cultural polarization and setting the stage for Vichy's collaboration with Nazi Occupation four decades later (Griffiths 1991; Marrus and Paxton 1981). In Germany, where Jews had been even more rapidly incorporated than in France, the backlash was much more brutal. The societalization of antisemitism had the perverse effect of inflaming Jew-hatred, significantly contributing to the destruction of the German civil sphere, which in turn allowed the annihilation of German Jewry itself.

Yet, despite the obdurate divisions that block the possibilities for societalization and vitiate its effects, it is the premise of this chapter – and, indeed, of this entire book – that civil spheres remain a vigorous cultural and material presence in modern societies and that, insofar as they sustain an independent power, they can challenge the particularistic discourses and institutional demands of separate spheres. The discourse of civil society is utopian and solidaristic, and the civil sphere's communicative and regulative institutions have the power to project this moral language beyond the boundaries of separate spheres and powerfully reconstruct them.

Yet, even as societalization gives way to the illusion of steady state, the civil sphere remains restless, ready to fight another day. Societalization revives what Plato called the memory of justice. For the philosopher, justice is an ideal form implanted inside every human being. For the sociologist, the memory of justice is not born but made.

#MeToo

#MeToo societalized sexual harassment in the workplace. For the entire history of modern society, such sexual mistreatment had been insulated from the civil sphere, safely hidden from its reach. This compromised the civil sphere, in turn delimiting its utopian qualities – freedom, equality, and solidarity – by defining them in a gendered manner that gave men sexual power over women.

For most of the civil sphere's history, women were not part of it. They participated almost exclusively in the domestic sphere of emotional intimacy, parenting, and reproduction, and inside this non-civil sphere they were subject to the authority of men – an institutional elite, a class, a status group, a patriarchy that defined values, dominated subordinates, and regulated their actions and interests. Not only work outside the home but sexual relations inside it were male prerogatives. If women suffered, and they often did, sometimes quite horribly, their cries were not heard by the wider society. Because they were marginalized, their suffering could not be societalized. Even when female subalterns were beloved, as frequently they were, their male devotees deemed them as thoroughly non-civil: irrational, hysterical, weak, dependent, and secretive. Without civil standing morally and legally, much less institutionally, women were not accorded a role in determining their sexual relations. They could not speak publicly or even privately about their sexual lives. When they made efforts to resist male sexual domination, their efforts were routinely dismissed as insincere, as strategic, perhaps even as seduction in disguise.

Feminism initiated the civil repair of patriarchy, breaking through the wall that had been erected between civil and intimate spheres, and reconstructing the status of women (Chapters 1 and 2, above). First and second-wave feminism were not only political movements concerned with mobilizing power, or legal efforts to expand citizenship; they were also, and perhaps above all, cultural efforts to redefine the nature of womanhood, among marginalized women and also for the male core group itself. If women were conceived as rational, they would be allowed to vote; if autonomous, they could own property; if open and honest, they could enter into public life; if strong, they could work outside the home. Feminism challenged the civil representation of masculinity, creating counter-narratives that polluted male domination. Claiming men were less paternal than patriarchal, less concerned with loving and caring than exercising power and control, feminism created affecting, melodramatic stories about the pathos of sexism, about women as an oppressed class, and about courageous female heroes fighting against it.[7] Feminism sketched a new utopia of gender civility, of a world defined, not by hierarchy and coercion, but by horizontal and consensual relations between women and men.[8] Feminist political and cultural performances transformed the consciousness not only of women but of many men as well. Those who scripted and acted out these performances became honored, not only as successful strategists but as civil heroes – Elisabeth Cady Stanton, Betty Friedan, Gloria Steinem, to name only a few.

Workplace Sexual Harassment in the Steady State

If the second-wave feminism of the late twentieth century effected revolutionary transformations, however, its success was far from complete. Feminist social and cultural movements became routinized, and the societalizing episodes that marked effervescent moments of civil repair eventually returned to steady state. Feminism allowed women to move out of the domestic sphere and into the workplace, but social problems associated with patriarchy remained. In the economic arena, women were still broadly subject to male power and frequently to sexual taunts, threats, coercion, and physical violation. Women were in the workforce, but they were still not fully fledged members of the civil sphere. In principle, they had access to legal rights and other protections of civil regulation; in practice, they remained second-class citizens, vulnerable to arbitrary practices that violated democratic principles. Female employees were often represented as intellectually inferior and emotionally immature, rationales that allowed male supervisors to slight them as workers and focus on their sexuality. Women's accounts of their mistreatment were usually ignored; when their stories were attended to, they were rarely believed. Male domination had moved from the sphere of intimacy to the institutions of economic life, and it remained largely insulated from civil surveillance. Men occupied most of the higher positions, made the big bucks and the big decisions; women were underneath, supposedly fortunate to be there at all.

In the 1980s and 1990s, women appearing before the Georgia state legislature were subject to catcalls and whistles, a practice so routine that women created an idiom for it – "talking under your dress" (*Atlanta Journal Constitution* 3/16/18). As a female state legislator who had served since the 1980s recounted, "it was almost an unspoken rule [that] it was no big deal, it was just for fun. It was always couched as a joke. At that time, sexual harassment was not really a word" (ibid.). Sexual harassment wasn't a "word" because male prerogative in the workplace – mental, moral, organizational, and sexual – was considered mundane and routine. "The fact that this is so prevalent," a Colorado woman complained, "so pedestrian that it no longer stands out when it happens, is inherently wrong" (*Colorado Springs Independent* 11/8/17a).

In the decades preceding #MeToo, everyday male behavior inside workplaces was episodically polluted as sexual harassment. A scattering of powerful men in politics (*WP* 12/7/17), entertainment (*Hollywood Reporter* 5/3/18), and science (*Huffington Post* 4/7/11) were exposed, morally sanctioned, and forced out of public life. They were represented as a few rotten apples, men who had stepped over the line, the very sanctioning of whom demonstrated that the bushel was mostly filled with good fruit. Sexually aggressive men who stepped up to the line but not over it continued to be described, with envious, barely muted admiration, as "womanizers." Women's stories of outrage and injury, let alone efforts at legal redress, continued to be routinely pushed aside. In New York City, in 2015, Ambra Battilana Gutierrez came to the police with an inflammatory accusation against Harvey Weinstein. Wired for her next meeting with Weinstein, Gutierrez returned with incriminatory audiotape (*NYT* 10/17/17). Yet the office of the Manhattan District Attorney, Cyrus

Vance, Jr., declined to press charges. "We had the evidence," attested an official who had been involved in the investigation, "more than enough evidence to prosecute Weinstein," adding it "as a case that made me angrier than I thought possible, and I have been on the force a long time" (*New Yorker* 10/10/17).

Such was the insulation of the steady state. Only societalization could transform such routine behavior into something polluted and profane.

Code Switch

The regulatory institutions of the American civil sphere remained quiescent, but the communicative institutions began to bridle with resentment and to stiffen with investigative ambition. In winter and spring 2016, as Donald Trump vanquished his rivals for the Republican presidential nomination, the incendiary far-right politician unleashed venomous attacks on mainstream news media, accusing them of creating false facts, threatening them with bankruptcy, even offering support for physical assaults on journalists. As the ideal and material interests of the communicative elite came under increasing threat, the media publicly interpreted some right-wing leaders not merely as anti-civil in the political-ideological sense but as exercising sexual domination.

Polarization blocks societalization

Candidate Trump dragged behind him a kite's tail of brazen womanizing, represented in mainstream journalism as part of his bullying, bragging, and abusive anti-civil persona. In early October 2016, the *Washington Post* revealed a decade-old tape recording of Trump boasting to a celebrity-news reporter, "When you're a star, they let you do it. You can do anything . . . Grab 'em by the pussy. You can do anything" (*NBC News* 10/7/16). These misogynist boasts were immediately denounced not only by leading Democrats but by mainstream Republicans as well. Yet in the thermonuclear heat of the Presidential election campaign, the controversy had the unexpected effect of allowing charges of anti-civil sexuality to be plausibly contextualized as expressions of political polarization.

The October revelation about Trump's malevolent misogyny sat between two explosive news investigations that appeared to confirm the connection between ideology, sexual abuse, and media accusation. In July 2016, an investigative journalist at *New York* magazine documented decades of workplace sex abuse by Roger Ailes, the legendary founder and President of the conservative television channel Fox News. Reporting on lawsuits Fox News employees had launched against Ailes, the exposé depended on gumshoe investigation and lengthy, first-time-ever interviews. When Ailes was forced to resign in late July, members of the journalist elite hailed it as a professional coup, but also as a victory for journalism's civil ambition. "Journalists are highly competitive, but every once in a while, a reporter is so far out ahead on a continuing story that all the rest of us can do is acknowledge the obvious," the *Washington Post* effused (*WP* 8/2/16), adding that the ramifications of this highwire performance went way beyond individual recognition. For the first time, journalism was breaking through the wall insulating workplace sexual abuse from civil evaluation. "Fox News has been notoriously secretive about its inner workings, aggressively managing its public image," the *Post* opined, and the reporter who had broken the story asserted, "now the curtain is fully open and it's incredibly creepy, dark and disturbing" (ibid.). Combining the personal with the institutional, *New York*'s executive editor attested to the courageous agency of the reporter: "It's really remarkable what he's done – he's exposed a corporate culture of sexism, harassment and misogyny" (ibid.).

This exposure, however, was taken as a window into the sexual abuse of power at Fox News, not as illuminating a systemic social problem. It was widely interpreted as an attack on right-wing media by a liberal media institution under siege, and this framing seemed only to be confirmed by the *Post*'s anti-Trump revelations three months later during the heart of the campaign. If media exposure of abuse were equated with partisan wrangling, then the possibility of *generalizing* workplace sexual harassment – of attacking it as a broad social problem, and of making efforts at civil repair – was blocked.

That polarization blocked societalization was further evidenced the following spring, in April 2017, when the *New York Times* revealed that Fox News had secretly paid out $13 million to protect its immensely influential conservative talk show host, Bill O'Reilly, from sexual harassment charges leveled by female Fox employees (*NYT*: 4/1/17). While O'Reilly was forced to resign, the event was reconstructed in a highly partisan manner. For the left, O'Reilly's wrongdoing seemed like an object lesson in right-wing sexual politics. The inverse was true for the right, who viewed the exposure of O'Reilly as yet another underhanded, distorted leftist political play.

Spread over ten months, these three exposés had breached the wall separating civil from non-civil spheres, repeatedly exposing the social problem of workplace sexual domination. Yet polarization prevented this newly visible social problem from being societalized, from being broadly understood as a deep and systemic danger, one that threatened the premises of the civil sphere itself.

The Weinstein exposé breaks through

On October 5, 2017, all this changed. The *New York Times* published the results of a year-long investigation into sexual misconduct inside the heart of Hollywood (*NYT* 10/5/17), a geographical location, a factory of globally influential art and fancy, and an ideological confabulation for liberal writers, producers, and actors that conservatives loved to hate. Not only was Harvey Weinstein, the object of the *Times* investigation, the most influential and highly visible mogul in this privileged and powerful world, but he was famously liberal, an activist with close ties to leftist causes and leading Democratic politicians, financially and personally. Eight months into the vituperatively anti-liberal Trump presidency, in the midst of the left's furious anti-Trump resistance, the *Times*' takedown of Weinstein seemed to expose the hypocrisy of preachy and self-righteous liberal ideas. Many conservative commentators jumped on the #MeToo bandwagon, gleefully claiming that liberals had always been among the worst sexual offenders. "The whole 'forgive me, I'm a liberal' thing won't protect him [Weinstein] now," wrote conservative *Times*' columnist Ross Douthat, "but it was part of his carapace for decades" (*NYT* 10/7/17). Conservative polemicist Anne Coulter claimed that "the breakthrough of the #MeToo movement was that it was finally acceptable to call out liberal sexual predators. Until recently, it was OK to rape and even murder girls – but only if your name was 'Clinton,' 'Kennedy' or 'Weinstein,' et al" (*Breitbart News* 9/19/18). Suggesting "those who shout the loudest are often times the ones most guilty," right-wing commentator Glenn Beck wrote that "Weinstein brought a nationwide spotlight on something that everyone in Hollywood already knew [but] didn't want out in the public ... until now" (*Glennbeck.com* 2018). Fox News star Sean Hannity opined: "It's great what Oprah did by standing up for victims of sexual misconduct and abuse. I think it's awesome. But we can't forget that misconduct is and has been rampant in Hollywood for decades . . . There's a lot of hypocrites out there on this specific issue" (*Hannity* 2018).

The *Times*' exposé had placed a famously liberal Hollywood mogul into the same boat as Ailes, O'Reilly, and Trump himself, portraying him, if anything, in a more decidedly savage way. But that, of course, was precisely the point. What the four men had in common, the sum of the four media exposés demonstrated, was not their political ideology, but their willingness to put their institutional power at the service of their hunger for sexual domination.[9]

The prize-winning investigation by *Times* reporters Jodi Kantor and Megan Twohey exposed the salacious and corrupt doings of a single, uniquely powerful Hollywood mogul. At the same time, the story represented Weinstein's insidious activities as ideal-typical, as a case study of how elites sustain intra-institutional control at the expense of the civil sphere. The reporters documented the sexual appetites of a powerful and predatory man, but they also described what happens when civil culture and institutions fail to exercise regulatory control. In the process, Harvey Weinstein became less man than object lesson, his story a parable about the dangers that male sexual desire, rampant still in the post-feminist workplace, posed to civil life. Kantor and Twohey exposed not only sex abuse but, perhaps even more centrally, "abuse of power" (*NYT* 10/5/17): as the *Los Angeles Times* editorialized, how "powerful men still believe they can get away with harassing less powerful women" (*Los Angeles Times*, 10/7/17). Kantor and Twohey documented what happens when male lust is uncontrolled by the morality of office and civil obligation. They devoted relatively little attention to the details of Weinstein's sexual predation, but a great deal of attention to how he managed to hide such heinous misconduct from the civil light of day. Their findings were nested inside the critical, judgmental binaries of the civil sphere's moralizing discourse. When *Times* executive editor Dean Baquet accepted the Pulitzer Prize for public service reporting in Spring 2018, he represented the newspaper's achievement neither in professional nor in political-ideological terms; instead, employing the language of the civil sphere, he spoke of gender and sexual justice. "By revealing secret settlements, persuading victims to speak and bringing powerful men to account," Baquet declared, "we spurred a world-wide reckoning about sexual abuse that only seems to be growing" (*NYT* 4/16/18). Baquet tied journalistic ambition to civil intervention. The *Times*' conscientious commitment to fact and neutrality, its skillful practice of the craft of journalism, had made possible its public service, its civil contribution.

Sexual harassment in the workplace could finally be societalized. The steady state long prevailing inside the Weinstein Company was reconstructed as a cruel, teeming caldron of anti-democratic domination. The man who held financial and managerial power over female workers had demanded not independence and productivity but sexual submission. This contrast between women as workers and women as sex objects permeated the *Times'* narrative. The first sentence of the October 5th story began with Weinstein's invitation to actress Ashley Judd to join him at the Peninsula Beverly Hills hotel "for what the young actress expected to be a *business breakfast meeting*" (*NYT* 10/5/17, italics added). Instead, Weinstein "had her sent up to his room where he appeared in a bathrobe and asked if he could give her a massage or she could watch him shower" (ibid.). What followed next was the story of Emily Nestor, "who had worked just one day as a *temporary employee*" before she became subject to Weinstein's depredations (ibid., italics added). Kantor and Twohey assured readers that their report was "documented through interviews with current and former *employees* and film *industry workers*" (ibid., italics added). Weinstein was described as preying on "vulnerable women who hope he will get them *work*" (ibid., italics added). His victims "reported to a hotel for what they thought were *work* reasons" (ibid., italics added). Weinstein's *production staff* facilitated the transformation of workplace into bedroom. Participating initially in encounters that created a pretense of business, staff would then escort victims up to Weinstein's private rooms, where he deployed his power to demand sexual submission: "He always came back at me with some new ask . . . It was all this . . . coercive bargaining" (ibid.).

Weinstein's predatory behavior had been widely known – inside the institution. "Everybody knew" – "It wasn't a secret to the inner circle" (*NYT* 11/5/17). "Dozens of Mr. Weinstein's former and current employees, from assistants to top executives, said they knew of inappropriate conduct while they worked for him" (ibid.). Outside the institution, by contrast, virtually nothing was known at all. "From the outside, it seemed golden – the Oscars, the success, the remarkable cultural impact," recounted a former president of Miramax, adding "but inside it was a mess" (ibid.). The inside mess was insulated by enforcing on victims and staff a "code of silence," English for the *omerta* that the Mafia imposed upon fear of death (ibid.). The voices of frightened, traumatized, and often angry and indignant women were silenced. Threatened not only with dismissal but career ruin, they were offered bribes conditional upon agreeing to non-disclosure agreements (NDAs) that forbade them ever to speak about "the deals or the events that led to them" (ibid.). Film star Asia Argento "did not speak out," the *New Yorker*'s Ronan Farrow attested, "because she feared that Weinstein would 'crush' her" (*New Yorker* 10/10/17). The threat was effective, Argento explained, because "I know he has crushed a lot of people before" (ibid.).

Weinstein publicly represented these silencing tactics, not as a strategy to hide his sexual domination, but as an effort to maintain institutional equilibrium. "In addressing employee concerns about workplace issues," he told the *Times*, "my motto is to keep the peace" (*NYT* 10/5/17). After being subjected to Weinstein's coercive bargaining, one newly hired female employee sent to company higher ups a note of bitter complaint: "I remain fearful about speaking up but remaining silent is causing me great distress" (ibid.). Weinstein and his staff offered her a financial settlement that required her to sign an NDA, after which, according to Kantor and Twohey, she "withdrew her complaint and thanked [Weinstein] for the career opportunity he had given her." Weinstein's spokesperson suggested, "the parties made peace very quickly" (ibid.). Rejecting this depiction of a mutually satisfactory steady state, Kantor and Twohey rendered these intra-institutional interactions as deeply anti-civil, as fundamentally threatening to democracy itself.

One day after the *Times'* exposé, a *Los Angeles Times* editorial demanded civil intervention, no matter the intra-institutional price. It was in part because Weinstein had made so much money and brought so much glory to his company that the board of directors had tolerated and shielded his sexual abuse, at the expense of Weinstein's victims and the larger civil sphere. After code switch, however, the lesson was now clear: Business "should no longer ignore or tolerate sexual harassment by the powerful against the powerless just because the harassers are making money for them" (*Los Angeles Times* 10/7/17). Another *Los Angeles Times* editorial, three days later, attributed such self-oriented abuse of power to the failure of office regulation: "Weinstein's behavior as described by the women is disgusting, but so are the allegedly widespread efforts on the part of others at his company to cover up for him" (10/11/17). Rather than civil-oriented oversight, those in power had engaged in a cover-up. There had been "collusion," efforts that "concealed" and "enabled," and "the company's entire leadership shares . . . blame and shame" (ibid.). Ronan Farrow, who shared a Pulitzer Prize with Kantor and Twohey, described a "culture of complicity" (*New Yorker* 10/10/17).

The October 5 *Times* exposé represented a massive civil intervention. It exploded like a bombshell in the American public sphere, shattering the wall between civil sphere and workplace, drawing back the curtain on male sexual behavior and condemning as deeply anti-democratic what was found inside. Once the code had been switched, the uptake was immediate and the fallout vast. The day of its online publication, *ProQuest* reported 33 take-ups of the story, across several continents and languages.[10] The next day, when the print version appeared, *ProQuest* reported 122 take-ups, and 26 other large circulation print-news sources featured reports.[11] Network news programs made it their lead, cable news provided blanket coverage, and blogs turned up the heat 24/7.

One week after the breakout story, on March 15, a television star and activist named Alyssa Milano sent out a Twitter message at 4: 21 (PDT) in the afternoon. It read:

> *Me too. Suggested by a friend: "If all the women who have been sexually harassed or assaulted wrote "Me too" as a status, we might give people a sense of the magnitude of the problem. If you've been sexually harassed or assaulted, write 'me too' as a reply to this tweet.*

By the next morning, Milano had received 55,000 replies, the hashtag trending #1 on Twitter (*Guardian* 12/1/17). During its first 24 hours, #MeToo was tweeted 110,000 times, spreading to Facebook with twelve-million posts, comments, and reactions by 4.7 million users worldwide (*PR News* 10/23/17).[12] Over the next four months, #MeToo tweets averaged 100,000 daily, an academic analyst describing the "constant buzz of #MeToo tweets" as "the new normal" (Cohen 2018). Before code switch, the social media presence of sexual harassment had been minimal, straight-lining for years. After code switch, its social media presence jumped three to four hundredfold and remained there, with hundreds of thousands of mentions daily and millions monthly (*WP* 10/22/18 – see the graphs below).[13] The hashtag was "meant for the public," a *Washington Post* blogger explained, "a massive show of scale to prove that the issue is unavoidable [and] that its audience is everyone" (*WP* 10/19/17).

Sexual coercion in the workplace had been insulated from the citizen-audience, a closely guarded intra-institutional secret. Now that this "invisible" social problem had become societalized, it was experienced as a dagger aimed at the heart of the civil sphere itself. Three weeks after the initial revelation, the *Monterey County* [California] *Weekly* (10/26/17) exclaimed, "the floodgates have been opened." Two months after that, a contributor to *Bloomberg/Businessweek* 12/20/17) observed, "the women who came forward with tales of rape and abuse by Harvey Weinstein set off a cultural earthquake," exclaiming the "ground is finally shaking" and "it feels at times as if our entire world has started to crumble." Nine months after

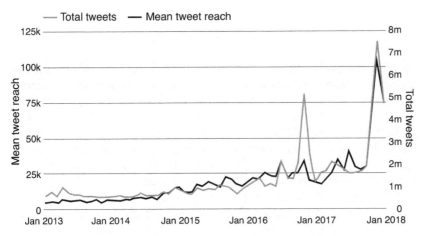

Graph 1 Mean Tweet Reach vs Total Tweet Volume
(Twitter Sexual Harrassment Conversation)
Source: Crimson Hexagon/George Washington University

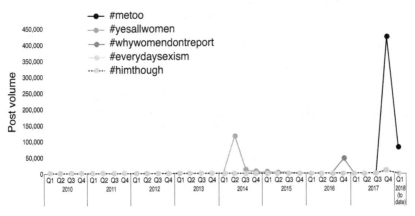

Graph 2 Sexual Harassment Hashtags Discussion Trend

the initial allegations, in "After #MeToo, the Ripple Effect," the
New York Times wrote that "nearly every woman seems to have a
#MeToo story" (*NYT* 6/28/18).

> One of the most sobering revelations – and one of the most powerful
> – has been the sheer universality of it . . . Harassment is pervasive in
> professions like finance and technology, as well as workplaces like res-
> taurants, factories, and hotels. It doesn't spare you if you're old, or rich,
> or privileged, or powerful. (ibid.)

79

Beyond the coasts and elites

In the very midst of this incendiary explosion, civil sphere agents, victim activists, and leaders on both the left and right wondered repeatedly whether code switch was an illusion, a teapot tempest limited to celebrities and bi-coastal elites from which the rest of the country, the "real" America, was left out and unaffected. Sometimes such doubts were ideological, adumbrating a gathering backlash against #MeToo. Often, the doubts expressed heartfelt concern that a wider civil solidarity had not been truly engaged.

Whether strategic or sincere, such concerns were off the mark. Certainly, the name recognition and long "friend" list of television and movie stars had greatly enhanced hashtag circulation, but code switch had already been triggered, by the publication of the *New York Times*' October 5 investigation. With deep financial pockets, a massive reportorial staff, and a proud tradition of critical journalism, the *Times* had, for decades, been America's most influential everyday generator of civil judgment, and more recently the global civil sphere's as well. With one million print readers and two million unique digital subscribers, its news reporting set the national agenda of the day, for newspapers and also for television, radio, and social media.[14] The Kantor-Twohey story triggered such a massive circulation of civil grievance that social media subsequently intensified, expanding social solidarity throughout the American civil sphere, among groups and individuals otherwise separated by religion, region, and class.

Religion

On October 19, the *New Jersey Jewish News* (10/19/17) reported on the "furious backlash" among orthodox Jewish women against an orthodox male leader's widely publicized advice to Jewish women that they wear modest clothing to protect themselves against sexual harassment. Such blaming the victim, the women complained, ignored the "Weinstein-like behavior" of orthodox men, in the workplace, on dates, and on the street (ibid.). The angry responders drew a parallel between "male-dominated" Hollywood and the "rigid hierarchy and patriarchal structure" of the orthodox Jewish community (ibid.). They found the same "code of silence . . . in insular religious circles," one that allowed "seemingly pious men [to] have free and unfettered rein" to commit "aggression" against powerless and constrained women (ibid.).

Two months later, the *Jacksonville Free Press* (12/7/17), identified on its masthead as "Florida's First Coast Quality Black Weekly," wrote about women using "the #ChurchToo hashtag to shed light on countless disturbing experiences." "Hundreds of women," it reported, "have been revealing stories of rape, sexual abuse, and harassment that they suffered inside the church or at the hands of Christian men in leadership" (ibid.). One churchgoing woman complained:

> I CANNOT COUNT the number of times I've heard guys in church PUBLICLY admit to molestation, harassment, assault, etc., only to be praised for their bravery and honesty. No consequences. The church's legacy of protecting abusers is sickening . . . (ibid., capitals in original)

Region

On October 17, under the headline "Houston Women Join #MeToo Movement," the website of KHOU11, a leading local news radio, reported that "women from all over the country are joining forces to speak out against sexual abuse [and] now hundreds here in Houston are doing the same" (*KHOU11* 10/17/2017). A week later, Connecticut's *Hartford Courant* headlined, "#All of Us: Why #MeToo Is Taking Off" (10/22/17). Suggesting "the case of Harvey Weinstein [has] resonated in a moving and profound way with women across the state and the nation," the state's leading newspaper published responses to its Facebook query for readers to "tell us why #MeToo took off and what they hoped it would achieve" (ibid.). Laura Mahon from Tolland, CT, asked, "Is there a woman out there who has NOT been harassed/assaulted?" (ibid.). Lucy Ferriss, from West Hartford, saying "so much has led up to this," eloquently enumerated "the pat on the fanny by the senior manager; the inappropriate familiarity of the HS teacher; the coercive boyfriend; the stranger in the deserted subway who exposes himself; the boss who offers a promotion but only in exchange for sex; the boss who threatens firing if you don't have sex; the doctor who gropes; the date rapist; the violent husband; the violent rapist." Ferriss concluded: "None of it is OK anymore . . . Women have been pushed too far, gotta push back hard" (ibid.). From Jill Fletcher in Wethersfield: "At last something pushed through the seemingly impenetrable. #MeToo creates an avalanche of solidarity for all the hurts that have been buried and [it] resonates . . . It took many voices to actually break through" (ibid.). From Marianne

O'Hare in Stonington: "Weinstein et al. are merely the top of the pyramid. I think the greatest tragedies occur systematically as we go down that pyramid to women who have no power at all" (ibid.).

Days later, the *Santa Barbara Independent*, headlining "Schools on #MeToo Track" (10/26/17), reported that "high-school girls [are] increasingly concerned with sex crimes and misconduct." In early November, the *Colorado Springs Independent* (11/8/17a) described "The Profound Prevalence," bemoaning that workplace sexual harassment had become so "pedestrian that it no longer stands out when it happens." Later that month, an anonymous contributor to the *Miami Times* warned, "We in Miami should not get on our high horses and proclaim this as a problem of the Washington Beltway or the entertainment capitals of Los Angeles and New York," predicting that "#MeToo will show up in sunny South Florida" (11/19/17). Four months after that, in March 2018, the *Atlanta Journal Constitution* published another installment from its months-long investigation into sexual harassment in Georgia's state government. Noting that Georgia's capital was "largely run by men," one of the American South's most influential newspapers reported that an "imbalance of power" had created a "cesspool of misogyny" (ibid.). The investigation documented how "the public is kept from knowing [the] misdeeds of elected officials," describing how "complaints are handled behind closed doors by a small group of lawmakers whose processes are unknown" (ibid.).

Class

On October 16, under the headline "#MeToo Brings Dallas Stories of Sexual Assault to Social Media," the *Dallas News* (10/16/17) printed the story of "Liz Landry's first job at a grocery store," which "became a nightmare the morning a manager came up from behind and pressed his pelvis against her, massaging her shoulders."

> At 19, she didn't feel she could bring legal charges in the mostly male corporate environment of the 1990s. Today, the 38-year-old who works as an advocate for those affected by sexual abuse in Dallas used #MeToo to speak out on that long-ago incident. (ibid.)

Early the next month, the *Colorado Springs Independent* (11/8/17b) published a firsthand testimonial under the headline "#WhoHasn't."

> I was 22 years old. I was a waitress at a popular downtown restaurant and had finished my shift. I decided to stick around and listen to the

band that was playing for the Halloween weekend. One of our regulars, a banker, came up and put his hand on my ass and said something like, "This is a great pumpkin you've got here." He kept his hand right there, squeezing. I turned to him and said, "Take your hand off my ass, they're not paying me to let you do this" . . . Of course, I could have walked into the managers' office and reported things, right? Oh sure, the office where they had a photocopied sign pinned on the corkboard that read, "Sexual harassment will not be tolerated here, but it will be graded." What would I have said? "Surprise grab, firm grasp, cheesy line? C+ at best." No, I didn't say anything and I'm sure I waited on the same man more times with a smile on my face.

"Until Celebrities Said 'me too,' Nobody Listened to Blue-Collar Women about Assault," headlined the *Chicago Sun Times* in March, 2018, over an op-ed by an anti-harassment activist. The author, a labor attorney, argued that #MeToo had shed an "overdue spotlight on workplace sexual violence . . . in blue collar industries" (*Chicago Sun Times* 3/21/28), reporting that one working-class woman told her, "Finally! It's not just us – it happens to rich people too." In September 2018, the *Guardian* devoted a story to "the protest and outcry of ordinary women" (9/18/18).

Last Tuesday, McDonald's workers in 10 U.S. cities walked off the job to protest against pervasive sexual harassment. A week earlier, female janitors in California marched 100 miles from San Francisco to the state capitol in Sacramento to support anti-harassment legislation. The janitors' union, SEIU, in partnership with the East LA Women's Center, has been quietly training women in self-defense and promoting peer-to-peer anti-harassment workshops and an assault crisis hotline.

(ibid.; cf. *NYT* 9/19/18)

Civil Repair as Culture (Re-)Structure

The first and perhaps still most significant civil repair that societalization effected was to create a new set of social meanings. A radically altered culture structure emerged, a public, sharply critical but also emancipatory collective representation of sexual harassment in the workplace and the struggle against it. The abstract ethical binaries marking civil sacred and profane now became specified in a gender-inverted way. Sexually aggressive men came to be seen as untrustworthy, secretive, dishonest, anti-civil, and their female victims as trustworthy, open, honest, and civil. These newly re-signified characters became protagonists and antagonists in a liberation narrative about defeating oppression and creating justice in the workplace.

Men, once admired as macho heroes in the battle of the sexes, became vilified as perpetrators. Women, once depicted as weak and help-less, were now hailed as heroes, whose courage and bravery were praised, for example by serial celebrities in the *Washington Post* (WP 10/13/17) six days after the Weinstein revelations:

> "It's wonderful they have this incredible courage and are standing up now." (Matt Damon)

> "Their bravery in speaking out." (Gretchen Mol)

> "Their bravery to come forward." (Jennifer Lawrence)

> "The intrepid women who raised their voices to expose this abuse." (Meryl Streep)

> "Incredibly brave." (Kate Winslett)

> "Forever in awe of the bravery of those who spoke out." (Lin-Manuel Miranda)

With the code shifted and an emancipatory narrative in place, aggrieved women who cried foul and pointed fingers were accorded a newly civil status, allowing them to become respected narrators of their own social suffering. "Telling their own stories" was the red thread that ran through the many months and tens of thousands of #MeToo testimonies. "The story isn't that Mr. Weinstein has been fired," wrote Roger Ailes, former accuser Gretchen Carlson in the *New York Times* on October 10, but "that women's voices are finally being heard" (*NYT* 10/10/17). Six days later, the once abused grocery clerk turned sexual abuse advocate attested to the *Dallas News* (10/16/17) that "telling your story is powerful [because] talking about it is the only way we start creating what it looks like." Half a year later, an ethicist at *Barron's*, the business magazine, reiterated the argument in a more intellectual way:

> Women ... have had the opportunity to tell their stories. Part of what is happening as a result of this movement is a re-imagining of the boundaries ... Unwelcome sexual comments and physical attentions previously dismissed as "boys being boys" or "locker-room talk" have been redefined as harassment. Women whose accounts were belittled or trivialized now have the space to reclaim their narrative.
>
> (*Barron's* 4/24/18)

Time magazine awarded its 2017 Person of the Year award to the "Silence Breakers" (*Time* 12/18/17).

Women telling personal stories about sexual abuse had become serious public business. Such performances of civil indignation projected not only deep pain but also authenticity, and they were widely believed. Audiences in the civil sphere listened carefully and often reported piercing experiences of emotional identification, seeing in such stories not just the victims but they themselves, and their friends and family members as well. Empathy extended, solidarity deepened, and civil feeling stretched, not only to other women but also to men, who contributed 37 percent of the tweets during the first three and a half months of #MeToo (Cohen 2018). A 41-year-old Dallas resident named Marty Yudizky wrote that, while "I have not personally been a victim of sex assault," he was tweeting "to show solidarity and compassion with the women posting 'metoo'" (*Dallas News* 10/16/17). After tweeting about her own abuse experiences, a Colorado woman posted: "I witnessed the reaction of male friends discovering their eighth of eight female relatives had posted these two words. I saw another male friend's breakdown when he found that post [#MeToo] on his sister's page. It was powerful – too powerful" (*Colorado Springs Independent* 11/8/17a).

"Her story" was not just hers, not just a personal account, but something that had the ring of a broader truth, about power and trauma – and survival. Indeed, women telling their #MeToo stories were accorded the sacred status of "survivor." According to post-Holocaust morality (Alexander 2003a), being a survivor provided precious authenticity, allowing personal testimony to be taken as moral truth.

Material Regulation

Societalization had barely commenced when activists and critics began wringing their hands that nothing was really going to change. These worries took the form of a binary that expressed itself in such contrasts as talk-versus-action, soft-versus-hard, feeling-versus-structure, individual-versus-system, and belief-versus-organization. On October 16, just one day after the hashtag began circulating, at the very center of the gathering firestorm, a postdoctoral fellow in Vancouver posted, "I don't think #MeToo signals some kind of 'watershed moment'," but "I am hoping that it serves as another link in the chain to some concrete, systemic change" (*WP* 10/16/17). After three months of societalization, a *Washington Post* contributor declared "the #MeToo movement will be in vain if we don't make ... changes [in] our legal system," that "without substantial reforms [the] movement may be all for naught" (*WP* 1/25/18). On the six-month anniversary of her and Twohey's code-shifting *New*

York Times investigation, Jodi Kantor crystallized these fears in a deeply pessimistic survey and retrospective. While she acknowledged "the #MeToo moment" had "shifted social attitudes" and "resulted in unprecedented accountability," Kantor rued that there had merely been "revelations about the pervasiveness of harassment" but nothing systemic and structural – no "legal and institutional" measures to prevent or punish it (*NYT* 3/24/18).

Those in the midst of a radical social change often fail to fully comprehend it. Inside the messy contingency of protest, it is hard to see the forest for the trees. Their restless energy is devoted to making things happen, more stuff and faster, not to looking back on what may already have changed. Those with less of a stake in the struggle can sometimes be more reflexive, recognizing that the forest itself has been changed. One month after Kantor's anxiety and regret, on April 19, 2018, *The American Conservative* got it much more right: "It's six months since #MeToo began trending on social media. Since then, these two little words have sparked a conversation about sexual harassment in work that has spread across the globe and into every walk of life" (*The American Conservative* 2018).

Societalization had produced new cultural understandings that were structural, systemic, and collective. These shifted the course of social action. But there was more, for when ideas change, materiality often follows.

Toppling the male élite

The most visible material effect of code switch was the physical inversion of gender power, the objective destruction of the careers of hundreds of rich and powerful men who composed the intra-institutional elite. The aroused civil sphere, having re-signified these men as abusive perpetrators, entered into their institutions and forced them to leave. This material effect did not take place via police action; few accused perpetrators were arrested, and, among them, Harvey Weinstein was the only one imprisoned. Yet a new phase of the gender revolution was nonetheless unfolding; it was a time to *couper le tête de la bourgeois*: "Another Executive's Head Rolls at Besieged CBS" (*NYT* 9/13/18). Taking stock of #MeToo after one year, *Times* journalists found that, despite a "crackling backlash," the movement had shaken, and was "still shaking," the "power structures in society's most visible sectors," and that, as a result, the "corridors of power" had been remarkably changed (*NYT* 10/23/18). "After public allegations of sexual harassment," more than two hundred extraordinarily "prominent men" had lost their jobs, and nearly half had been replaced by women (ibid.). It was not only that the civil sphere had entered into the workplace and ejected anti-civil men from power; it was that a form of power now construed as more civil – female power – had taken its place. "Research has repeatedly shown," the *Times* reported, "that women tend to lead differently [by] creat[ing] more respectful work environments, where harassment is less likely to flourish and where women feel more comfortable reporting it" (ibid.). In the corporate world, women managers "hire and promote more women" and "pay them more equally." In government, "women have been shown to be more collaborative and bipartisan" (ibid.). A law professor from the University of California, Hastings, interpreted the gender transformation of power in terms of contrasting risks: "Women had always been seen as risky, because they might do something like have a baby. But men are now being seen as more risky hires" (ibid.) – because of what was now construed as their anti-civil proclivity for sexual domination. With societalization, women "are starting to gain power in organizations," with "potentially far-reaching," decidedly civilizing effects (ibid.).[15]

Reconstructing organizational insides

#MeToo "touched almost every industry" (Pew Stateline Blog 7/31/18). If the U.S. had become "a vastly different country with sharply different values," as the *Los Angeles Times* contended (9/17/18), and "the public's definition of what constitutes acceptable [sexual] conduct" had been deeply changed (ibid.). Organizations whose material interests depended on staying right with public opinion had to adapt.

The *New York Times* reported that, in the wake of #MeToo, companies felt they were exposed to "a serious reputational and business risk" (*NYT* 3/24/18), and that, in response, a "fear-driven shift" in intra-institutional policies had begun (cf. *Market Watch* 7/14/18). Corporate boards, managers, and investors "from Wall Street to Silicon Valley are going on the offensive, probing for problems to avoid being surprised" (*NYT* 3/24/18). Shareholders tried to ascertain whether or not companies had instituted appropriate anti-harassment controls. "While sexual violence in the workplace endangers those who endured it," *Market Watch* (2/16/18) reported, it "might make the predators' companies a bad investment too." Cornerstone Capital, an investment advisory and wealth management firm, employed the discourse of the civil sphere to measure the capacity for profitability. Warning prospective investors against "structural complicity" with harassers, the firm declared "sexual and gender-based violence" to be an "emerging investment risk" (ibid.), concluding "it is incumbent upon investors to demand greater transparency on issues of SGBV – to hold companies accountable." If capital markets did not hold companies to such civil standards, according to the advisory firm, companies would be regarded as "complicit" in abuse (ibid.). The outplacement and executive coaching firm Challenger, Gray, and Christmas (2018) urged employers "to get ahead of potential problems," and to become "more aware of power dynamics" (ibid.). *Fortune* quoted a University of New Haven expert on workplace romance, who suggested, "the underlying message of top management must be that their workplace is one of civility where employees get by on their merits" (*Fortune* 7/18/18).

Forbes magazine analyzed what had gone wrong at CBS, the television and entertainment company that had been hugely embarrassed by a series of accusations and forced departures in the months after code switch. CBS's board had been "far too detached and passive," *Forbes* (9/17/18) reported, suggesting that "an independent internal investigation" had been far too late responding to what the *New York Times* characterized as CBS chairman and CEO Les Moonves' "deceit" (*NYT* 9/13/18). The CBS board "was too slow to be transparent," agreed the female CEO of The Santa Fe Group (ibid.).

Reporting on a survey of 150 Human Resources executives, *Workforce* found "HR departments [were] stepping up their responses," hiring outside contractors to "perform workplace culture audits," providing "independent whistleblower services," and "increasing sexual harassment training" in house (*Workforce* 4/3/18). The founder of the field of sexual harassment training testified, "I would be booked between now and ten years … and still not fulfill the demand" (*NYT* 3/23/18). According to business cable channel CNBC, companies were turning to private investigators "to identify predators," not only inside their own institutions but inside their rivals' as well; such a practice of "weaponizing feminism" often involved "massive intrusions into businessmen's private lives" (*CNBC* 5/31/18). Advertising agencies dramatically revised employee dating policies (*Digiday* 2018). After twenty thousand Google employees walked off their jobs to protest the company's handling of sex harassment complaints, the tech giant announced it would no longer force employees to accept private arbitration of such claims. The next day

Facebook did the same (*NYT* 11/9/18). Microsoft had changed its arbitration policy a year before, eliminated FAAs (Federal Arbitration Acts), and began lobbying for similar changes in Federal law (*Fortune* 12/19/17). After UBER ended forced arbitration, it hired former Attorney General Eric Holder's law firm to conduct a wide-ranging internal examination (*Time* 2/21/17). Condé Nast announced new rules about "nudity and touching" (*NYT* 10/23/17).

Barron's featured an influential business ethics expert responding to "knotty questions from people in the advisory industry" (*Barron's* 4/24/18).

> I am the leader of a large practice [and] recently held a team-building event for my financial advisors and administrative support staff. At this event, one of the top producers, a male in his early 50s, was overheard making several jokes about the "#MeToo" movement . . . Several people witnessed this and were offended by the remarks . . . I'm not sure of the best way to respond now.

The ethicist responded that, "as a leader, you should immediately bring the team together" and make clear "the conversation mocking the #MeToo movement violated" company values, that it was "harmful to the organization," and that "people who violate these values will not be permitted to harm the cohesion of the unit." Stressing it was important "to take a strong tone," she advised the executive to "meet with the 'ringleader' alone, and ask him if he agrees with what you've said" to the group. "If he agrees," then you "can ask for his support," in which case he may become "an influencer within the organization." If, however, the ringleader "is non-committal," then "you have an important decision to make," for it has then become "a decision about who will dictate the culture of the firm – him or you."

Gaining legal traction

In the midst of societalization, the conviction was continually expressed that sexual harassment in the workplace was rampant because laws to prevent it had not been put in place, and that civil repair would need to center on legal reform. Quite the opposite turned out to be the case. Already in 1964, the Civil Rights Act had established a powerful foundation for constructing anti-harassment law, and in 1980 the Equal Employment Opportunity Commission (EEOC) declared specifically that workplace sexual harassment violated Title VII, which prohibited harassment based on sex, race, and national origin (*WP* 1/25/18). In 1986, the Supreme Court ruled that hostile work environments also violated Title VII, and in 1991 Congress made compensatory and punitive damages available under Title VII as well. During these decades and after, a thick web of sex discrimination law developed (ibid., cf. *Time* 4/11/16; Siegel 2003).

Strong legal protections were in place before the societalization of sexual harassment began. Here is the policy of the EEOC, which defined normative workplace behavior and prosecuted departures from it:

> It is unlawful to harass a person (an applicant or employee) because of that person's sex. Harassment can include "sexual harassment" or unwelcome sexual advances, requests for sexual favors, and other verbal or physical harassment of a sexual nature [if] it is so frequent or severe that it creates a hostile or offensive work environment or when it results in an adverse employment decision (such as the victim being fired or demoted). (*Equal Employment Opportunity Commission* n.d.)

In early January, 2018, a powerful Florida law firm specializing in employee rights noted that it had "been a long road [making] sexual harassment illegal in the workplace," and listed sixteen critical legal decisions between 1964 and 2005. Declaring "there are laws that are now in place to help protect employees from unwanted sexual advances and conduct of a sexual nature that can affect their ability to do their job," the firm assured prospective clients, "if you've been a victim of sexual harassment and/or wrongfully terminated or retaliated against for reporting sexual harassment, you are protected under federal and state laws" (*Wenzel Fenton Cabassa, P.A.* 1/1/18).

What, then, was the problem? Why had sexual harassment in the workplace continued, relatively unabated, during the same period as such a legal network emerged? Laws are external constraints on action; they must be activated internally, by will and imagination, and this happens only if legal regulation is connected with a shared cultural core. Energizing such a core is what code switch is all about. Four months after societalization began, Catharine MacKinnon, the pioneering feminist legal scholar whose decades of work helped build the legal lattice against sexual harassment, declared in a *New York Times* op-ed that "the #MeToo movement is accomplishing what sexual harassment law to date has not" (*NYT* 4/4/18). The "disbelief and trivializing dehumanization of its victims," MacKinnon wrote – the "denial by abusers and devaluing of accusers" – had long prevented sexual harassment law from having significant effect (ibid.). Because women's "complaints were routinely passed off with some version of 'she wasn't credible' or 'she wanted it'," many "survivors realistically judged reporting pointless" (ibid.). While "it is widely thought that when something is legally prohibited, it more or less stops," MacKinnon cautioned, "it is not true for pervasive practices like sexual harassment" (ibid.). It is *cultural* inequalities" that count, and they can be broken only when "publicly and pervasively challenged by women's voices" (ibid., italics added).

> No longer liars, no longer worthless, today's survivors are initiating consequences none of them could have gotten through any lawsuit . . . They are being believed and valued as the law seldom has. Women have been saying these things forever. It is the response to them that has changed.   (ibid.)

Men who harassed women had been re-signified. There was now a "revulsion against harassing behavior" and "men with power [are] refusing to be associated with it" (ibid.). Women's stories, now seen as authentic, were fusing with citizen audiences. When these storytellers identified male behavior as predatory and polluted, those listening and looking, including many men, saw it that way too. Laws are essential to maintaining civil behavior and extending solidarity, but such regulative power must be communicatively intertwined. Only if anti-harassment laws were infused with social meaning would they be able to exercise regulative power.

None of this meant that anti-harassment law could not be strengthened. Indeed, the prospect of existing law finally gaining traction made gaps and lacunae more evident. If egregious episodes of earlier harassment were to be prosecuted, statutes of limitations would have to be lifted. For victims to speak more freely, non-disclosure agreements should have to be scrutinized and eliminated. Forced arbitration could be neutralized and private litigation costs underwritten to neutralize upfront attorney fees. Monetary caps on pain and suffering might be raised. Should companies be required to report harassment claims to the federal government, for example, as part of the Labor Department's annual Survey of Occupational Injuries and Illnesses? In the interests of fairness, should legislation address the issue of proportionate punishment for different levels of severity (PEW Stateline Blog 7/31/18; *BillTrack50* 2/15/18; WP 1/25/18)? In the first five months of 2018, according to the National Conference of State Legislators, 32 states introduced over 125 different pieces of legislation, "an unprecedented amount of legislation on sexual harassment and sexual harassment policies" (*National Conference of State Legislatures* 6/6/18). By year's end, many of these bills had been signed into law, not only in such high population centers as

New York state, New York City, California, Illinois, and Maryland, but in states like Vermont, Maine, Delaware, Connecticut, and New Mexico as well (*Real Estate In-Depth* 10/18; *Pillsbury Insights* 10/8/18; *Winston & Strawn LLP* 6/14/18).

Backlash

The societalization of workplace sexual harassment unfolded in the midst of one of the most poisonously polarized political periods in living memory, which made the civil expansion it effected that much more remarkable. That during the second year of Donald Trump's presidency women and men were so powerfully resignified; that women were accepted as authentic narrators of their own stories; that citizen audiences identified with their trauma, expressing a revulsion that destroyed the careers of powerful men and put women in their place, restructuring the internal environments of institutions and allowing anti-harassment law to gain more traction. Sexual harassment in the workplace became societalized because it was constructed not as a matter of political right or left but, rather, as a problem of society itself. That men shared in this newly extended solidarity was symbolized by the performance of public apology. Many accused men engaged in such performances, even when they were tepid, starting with Harvey Weinstein himself: "I appreciate the way I've behaved with colleagues in the past has caused a lot of pain and I sincerely apologize for it. Though I'm trying to do better, I know I have a long way to go" (*NYT* 10/5/17).

Yet the very success of societalization – the indignation that triggered it, the civil repair it created – triggered a backlash. #MeToo had from the beginning sparked resistance among members of the male elite, but for many months such pushback did not express itself in a politicized, right-versus-left way. Running just below the visible surface of apologetic rituals of degradation, there were rivulets of resentment. Even as the public narrative of accusation, punishment, repentance, and restructuring became hegemonic, many of the men who were exposed and humiliated failed to publicly accept responsibility. A rough survey between October 5, 2017, and May 23, 2018, revealed that, while some 40 percent did stage an apologetic performance, 60 percent did not apologize, even tepidly.[16]

The pushback against civil intrusion into workplace sexuality actually began before societalization, before massive code shift was even on the social horizon. When communicative agents of the civil sphere began investigating the sexual behavior of men who held key institutional positions, members of the male elite deployed their power in an effort to prevent news stories from being written and published. In February 2017, as *New York Times* reporter Emily Steel began looking into contentious issues at Fox News, Bill O'Reilly called, telling her, on the record: "I am coming after you with everything I have," and "you can take it as a threat" (*NYT* 10/15/17). When the *Times* first began sleuthing into the intra-institutional behavior of Harvey Weinstein, Jodi Kantor recounted, the Hollywood mogul threatened to sue the newspaper – "he had one high-priced consultant or lawyer after another" (*WP* 1/25/18); her co-author Megan Twohey recalled "an army – it was an army attacking us." After code switch was triggered, and a CBS News reporter asked Jeff Fager, the powerful executive producer of *60 Minutes*, to respond to harassment accusations leveled against him, he warned her to "be careful," threatening "there are people who lost their jobs trying to harm me, and if you pass on these damaging claims without . . . reporting to back them up that will become a serious problem" (*NYT* 9/13/18). "They throw up as many hurdles as possible [and] many used threats," recalled the *Times* editor who had supervised the paper's investigation into sexual harassment in Silicon Valley (*NYT* 10/15/17).

As published investigations began intruding into the workplace, many of the men exposed as male predators, despite performances of apology, professed to disbelieve many particulars of the exposés. "I don't know anything about that," Weinstein responded to the *Times* account of his years-long harassment of a long-time employee (*NYT* 10/7/17). Investigating how "#MeToo has changed the DC power structure," the *Washington Post* reported that, among the nineteen powerful political figures who had been forced from office, "the majority were defiant, accusing women of lying" (*WP* 9/26/18). Supporters of stigmatized men often pushed back as well. Responding to explosive charges against CBS chairman and CEO Les Moonves – accusations that eventually drove him from office – board of director's member Arnold Kopelson, the 83–year-old movie producer who had won an Oscar for *Platoon*, pledged institutional loyalty: "I don't care if thirty more women come forward and allege this kind of stuff, Les is our leader and it wouldn't change my opinion of him" (*NYT* 9/13/18, A1).

As the #MeToo crisis deepened and societalization gained tsunami strength, isolated acts of resistance began to be stitched together, forming a "rhetoric of reaction" (Hirschman 1991) that, while circulating mostly on right-wing websites and Fox News, created a profile on the public scene. The civil sphere remained central to this backlash discourse, but its relation to #MeToo was radically changed. Rather than expanding civil solidarity, the societalization of sexual harassment was here construed as endangering it. Backlash challenged the truth-telling status of female victims. "Women should not be reflexively believed," one *Breitbart* critic wrote (*Breitbart News* 2/14/2018). Because "facts have been readily sacrificed for the good of the cause," we should no longer "automatically take woman's words as the truth" (*The American Conservative* 4/19/18). "I don't believe a word of it," the famous fashion designer Karl Lagerfeld proclaimed, adding "if you don't want your pants pulled about, don't become a model! Join a nunnery, there'll always be a place for you in the convent" (*Numéro* 4/12/18). The rising force of anti-harassment public opinion was attacked as a form of mass hysteria, as "a mob mentality" that had left reason aside (*Breitbart* 2/14/18). #MeToo was "driven by the mainstream media that is calling for public stoning" (ibid.). "Infantile and authoritarian" (*The American Conservative* 4/19/18), #MeToo had become a "witch hunt" that smacked of "McCarthyism" (*RedState Blog* 11/29/17). A French petition of protest, signed by 100 leading female figures in the arts and entertainment, blamed #MeToo for trying to create a "climate of totalitarianism":

> We are all being told what is proper to say . . . Women [are] enslave[d] to a status of eternal victim [and those] who refuse to fall in line are considered traitors. [There are] public confessions. (*NYT* 1/9/18)

Despite its libertine animus, this French protest was eagerly taken up by the emerging backlash line (e.g., *The American Conservative* 4/19/18).

"#HimToo" soon popped up as a hashtag (*NYT* 12/14/17). Declaring "tropes of predatory men and vulnerable women are outdated" (*The American Conservative* 4/19/18), backlash turned the #MeToo narrative upside down. Women making accusations were now described as predators, and men the victims – of women's false accusations. Complaining that "the current climate" had led "many men to resent and be angry toward women," Andrew Yarrow claimed, #MeToo "hinders teamwork" (*Forbes* 9/17/18). Fox News senior analyst Brit Hume tweeted, "Mike Pence's policy of avoiding being alone with women other than his wife looking better every day" (*Newsweek* 11/17/17). "Men are going to be afraid of working with women," *Breitbart News* (2/14/18) warned. "Male managers . . . have grown significantly more uncomfortable mentoring women than before," LeanIn.org reported (*USA Today* 10/8/2018).

The civil sphere had to be protected from #MeToo if democracy were to survive. Newly emergent cultural structures were anti-democratic; they must be avoided and, if possible, destroyed. Female subjectivity could not be trusted. Women were abusing men. #MeToo women were dangerously anti-civil, making use of corrupt communicative institutions to conduct witch-hunts. To protect themselves, victimized males would need to rely on other civil sphere institutions, especially the law. Only due process – the fair, balanced, and objective evaluation of material evidence in a court of law – could protect men's democratic rights (*American Conservative* 4/19/18; *Breitbart News* 2/14/18). Unless there were objective "proof," male guilt could not be proclaimed. In lieu of such legal documentation, women's stories didn't matter, their voices would be silenced, their truth denied, and their invidiousness, not their authenticity, proclaimed.

It was with this gradually congealing rhetoric of reaction that the confrontation between Judge Brett Kavanaugh and Dr. Christine Blasey Ford collided in the late summer of 2018. Conservative ideologues had chipped away at the new culture structure of societalization, yet they had not managed to link their backlash construction to the nation's intensifying left–right polarization. President Trump, for example, had barely been mentioned throughout the many months of gender confrontation; neither he nor the conservative movement had been objects of #MeToo. When Blasey Ford retrospectively accused Brett Kavanaugh of having sexually abused her at a high-school party, this all changed. President Trump had nominated Kavanaugh to the Supreme Court, an appointment that, if confirmed by the Senate, would help ensure a conservative majority for decades to come. With the help of liberal Democratic Senator Dianne Feinstein, Ford publicly launched her accusation just days before Kavanaugh's nomination was to have come up for a vote in the Republican controlled Senate Judiciary Committee, where support for confirmation had seemed assured. Ford's claim that Kavanaugh had tried to rape her exploded as a "#MeToo moment"; with the winds of societalization at its back, the accusation threatened to upend Kavanaugh's confirmation and undermine an imminent conservative triumph. President Trump became enraged, as did most Republican Senators and conservatives throughout the nation.

Sexually abused women had overcome marginalization, and the societalization of their plight had managed largely to escape the invidious effects of contemporary polarization. This generalized status was now being torn away. "The movement originally founded to help victims has become weaponized as a political tool," the conservative blog Red State exclaimed in late September 2018 (*RedState Blog* 9/24/18). "For many conservatives, especially white men who share Mr. Trump's contempt for the left and his use of divisive remarks," the *Times* reported on the eve of the Senate hearings, "the clash over Judge Kavanaugh's confirmation has become a rallying cry against a liberal order that, they argue, is hostile to their individual rights, political power and social status" (*NYT* 9/30/18, A23). That same day, from the other side of the political chasm, a female member of the *Times* editorial staff, in a signed editorial "What America Owes Women," stressed the supra-political level of civil solidarity, reminding Americans that "Dr. Blasey said she shared her story out of a sense of civic duty," and asserted "now it's up to the men of this country to hear us," that this "is what we are owed, as citizens and as human beings" *(NYT* 9/30/18, SR8). Would #MeToo become identified with leftist critique rather than with systemic social problems? If so, the societalization of sexual harassment would be blocked and civil repair halted.

In a front-page story headlined "Fight over Kavanaugh Shows the Power, and Limits, of #MeToo," the *Times* suggested that "the fight over [Kavanaugh's] nomination shows how the dynamics of the #MeToo movement have threaded their way into American life" (*NYT* 9/30/18, A1a). Twenty years earlier, the all-male Senate Judiciary Committee had greeted with demeaning incredulity Anita Hill's charges of sexual harassment against Supreme Court nominee Clarence Thomas. Now, in sharp contrast, even most conservative senators went out of their way to exhibit elaborate courtesy to Kavanaugh's accuser, exercising great care not to appear publicly to challenge her story, allowing that it was her "truth." The Republican chair of the Judiciary Committee put off the date of Ford's required appearance, acceding to her request for more preparation time. When the hearings finally unfolded, the Republican side's questioning of Dr. Blasey was handled by a Deputy County Attorney from Arizona, a female expert on sex crimes hired especially for the occasion – to avoid the appearance of male bullying.

Despite these efforts to prevent Kavanaugh's Senate confirmation from becoming ensnared by societalization, the hearing became "an explosive collision between #MeToo – the cultural movement shaking the country – and the politics of outrage that drive President Trump's Republican Party" (*NYT* 9/27/18). Ford's tearful recounting of her sexual harassment appeared authentic, a moving representation that encapsulated #MeToo coding and narration. Kavanaugh's testimony

was represented, by mainstream media, as an angry, bitter, and accu-
satory response from the backlash side.

> Republicans [had] outsourced their questioning of Dr. Blasey to a female
> lawyer because they worried about the optics of an all-male panel quiz-
> zing a woman about sensitive matters. But by the time they got to
> Judge Kavanaugh, Republicans could no longer hold their tongues.
> They treated him as a victim, treated unfairly by a society eager to sym-
> pathize with women's allegations. In a tirade, Senator Lindsey Graham,
> Republican of South Carolina, called the accusations "crap" and "the
> most despicable thing" he'd seen in his time in politics.   (ibid.)

The Republican majority on the Judiciary Committee approved
Kavanaugh's nomination, and their Senate majority soon confirmed
it. When Donald Trump swore Kavanaugh into office on October
8, the President pointedly apologized to him and his family "for the
terrible pain and suffering *you* have been forced to endure" (*NYT*
10/24/18, italics added).

Republicans won the battle, but they lost the war. Forty days after
11 Republican Senators on the Judiciary Committee voted to approve
Kavanaugh, some 113 million Americans entered voting booths to
participate in the biannual, nation-wide Congressional elections.
Trump had tried making the election turn on *Ford v. Kavanaugh*,
hoping the conservative Senate victory had so stoked the backlash
against #MeToo that it would neutralize the Democratic "Blue Wave"
threatening Republican control of the House of Representatives. "For
a while," the *Times* reported, the President "said that 'this will be
an election [about] Kavanaugh, the [immigrant] caravan, law and
order, and common sense'" (*NYT* 11/7/18). For a while, perhaps,
but soon the President changed his mind. "Kavanaugh" was not a
winning hand. A majority of Americans told pollsters that they sym-
pathized with Blasey Ford, not Kavanaugh, believing her story, not
the judge's putative recollections (*NPR* 10/3/18). Far from fueling
Republican electoral victory, the Senate confrontation had backfired,
enraging not only liberals but centrists, driving women and younger
voters to the polls in record numbers. Yes, Republicans had been
"able to narrowly seat Judge Kavanaugh," the *Times* reported, but in
doing so they had energized "many Democrats and a share of inde-
pendents in suburban congressional districts and big-state governor's
races where female voters were already enraged" (*NYT* 9/29/18). On
November 6, Democrats took back control of the House, winning
more new seats than they had in any election since the party's 1974
post-Watergate landslide. Among the Representatives elected were

more than a record one hundred women (*NYT* 9/30/18, A1b; *NYT* 11/26/18).

The societalization of sexual harassment in the workplace would not be blocked by polarization. #MeToo had become deeply imbedded in American collective consciousness.

Returning to Steady State

The societalization of sexual harassment in the workplace – the "#MeToo moment" – took years to subside from effervescence into steady state. In the wake of "Kavanaugh," a handful of men who had been stigmatized as predators and ejected from their positions of power made efforts to return to the mainstream, presuming that there should be a return to normalcy, indeed that there already had been. Each effort, however, ignited a firestorm of passionate reproof. Jian Ghomeshi, a disgraced former Canadian Broadcasting Company star whom more than 20 women had accused of assault and harassment, published "Reflections from a Hashtag" in the *New York Review of Books* (*NYRB* 2018), a barely concealed plea for pity, sympathy, and exoneration. Its appearance on the website of NYRB, the Anglophone intellectual world's most influential intellectual magazine, immediately triggered widespread revulsion. The *Review* felt compelled to open its back pages to outraged letters expressing "shock," "utter horror," and "disgust" from readers explaining how "appalled" they were at an "absolutely disgraceful" editorial decision that brought "shame to the organization" (*NYRB* 10/25/18).

> To the Editors: I, like many others, am writing to express my distaste for the recent essay you published by Jian Ghomeshi. I have never had such a strong physical reaction of disgust while engaging in a sedentary activity like reading. It's clear that Jian still thinks *he* is the victim . . . Good lord! It's honestly just so embarrassing that you published [it].   (ibid.: 56)

NYRB's editorial staff apologized for "our failures" (ibid: 54), and its powerful editor, Ian Buruma, appointed with great fanfare only months earlier, was forced to resign (*NYT* 9/19/18; cf. Kudla and Stokes 2024).

"Only one of my accusers reached out or responded to my heartfelt queries," complained John Hockenberry, the former National Public Radio host, in "Exile," another long and self-absorbed mea culpa, this one published in *Harper's Magazine*. Immediately controversial, the essay generated angry pushback and critical debate (*The Cut* 2018). On his eponymous weekly program "Real Time with Bill Maher," the popular comedic commentator Bill Maher defended Al Franken, who had resigned from the U.S. Senate amid groping allegations, questioning the credibility of his female accusers and joking, "You know when you're a politician, being touch-feely is kind of part of the job." Maher was ridiculed as out of touch (*Is it Funny or Offens ive*.com 2018). The comedian Norm Macdonald told *The Hollywood Reporter*: "It used to be, 'One hundred women can't be lying,' . . . and then it became, 'One woman can't lie' and that became 'I believe all women.' And then you're like, 'What?'" (*Huffington Post* 9/12/18). Macdonald's appearance on "The Tonight Show" was canceled and his career endangered (*CNN* 9/12/18; *Vanity Fair* 9/12/18). When Louis C.K. – "the onetime king of stand-up who admitted to sexual misconduct with multiple women" (*NYT* 10/31/18) – returned to per- forming one year after his #MeToo humiliation, he was confronted with protestors holding angry signs, one of which read, "When you support Louis C. K., you tell women your laughter is more important than their sexual assaults and loss of their careers" (ibid.).

On the front page of the *New York Times*' "Sunday Review," feminist author Jennifer Weiner worried that "over the past few weeks it's felt like someone fired a start pistol [and] one by one, like bad dreams, the #MeToo men have come back" (*NYT* 9/23/18). They were now being allowed to publish their own stories, and Weiner protested it wasn't right.

> Stories matter tremendously. They're how we learn about who is real and who's less consequential; whose pain is important and whose, not much; who is the hero and who is merely the hero's reward . . . *Do men know how to be sorry?* (ibid., italics added)

These reactions highlighted the powerful existence of a newly gendered civil sacred. Like earlier hard-fought expansions of civil sol- idarity, this one would have to be fiercely protected against threats to undermine it, to demonize it, or even simply to make it seem mundane. If women's truth were to continue to be respected, it was their stories, not men's, that would need to be heeded. Hockenbery "demands that we consider his misery and embarrassment," the *Times*' feminist columnist Michelle Goldberg angrily observed, but "he never really grapples with the misery and embarrassment he caused, never thinks deeply about how he affected the lives of the women who changed jobs to escape his advances" (*NYT* 9/16/18). Goldberg freely admit- ted that she, too, "mourns the loss of Franken in the Senate," but she excoriated Maher for "seem[ing] to lack empathy for the woman who is discombobulated by suddenly feeling the hand of a man she admires on her backside." Claiming "the discussion about #MeToo and forgiveness never seems to go anywhere," Goldberg suggested, it's "because men aren't proposing paths for restitution [but] asking why women won't give them absolution." It's not men but the gendered expansion of civil solidarity that is being betrayed.

When steady state finally returned, it did not mean returning to what existed before #MeToo seized the day. Societalization had produced, not only a new culture structure, but reconstructed social organization. The boundaries separating civil and non-civil spheres had shifted; the civil/anti-civil binary was now applied to sexual behavior in the workplace in strikingly more democratic ways. There were new protagonists and antagonists, a new female hero, a new narrative about survivors telling their truths, an expanded vision of civil solidarity inside the workplace.

Short of some "Thermidor" that brings into being a "Handmaid's Tale" dystopia, sexual harassment will join such other master signifiers of social evil as racism, antisemitism, and homophobia, things that cannot be said or done without powerful profanation. Which does not mean that the behaviors themselves have ceased. Sexual harassment in the workplace continues. As long as men hold asymmetrical power, there will be not only the motive but also the means and opportunity for them to take advantage of female subordinates in a sexual way. When they do, however, men now face the likelihood, or at least the very real possibility, of public sanction, of being humiliated and punished. Revelations of sexual harassment will still trigger moral revulsion and organizational and legal action – just not on the front page.

— 4 —

FROM CIVIL RIGHTS TO
BLACK LIVES MATTER

Since their first institutionalizations in the seventeenth century, the universalistic promises made by the civil spheres of even formally democratic nation-states have been mocked by gross exclusions and inequalities. With the help of the bifurcating discourse of civil society, these "destructive intrusions" have entered into the very construction of the civil sphere, distorting its norms, institutions, and interactions. Yet, insofar as the universalizing ideals of the civil sphere have retained some independence and force, and they often have, there has always remained the possibility, in principle, for civil repair.

In this chapter, I wish to suggest that social movements against racial oppression in American – from the civil rights movement of the mid twentieth century to the Black Lives Matter movement in the early twenty-first – should be regarded, among other things, as efforts to repair America's compromised civil sphere.[1] In social systems that include a partially independent civil sphere, every actor might be said to occupy a dual position. He or she is a subordinate or superordinate actor in a whole series of vertical hierarchies and, at the same time, a member of the putatively horizontal community of civil life. Even for a dominated and marginalized minority, duality allows the possibility, in principle, of struggles for empowerment and incorporation. One metaphorical way of putting this is to say the vertical relationships of the non-civil spheres – economic, political, religious, familial, ethnic, and scientific – are challenged by membership in a horizontal, civil "environment" that, in principle, surrounds them.

Duality is missed by social movement theories that focus exclusively on resistance to domination and the accumulation of scarce resources. It is not only the system of resource allocation that is crucial for stimulating social movements but also the system of normative integration, however that may be defined. If this integrative environment is at least partly a civil one, conflicts against domination become more than simply Gramscian "wars of position" whose outcomes depend on which side accumulates more power and more effectively threatens, and sometimes exercises, coercion and force.

Duality means that social movements also involve demands for recognition and for the expansion of civil solidarity that recognition implies. Achieving power remains vital, but it can only be gained by civil means. Organizations and resources remain crucial for social movements, but what they provide, in the first instance, is access to the "means of persuasion." In a social system that contains a substantial civil sphere, it is communicative institutions that provide leverage for affecting regulative institutions – the legal codes, the office obligations, and the electoral outcomes that effectively control the allocation of the state's money and force.

The Civil Rights Movement in the Mid Twentieth Century

It goes without saying that there was little civil mediation in the vertical relationship between Black subjects and white dominators in the American South. Because there was no civil mediation, Blacks often felt compelled to try to seize power directly, through revolts and other kinds of violent confrontations. When they did so, their efforts were invariably put down with overwhelming force.

As the notion of duality suggests, however, even in the Southern states the vertical relationship of racial domination was surrounded by implicit, not yet articulated constraints that emanated from the more horizontal civil sphere of the North. It was this duality – not the accumulation of instrumental power and the exercise of direct confrontation – that promised the possibility of justice for dominated Southern Blacks. How could this duality be activated? The challenge was to find a way to reach over the anti-civil domination of white Southerners to the other, more civil side in the North.

Contemporary American historians and sociologists have tended to portray the civil rights movement simply as a power struggle between Blacks and whites, emphasizing grassroots organizing and direct, face-to-face confrontations between organized masses of African Americans and their immediate oppressors on the local scene (Morris 1984, 2007). As I see it, however, the civil rights movement must be understood in a different way. Certainly, its ambition was to lever-

102

age the power of state intervention. In order to do so, however, the movement concerned itself, first and foremost, with persuasion. Its goal was to achieve a more influential and hence more dominant position in the "national" civil sphere directed from the North. Only after achieving such civil influence could movement leaders, and the masses they were energized by, trigger regulatory intervention and accumulate power in the more traditional sense.

There were many so-called structural factors that made such communicative mobilization possible, and these have been the focus of various empirical studies. Theorists and empirical social scientists alike have identified such factors inside the Black community as industrialization and urbanization; increasing secondary and higher education; the independence, wealth, and power of the Black church; and the significance of Black newspapers. What facilitated the emergence of the Black counter-public in more contingent, historically specific terms was the massive African American participation in World War II, which heightened expectations for full empowerment.

The force of structural factors outside the Black community has also been frequently noted, most often the increasingly responsive legal order of the surrounding Northern civil sphere. This new legalism was itself stimulated, in no small part, by the growth of the National Association for the Advancement of Colored People (NAACP), which constituted a kind of "shadow" regulatory institution *vis-à-vis* white civil society. The NAACP initiated the U.S. Supreme Court's *Brown v. Board of Education* decision, which made school desegregation illegal in 1954. To these widely recognized structural factors, I would add the emergence of Northern news journalism as an independent profession with its own universalizing and increasingly idealistic ethics. Once Northern white news reporters entered the South to cover the nascent civil rights movement, in the mid 1950s, they functioned as the eyes and ears of the Northern civil sphere. Without this organizational feature, there would have been no success for the Black movement for civil rights.

Such structural-institutional factors – resources and capacities – made possible the emergence of the Black movement for civil rights. But what was also crucially important – and what has remained virtually unstudied – was the process of communicative mobilization itself, the cultural-symbolic process that these structural factors facilitated but did not determine in a causal sense. By communicative mobilization, I refer to the ability of movement leaders to frame and reframe their complaints, their selves, and their groups in a manner that allowed their demands to leapfrog Southern officials and Southern media and to gain the serious, eventually the rapt, attention of less racist whites in the Northern civil sphere.

From this perspective, the Black leaders of the Southern movement, the "movement intellectuals" (Eyerman and Jamison 1991), can be understood as enormously skillful mobilizers of communication. In effect, they functioned as translators, reweaving the particular concerns of the Black community by stitching them together with the tactics of Ghandian nonviolence, Christian narratives of sacrifice, and the democratic codes of the American civil sphere. In order to establish a relationship with the surrounding civil sphere, the Black movement was compelled to engage not only in instrumental but in symbolic action. It aimed not only at accumulating and leveraging structural power but also at creating performative power, which depended on producing an arresting, existentially and politically compelling narrative. The movement would succeed to the degree it could create a "social drama" with which the Northern civil audience could identify and vicariously participate in the struggle against racial injustice in the South. In the late 1970s, James Bevel, one of the movement's most effective non-violent leaders, retrospectively explained movement "action" in precisely these terms. "Every nonviolent movement is a dialogue between two forces," Bevel said, "and you have to develop a drama, [you have] to dramatize the dialogue to reveal the contradictions in the guys you're dialoguing with."

This dramaturgic element provides the elusive key to understanding how duality was triggered during those years of heightened mobilization and structural reform. How could white Northern civil society be there, in the South, yet not be there at the same time? When its physical presence was barely tangible, how could its moral presence eventually become strongly felt? How could the North's representative officials be compelled to intervene in a society toward which they had earlier evinced so little interest and against which they had so often claimed to exercise so little control?

Duality was activated because the Southern Black movement created a successful social drama. Only such a symbolic vehicle could break through the structural constraints on the local scene. The symbolic power of the civil rights drama facilitated emotional and moral identification between Northern whites and Southern Blacks. Eventually, these intertwined processes of emotional identification and symbolic extension created a historically unprecedented widening of civil solidarity, one that extended for the first time significantly beyond the color line. Insofar as solidarity expanded, Northern whites reacted with indignation and anger to the violation of Black civil rights, especially to the anti-civil violence that white Southern officials often unleashed against the nonviolent protest activities of Southern Blacks. This white outrage eventually affected Northern officials, who felt compelled, finally, to begin to repair the destructive intrusion of race into the Southern civil sphere, and eventually, with much more ambivalence, in the Northern civil sphere as well.

Only through the concepts and methods of cultural sociology can we observe, and begin provisionally to explain, power processes of this kind. I am not suggesting that other approaches to power should be abandoned, but that conventional understandings of power – as consisting of resources and capacities – must be modified in a fundamental way. In the *Poetics*, Aristotle explained that drama compels identification and catharsis. Tragic drama, he wrote, excites in the audience pity and terror, and sympathy for the protagonists' plight. The progression of protagonist and antagonist eventually allows catharsis, the emotional working through that affirms not only the existence but the force of higher moral law. Of course, the civil rights movement was not scripted; it was a social movement, not a text. Nonetheless, the contingent, open-ended nature of its conflicts was symbolically mediated and textually informed. Life imitates art. In the dramas created by the civil rights movement, the Black civil innocents, who were weak, were pitted against the white anti-civil antagonists, who were strong. The forces of civil good unexpectedly but persistently emerged triumphant. If such an outcome made the process ultimately more melodramatic than tragic, melodrama shares with tragedy an emphasis on suffering and the excitation of pity and terror (Brooks 1976).

Civil rights leaders became heroes only because they first were victims; they gained repeated triumphs only after repeated experiences of tragedy. As the movement gained experience, its organizers learned how to dramatically display their victim position more effectively. What they knew from the very beginning, however, was that Southern Black protestors could redeem their suffering only if they maintained their civil dignity in the midst of defeat, if they refrained from anti-civil violence, aggression, dishonesty, and deception. The protestors had to be viewed by the Northern audience as keeping faith with civil good in the face of anti-civil abuse and the temptations of despair.

The modern civil rights movement began with the Montgomery bus boycott in 1955–1956, a drama that brought Martin Luther King into the spotlight and captured the attention of Northern communicative media and citizens. After Montgomery, King and his colleagues formed the Southern Christian Leadership Conference (SCLC). For the next four years, this strongly networked organization devoted itself to winning voting rights by launching campaigns to register and educate potential Black voters. These campaigns were bound to fail. They aimed at achieving regulatory intervention and political power directly in the South without first addressing communicative institutions and achieving influence in the North. Movement leaders learned the hard way that they would have to put first things first. They would have to mount a full dress, years-long social drama for the benefit of the civil audience in the North. Only if they succeeded in this communicative effort could they produce the regulatory intervention – first via voting, then via positive law and office regulation – that, eventually, would give them political power on the local scene.

The critical learning experience that changed leaders' minds was the sit-in campaign that Black college students launched in 1960. As a result of this spectacularly successful movement, lunch counters were desegregated in Greensborough and Nashville and hundreds of other Southern cities. The most important effect of the sit-ins, however, was to introduce what came to be called "direct nonviolent action." With this new tactic, the civil rights movement's understanding of itself was permanently changed. Without ever explicitly acknowledging it, leaders discarded the Ghandian approach to nonviolence. For Ghandhi and early movement leaders, non-violence had been an end in itself; they believed that love and tolerance could alter the consciousness of the oppressor. After 1960, nonviolence became a tactic, a means to a dramaturgical end. Its function became not to efface the anti-civil violence of racist officials but, rather, to provoke it, allowing movement activists to draw attention to their own civil composure in turn.

The drama-producing status of direct nonviolent action became evident in the next year, in the "Freedom Rides" of 1961. For several weeks, the leaders of CORE (Congress for Racial Equality) and SNCC (Student Non-Violent Coordinating Committee) organized a "protest bus" to test laws outlawing discrimination in public transportation throughout the South. Every few days, the riders on the Freedom bus would be brutally beaten, sometimes nearly to the point of death, by the white vigilante posses that gathered to confront them when they arrived to the bus stations in the deep South. This campaign did not succeed in making the South enforce its antidiscrimination laws. It did succeed, however, in providing for Northern whites an extraordinarily compelling melodrama about racial power, suffering, and heroic justice. This dramaturgical power was suggested by the fact the

Freedom bus eventually came to be filled with more journalists and national-guard members than movement activists, and was trailed by many more carloads of the same.

The endgame of these serial civil dramas was to so deepen emotional identification and symbolic extension between Southern Blacks and Northern whites that powerful national officials were compelled to undertake the very serious political costs of what came to be known as "the second Reconstruction." The 1963 Birmingham campaign marked the tipping point, after which the Northern civil sphere became so communicatively engorged that it did indeed transmogrify public feeling into regulative intervention.

The year before Birmingham, in 1962, the movement had suffered a disastrous political and symbolic defeat in Albany, Georgia. Black protest leaders learned from this experience. In their effort to penetrate the symbolic space of the Northern civil sphere, they vowed that, in the future, they would leave much less to chance. Until Birmingham, King and his organization had entered local civil rights contests rather haphazardly, leveraging the Black hero's national prestige and the civil deference he commanded into dramatic power over an ongoing flow of events. After the Albany fiasco, protest leaders realized that, in order to frame white violence effectively, they would have to exert significantly more control over their own performance and, if possible, over that of their antagonists as well.

The very choice of Birmingham as the target for this exercise in systematic provocation reveals the movement's heightened self-consciousness. Birmingham was picked, not because of its potential for progressive reform, but for the opposite reason. As a deeply reactionary city, its chief law-enforcement officer, "Bull" Connor, was known to have a serious problem containing his temper and maintaining self-control. Only if there were a clear and decisive space between civil good and anti-civil evil could the conflict in the street be translated into a symbolic contest, and only if it became such a symbolic context could the protest gain its intended effect. Agonism is essential to the plot of every successful performance.

In the days leading up to the campaign, the dramatic tension between protagonists and antagonists reached a fever pitch. Ralph Abernathy, King's principal assistant, promised "we're going to rock this town like it has never been rocked before." Bull Connor retorted that "blood would run in the streets" of Birmingham before he would allow protests to proceed.

Providing an overarching narrative for this imminent clash, King drew upon the book of Exodus, the iconic parable of the Jews'

107

divinely inspired protest against Egyptian oppression. The SCLC leader publicly vowed to lead demonstrations until "Pharaoh lets God's people go." Despite elaborate preparation, however, the social drama initially failed to ignite, and the performance did not develop as planned. The demonstrations began on cue, and King went to jail. Yet Birmingham's Black civil society did not rise up in solidarity and opposition, and the surrounding white civil sphere in the North became neither indignant nor immediately involved. Even King's "Letter from the Birmingham Jail," later accorded canonical status in American protest literature, failed to generate any significant response from the Northern media, much less from their audience.

The routine of daily marches, arrests, and nightly mass meetings continued, but the national reporters begin to drift away from Birmingham for lack of "news." It became increasingly difficult to mobilize support beyond the small core group of dedicated activists. The problem was that the sequence of demonstration, arrest, and mass meeting was becoming routine. It would have to be disrupted by something "abnormal." An event would have to be staged of such performative power that it could create a breach.

After intensive discussion and self-doubt, movement leaders made the decision to allow Birmingham's school children to enter the fray. In the historical literature, the motivations and the repercussions of this decision are typically represented in quantitative and material terms, as making up for the falling numbers of adult participants. Much more significant, however, was the potential for altering the *moral* balance of the confrontation. Children would appear more well-meaning, sincere, and innocent than the movement's nonviolent but powerful and determined adults, and this greater vulnerability would provide an even sharper contrast with the irrational, violent repression that the movement intended to provoke from Southern officials.

When the "children's crusade" began, and hundreds of young people were herded off every day to jail, the drama did, in fact, markedly intensify. Attendance skyrocketed at the nightly mass meetings, and a sense of crisis was in the air. Birmingham was back on the front pages, and the local confrontation had succeeded in projecting itself into the attention space of the wider civil sphere. As the long-time local leader of Birmingham's freedom movement, Fred Shuttlesworth, proclaimed to the overflow crowd who showed up in his church the evening after the children were first jailed, "the whole world is watching Birmingham tonight."

It was the pressure created by this intensifying external scrutiny, not simply the material constraint of the city's jails being filled to overflowing, that managed, finally, to incite Birmingham's bad-tempered sheriff. Bull Connor unleashed the repressive violence that underlies white domination. Stepping outside the constraints of civil society, he ordered his men to use physical force, turning fire hoses on the protestors, setting police dogs loose on them, and poking them with electric cattle prods. Because of his local power, the sheriff thought he could act with impunity. Yet, while he did succeed in gaining control of the immediate situation, he could not control the effect that this exercise of unbridled power would have on the civil audience at one remove. The sheriff ignored duality at his peril. Bull Connor won the physical battle but lost the symbolic war.

By unleashing public violence, these Southern white officials had allowed themselves to become antagonists in a civil drama written and directed by the Black protest movement. The melodrama presented Southern evil in an almost gothic way. Graphic reports of horrendous, lopsided physical confrontations between civil good and anti-civil evil were broadcast over television screens and splashed across front pages throughout the Northern civil sphere. Fiercely rushing water from high pressure fire hoses swept little girls and boys dressed in their Sunday best hundreds of feet across Birmingham's downtown square. As they were pinned against a brick wall, the civil interpreters from the North transmitted the children's screams of terror and their bathetic efforts to shield themselves from the violent force. Growling German shepherds and their police handlers in dark sunglasses lunged forward into the youthful crowd. Northern journalists, both reporters and photographers, recorded the viciousness of the animals and the arrogant indolence of the men, and they captured the fright, helplessness, and righteous rage of their nonviolent victims. The emotional resonance these photos generated in the Northern civil sphere was palpable and became only more profound with the passing of time. From being symbols that directed the viewer to an actual event, the photographs of the confrontation became icons, evocative embodiments of the fearful consequences of anti-civil force regardless of time and place.

It is important to see that these media messages were representations, not literal transcriptions, of what transpired in Birmingham during these critical days. Even if the events seemed to "imprint" themselves on the minds of observers, they did not do so literally; they needed to be interpreted first. The struggle for interpretive control was waged just as fiercely as the struggle in the streets, and its outcome divided just as cleanly along local versus national lines.

109

In their own representations, Birmingham's local media completely inverted the indignant interpretive frame being broadcast by media in the North. For example, when the *Birmingham News* reported on the fire hosing of demonstrators, it presented a photograph of an elderly Black woman strolling alongside a park, holding an umbrella to protect herself from the mist produced by the gushing fire hoses nearby. "Just another showery day for a Negro stroller," read the caption below the photo, offering the further observation that the woman "appears undisturbed by disturbances" from the riot nearby. Headlining statements by city officials, the local media broadcast the Birmingham mayor's condemnation of the "irresponsible and unthinking agitators" who had made "tools" of children and turned Birmingham's whites into "innocent victims."

For Northern communicative institutions and their audiences, however, the linkage of anti-civil violence to white, not Black power proved much more persuasive. Portraying the Black demonstrators as helpless victims at the mercy of vicious, inhuman force, these reports evoked feelings of pity and terror. For the audience in the surrounding Northern civil sphere, the narrative of tragic melodrama was now firmly in place. Northern white identification with the victims triggered feelings of civic outrage and moved many vocal protests. Angry phone calls were made to Congressional representatives, indignant letters fired off to the editorial pages of newspapers and magazines. In the *Washington Post*, an angry citizen from Forest Heights, Maryland, poured out her personal feelings of outrage and shame. Her simple and heartfelt letter provides an eloquent expression of the indignation she evidently shared with many other white Americans in the North. Revealingly, she explains her outrage as motivated by her identification with the Black protestors, to whom she seamlessly extends her own ethical and civic principles.

> Now I've seen everything. The news photographer who took the picture of a police dog lungeing at a human being has shown us in unmistakable terms how low we have sunk and will surely have awakened a feeling of shame in all who have seen that picture, who have any notion of human dignity. This man being lunged at was not a criminal being tracked down to prevent his murdering other men; he was, and is, a man. If he can have a beast deliberately urged to lunge at him, then so can any man, woman or child in the United States. I don't wish to have a beast deliberately urged to lunge at me or my children and therefore I don't wish to have beasts lungeing at the citizens of Birmingham or any other place. If the United States doesn't stand for some average decent level of human dignity, what does it stand for?

The experience of moral outrage was so widely shared in the days after Birmingham that it set the stage for regulatory intervention and fundamental civil repair. When King declared, "the hour has come for the Federal Government to take a forthright stand on segregation in the United States," President Kennedy responded by assuring the public that he was "closely monitoring events." The President sent Burke Marshall, the head of the Justice Department's Civil Rights Division, down to Birmingham. With Marshall's prodding, settlement negotiations were begun. In the eye of the hurricane of communicative mobilization, white and Black leaders for the first time spoke cooperatively face-to-face. As the local negotiations continued, high officials from the surrounding civil sphere – President Kennedy and his cabinet secretaries – placed calls to strategically placed local businessmen and to corporate executives outside the South who could exercise leverage on the local elite. These interventions eventually produced a pact detailing goals and timetables for ending Birmingham's economic segregation.

While these progressive local reforms certainly deserve praise, it was to the community beyond the city, indeed beyond the region, that the Birmingham demonstrations were aimed. It was their success in mobilizing the North's more democratic and, potentially at least, much more powerful civil sphere that made Birmingham into "Birmingham," a watershed in the history of the racial movement for civil justice in the United States. "Birmingham" entered into the collective conscience of American society more powerfully and more indelibly than any other single event in the history of the movement for civil rights. In the days immediately following the Birmingham settlement, a weary President Kennedy summed up this new world of public opinion in a complaint to his party's Majority Leader in the Senate: "I mean, it's just in everything. I mean, this has become everything." Three months later, a White House official remarked to the Associated Press, "This hasn't been the same kind of world since May." In 1966, Bobby Kennedy recalled those days during an interview. "Everybody looks back on it and thinks that everybody was aroused about this for the last three years," Bobby remarked. "But what aroused people generally in the country and aroused the press," he insisted, "was the Birmingham riots in May of 1963."

This dramatic deepening of Northern white identification with protesting Southern Blacks had political effect. The profound arousal of civil consciousness, which "Birmingham" simultaneously triggered and reflected, pushed the civil sphere's elected representatives in the direction of regulatory reform. That summer, the Kennedy

111

administration drew up far-reaching legislation, submitted to Congress as the Civil Rights Act of 1963. With this action, the symbolic space of communicative mobilization became transformed into the details of law and sanction that would eventually allow massive regulatory intervention in the Southern states.

It is a matter of historical debate whether this civil rights legislation could have been passed without Kennedy's martyrdom in November, 1963, and the accession to the presidency of Lyndon Johnson, the former Senate Majority Leader who was a master of the legislative craft (Caro 2012). That the very introduction of this far-reaching legislation represented a fundamental fork in the road, however, is beyond dispute. Johnson organized passage of the first major civil rights legislation in 1964. In March of 1965, Martin Luther King led the extraordinary "March on Selma," whose dialectic of tragedy and triumph triggered passage of the second civil rights bill, the *Voting Rights Act of 1965*. Yet, despite the momentous events that followed in the two years after Birmingham, they can be properly understood only if they are seen as iteration, as amplifying and filling in the symbolic and institutional framework that had become crystallized by the early summer of 1963. What began as counter-performance became a powerful core narrative for a less racist American way of life.

Black Lives Matter in the Early Twentieth Century

The iterative performances of the mid-century civil rights movement left behind a deeply ingrained culture structure of racial justice, an intensely redolent set of background representations upon which later Black protests would draw. Yet there is an enormous distance between background representations – the culture structures that provide the *langue* for symbolic action – and the concrete performances situated in time and space that are informed by them. The latter are more like pragmatic speech acts than emanations of cultural structures. To become successful, other elements of performance must be brought felicitously into play.

Between the Black protest tradition as crystallized in the mid twentieth century and the conditions of poor Black inhabitants of the inner cities in the early twenty-first century, there loomed the enormous challenge of forging new action-oriented scripts. These scripts would also have to be made to walk and talk, informing dramatic scenes that could appeal to, energize, and, in some significant part, unify citizen-audiences fragmented by race and class and demoralized by political fatalism. There would also have to be strong leaders, dramaturges who could produce protest performances and directors who could manage their *mise-en-scènes*. Successfully fusing audience, script, and actors would require, as well, access to the means of symbolic production; sympathetic interpretation of ongoing performances by critics, such as journalists and intellectuals; and sufficient leverage *vis-à-vis* material power that states would hesitate to use repression to prevent protest performances from taking place.

These disparate elements were finally brought into place by the Black movement against police violence that gathered force in the years between 2012 and 2016.[2] Skill, fortitude, and *fortuna* were required to weave them together into the iterative sequence that finally allowed Black Americans, once again, to seize the nation's political stage.

The Underclass Becomes an Acting Subject

It had been decades since they had been able to do so. If the victory of the mid-century civil rights movement had been decisive, it was also partial. The gates of the ghetto (Duneier 2016) had been pried loose for African American workers, clerks, professionals, and business people (Landry 1988). While these occupational groups remained subject to far-reaching racial stigma (Anderson 2012a, 2015), their freedom of movement was vastly expanded. Even as they left their ghetto confinement, however, the uneducated, unskilled, and unemployed stayed behind in the inner city. A racial underclass formed, an often desperate admixture of a dominated class and the most subordinated fragment of a still widely despised race (Wilson 1987). Racial and class prejudice built a cultural fence around this inner-city group (Patterson 1998); politicians, real estate agents, courts, police, and prisons exercised controls of an administrative, coercive, and material kind (Massey and Denton 1993). Young Black males were incarcerated at alarmingly high rates, often for acts that would not lead to imprisonment if the perpetrators had been white (M. Alexander 2012).

Working and middle-class African Americans had peopled the mid-twentieth-century movement for civil rights, supplying crucial cultural capital. They brought education and professional skills to the task of protest, and the Black church, with its powerful bonding and bridging institutions (Putnam 2000), provided not only generalized trust but protected spaces within which public performances could be rehearsed (Morris 1984). These kinds of resources were not nearly as

113

available to the racial underclass; as a result, its capacity for exercising political agency was severely curtailed.

In principle, if not in practice, the potential for social protest on behalf of the underclass remained, along with the possibility of leveraging widespread social criticism into civil repair of the institutions that have sustained its depredation. Despite fissures, contradictions, weak-kneed liberalism, and conservative backlash, the civil sphere in the U.S. remains relatively autonomous and potentially empowering, its ideals and institutions on call if the social forces can be rightly arranged. To create such arrangements a performatively powerful social movement is required, one that can so effectively dramatize underclass suffering that new networks of meaning can form – between marginalized racial groups excluded from the civil sphere and core groups who occupy secure and influential places within it.

It was in 2012 that such a performatively powerful Black civil rights movement began taking shape. Police shootings of Black men had been routine for decades, but they had rarely been publicly marked. This changed when online organizers created evocative, highly condensed slogans and visual symbols, circulating them virtually on their social networks. When their cell phones and computers lit up, tens of thousands of Black bodies took to the streets, producing choreographed demonstrations that evocatively contrasted Black innocence with police brutality. Once regarded as routine, police shootings now became dramatized as egregious, undeniable abuses of civil authority. A contemporary observer put it this way:

> Neither police violence in Black communities nor resistance to that violence are new. But something new *has* emerged: a new focus for anger and despair, a new source of critical hope, a new catalyst for social imagination and creativity. There are surely many reasons that a movement has developed at this particular moment. [One] factor has certainly been the skill with which organizers have deployed symbols, hashtags, chants, metaphors, and images in order to communicate – quickly and powerfully – the underlying values and goals of the movement. Every social movement develops a cache of symbols. These symbols give coherence to dispersed grassroots efforts. They tap into our emotions and encourage us to learn more. We use them to mark our collective identity and to capture the attention of media outlets, with their famously short attention spans.
>
> (Kuttner 2015, original italics)

"The Black Lives Matter movement," in the words of the *Huffington Post*, "has reframed the way Americans think about police treatment of people of color" (McLaughlin 2016). It began to seem that, for the first time, the lives of poor Black people began to matter.

> The Movement has managed to activate a sense of red alert around a chronic problem that, until now, has remained mostly invisible outside the communities that suffer from it ... Evidence does not suggest that shootings of black men by police officers have been significantly on the rise. Nevertheless, police killings have become front-page news and a political flash point, entirely because of the sense of emergency that movement has sustained. (ibid.)

The *New York Times* described the dramatic effect of the exploding new protests in a similar manner: "The swiftness with which the movement now acts, and the volume of people it can bring out to every protest, have turned every police killing into a national referendum on the value of black lives in America" (Kang 2015).

The impact of this newly powerful symbolic mobilization was an extraordinary increase in awareness of the precarious position of the Black underclass, and widening sympathy and identification with it. Until recently, according to Pew (2015), "public opinion was ... closely divided" on the question of whether significant changes were still needed to achieve racial equality. By July 2015, after three years of social mobilization, Americans who believed deep changes were needed outnumbered those satisfied with the status quo by two to one: "This shift in public opinion is seen across the board. Growing shares in all regions of the country, and across all demographic and partisan groups say both that racism is a big problem and that more needs to be done to achieve racial equality" (ibid.).

Performing Indignation and Extending Identification

How were such largely Black protest performances able to affect majority white American citizen-audiences? As they unfolded on television and computer screens, the unprecedented wave of demonstrations against police brutality seemed spontaneous, as if they were grassroots, springing up from the underclass victims themselves. Yet this was not the case. Certainly, the demonstrations were heartfelt. But their authenticity had to be carefully choreographed, the verisimilitude they projected enhanced by performative effect.

When 17-year-old high-school student Trayvon Martin was murdered by George Zimmerman, a Neighborhood Watch coordinator for a gated community in Sanford, Florida, on February 26, 2012, the national Black community and its white supporters filled the airwaves with outrage over racism and civil irresponsibility. When the local police chief refused to arrest Zimmerman, claiming Florida's Stand Your Ground statute allowed his exercise of armed self-defense, thousands protested, and their demonstrations surprised and riveted what turned out to be a broadly sympathetic nation. The reaction was as electrifying as it was unexpected, pushing the envelope of interracial moral responsibility and emotional identification further than it had extended since the mid-century period, sixty years before. When President Obama publicly crystallized this identification, dramatically avowing, "When I think about this boy, I think about my own kids . . . If I had a son, he would look like Trayvon" (Shear 2012), he was speaking not only for himself and other African American parents but for a much broader swath of white citizens whom he represented as President of the United States. The "Million Hoodies for Justice" protest group sprang into existence one month after the shooting, organizing a march in New York where protestors chanted "We want arrests!" and "We are all Trayvon," many clad in hooded sweatshirts "symbolic of the clothing Martin wore when he was killed" (Miller 2012). Two weeks later, Zimmerman was charged with murder by a special prosecutor appointed by conservative Republican Governor Rick Scott.

Fifteen months later, when Zimmerman was acquitted, civil outrage once again ignited, boiling over with the news that Eric Garner, an African American father of six, had died when a white NYPD officer put him in a twenty-second chokehold in the course of his arrest. In the days and weeks of protests that mushroomed across U.S. cities, highly theatrical "die-ins" were staged; protestors lay down in the middle of busy streets, and demonstrators publicly chanted Garner's final words, "I Can't Breathe." When, just one month after Garner's killing, on August 9, 2014, a white police officer in Ferguson, Missouri, shot another young Black man, Michael Brown, protests exploded again. Brown's last words were, "I don't have a gun, stop shooting!" This secular prayer of pleading and protest "became a national rallying cry," according to the *New York Times* (Healy, Stolberg, and Yee 2015). As protestors chanted these words in cities and campuses across the country, they also projected indexical gestures that would be immediately recognized as ritual re-enactment. For example, they raised their arms above their heads, in solidarity with Michael Brown, the Black teenager who, according to witnesses, was surrendering when he was shot.

In December 2014, when a grand jury refused to issue indictments for Eric Garner's murder, urban protests reignited. Facing the specter of police repression, Black Americans performed with anger and gumption, their dramatic words and choreographed movements were streamed live by social media and, reported by mainstream journalism, ricocheted around the nation. Chanting and raising their arms in archetypical gestures of solidarity and fear, demonstrators marched in public squares, blocked local and interstate highways, and interrupted shopping centers, religious holidays, and political events. Their slogans and gestures became totems – "Mike Brown is an emblem," a protestor in Philadelphia declared (Associated Press 2014) – and were circulated by iconic African American celebrities from music, film, sport, theatre, and politics. Across from the Broadway NYPD police station, African American actors staged a precision rap-and-dancing protest. Outside a Cleveland Cavaliers and Brooklyn Nets basketball game, thousands milled in protest, while, on the inside, superstar LeBron James donned an "I Can't Breathe" T-shirt, proclaiming to national media, "as a society, we have to do better . . . for one another no matter what race you are" (Zillgit and Strauss 2014). Another player, Nets guard Jarret Jack, explained to television audiences that it was a matter of civil, not racial, solidarity.

> We aren't just focused on ourselves as just athletes [. . .] We collectively understand that this is an issue that needs to be addressed. The more attention we can bring and awareness to it is great. It's not a color issue, it's a people issue. It's a citizen issue. (ibid.)

The demonstrators outside the Cleveland arena welcomed these gestures, seeing them as potentially connecting with a much wider audience beyond.

> "That's a result of them being educated brothers and having a slight moral compass," a protestor identifying himself only as L.B. said. "They know they're on their grand stage. Anybody that has any type of public voice needs to stand up and do something." (ibid.)

Projecting gestures and voices from these grand stages had impact. The ritual-like symbolic actions generated a collective effervescence that pulsated outward in great waves, and these were commented upon by political observers who gauged and influenced shifting opinion. Donna Brazile, an influential Black media commentator and Democratic Party strategist, declared:

> "Hands up, Don't Shoot" has become a larger symbol of the desire to prove one's innocence . . . In many ways, it will always resonate as a symbol of an unarmed dead teenager lying for hours on the street. Just

117

like "I can't breathe" will never go away. They are forever etched in the complicated story of racial bias in our criminal justice system.

(Healy et al. 2015)

Black Lives Matter Seizes the Stage

It was in the midst of the Ferguson protests that Black Lives Matter – the hashtag, the organization, and the broad eponymous movement – emerged on the public scene.[3] #BlackLivesMatter had been created the day George Zimmerman went free, but in the year following it was rarely evoked. After the murder of Michael Brown, the website #BLM helped organize the latter-day Freedom Rides that fed the conflagration in Ferguson, and the number of online visitors jumped a hundred times (Freelon et al. 2016). A breathless contemporary account by the activist Spanish-language website teleSUR is revealing. "A national coalition determined to challenge state violence will convene in Ferguson over the next three days," teleSUR reported, and described the purpose of the gathering in performative terms – "to re-envision a Black political platform in the United States." The group that would build this platform was Black Lives Matter. TeleSUR linked the organization to the sacred tradition of Black civil rights, providing one of BLM's founders a platform to declaim about repression, resilience, and destiny.

> On Friday, close to 600 people will gather in Ferguson, Missouri from across the continental United States, part of the Black Life Matters (BLM) Ride. "The Black Life [sic] Matters (BLM) Ride is the Freedom Ride of our generation," explains co-organizer Patrisse Cullors . . . The BLM Ride comes out of the spirit and history of the 1960s Freedom Rides to Mississippi that aimed to end racial segregation" . . . "The BLM Ride is a call to action for Black people across the country to come together and re-articulate our destiny," stresses Cullors . . . "We believe that in order to move this country out of a cycle of destruction and trauma, we have to rise up, both locally and nationally. Ferguson represents both the repression that exists in Black communities, and also our immense resilience," advocates BLM in their National Advocacy and Organizing Toolkit. (teleSUR 2014)

A UCLA graduate in religion and philosophy, Patrisse Cullors was a full-time organizer for the Ella Baker Center for Human Rights in Oakland, a nonprofit dedicated to social justice issues in the inner city (Cobb 2016: 36). She created the hashtag #BlackLivesMatter from a Facebook post by her friend Alicia Garza on the day of George Zimmerman's acquittal. "The sad part is," Garza wrote, "there's a

118

section of America who is cheering and celebrating right now. And that makes me sick to my stomach. We GOTTA get it together y'all." To this Garza later added:

> . . . btw stop saying we are not surprised. That's a damn shame in itself. I continue to be surprised at how little Black lives matter. And I will continue that. Stop giving up on black lives . . . black people. I love you. I love us. Our lives matter . . . (ibid., 35)

After studying anthropology and sociology at the University of California, San Diego, Garza worked as a special-projects director in the Oakland office of the National Domestic Workers Alliance, representing twenty thousand caregivers and housekeepers. It was the third member of #BLM's founding trio, Opal Tometi, a writer and immigration-rights organizer in Brooklyn, who built the social-media platform on Facebook and Twitter so that, in the words of *New Yorker* journalist Jelani Cobb, "activists" could use the hashtag to "connect with one another" (ibid., 26). Then, as Cobb put it, the three women "began thinking about how to turn the phrase into a movement" (ibid.).

Organizers, Producers, Directors, and Activists

Garza, Cullors, and Tometi became invisible dramaturges, writing scripts for the highly visible public performances of their organization. They were not on the scene, but behind it. Looking back, Cullors claimed the role of producer and director, distinguishing her responsibilities from participating in real time performances and handling the mise-en-scène.

> I identify as an organizer versus an activist because I believe an organizer is the smallest unit that you build your team around. The organizer is the person who gets the press together and who builds new leaders, the person who helps to build and launch campaigns, and is the person who decides what the targets will be and how we're going to change this world. (http://patrissecullors.com/bio/)

It was somebody from outside the founding group of invisible organizers, a Brooklyn-based activist and friend of Cullors named Daniel Moore, who stepped onto the public stage, coordinating the "freedom rides" to Missouri from New York, Chicago, Portland, Los Angeles, Philadelphia, and Boston. Moore was soon joined by DeRay Mckesson, a 28-year-old school administrator from Minneapolis who, transfixed by the images and texts unrolling on his Twitter feed, drove six hundred miles to Ferguson to immerse himself in the ongoing protest scene (Kang 2015). In Ferguson, at a street-medic training session, Mckesson met Johnetta Elzie, a 25-year-old St. Louis native who had studied journalism in college. The two became hands-on, all-in, street-level organizing partners, avidly sharing information, participating, and helping to project BLM events in the weeks and months ahead.

> Elzie [was] one of the most reliable real-time observers of the confrontations between the protesters and the police. She took photos of the protest organizers, of the sandwiches she and her friends made to feed other protesters, of the Buddhist monks who showed up at the burned QuickTrip. Mckesson, too, was live-tweeting [and] integrating video and referring to protesters and police officers alike by name. Mckesson's tweets were usually sober and detailed, whereas Elzie's were cheerfully sarcastic. (ibid.)

Elzie and Mckesson soon became "the most recognizable figures in the movement in Ferguson" (Cobb 2016: 36). As iterations of Black protest unfolded in response to later police shootings, the two became publicly visible persona standing out from the emerging, but still largely anonymous "Black subject" whose gathering power was increasingly seen and heard over television and computer screens.

> Pretty soon, Mckesson and Elzie were appearing regularly on TV and radio. The two cultivated appealing personas, becoming easily recognizable to their many followers. Mckesson had begun wearing red shoes and a red shirt to protests. Later, he replaced this outfit with a bright blue Patagonia vest, which he now wears everywhere he goes. (Someone created a DeRay's vest Twitter account.) Elzie often wore dark lipstick, a pair of oversize sunglasses and a leather jacket: the beautician's daughter channeling a Black Panther. (Kang 2015)

This passage is from a spread about Mckesson and Elzie in a 2015 issue of the *New York Times Magazine*, a lengthy account filled with appealing color photos and marked by an enthusiastic, even adulatory tone (Kang 2015). Mckesson later announced his candidacy to become Baltimore's mayor. Soon after, clad in signature red sneakers and blue vest, he made guest appearances on *The Late Show* with Stephen Colbert and *The Daily Show* with Trevor Noah.

The Double Movement

When journalists and social scientists began to examine the new BLM protest movement, they highlighted its online quality, as if software

120

savvy plus anger and grit were sufficient in themselves to initiate the shock waves pulsating throughout the broader civil surround. Beguiled by technology, such understandings truncate the performative process, eliding the chasm separating scripts and actors, on one side, from audiences, on the other – making invisible, in other words, the very "de-fusion" of performative elements that makes it so difficult to achieve dramatic success.[4]

That this gap was real, and immensely challenging, explains why the BLM protest movement was a series of interrelated but separated calls and responses, not one performance but several, each one temporally, spatially, and demographically independent even if topically interlinked. The triggering posts of anonymous leaders, such as Garza and Cullors, were elaborated by on-scene actors, such as Mckesson and Elzie, and retweeted to a network of hundreds of organizers who were viewed as "in place" and "ready to bring thousands of people into the streets with a tweet" (Kang 2015). These first responders in the layered audience (Rauer 2006) were primed and committed, waiting to be "re-fused." Mckesson put it this way: "When I tweet, I'm mostly preaching to the choir" (Kang 2015). He was confident the audience for his missives would become actors performing protest on the street. What this on-scene organizer was not quite as certain about, however, were the effects that such choreographed bodily displays would have on audiences at one layer removed, those watching and listening to the street performances via mainstream media. Mckesson hoped, of course, this more distant audience would identify with the dramas he was organizing, but he confessed that, in this second phase, he was actually preaching *against* the choir.

> The heart of the movement is . . . shutting down streets, shutting down Walmarts, shutting down any place where people feel comfortable. We want to make people feel as uncomfortable as we feel when we hear about Mike, about Eric Garner, about Tamir Rice. We want them to experience what we go through on a daily basis. (ibid.)

The BLM street protests did not aim to seize power; most did not even make specific demands. Their ambition, rather, was communicative, to create dramatic performances that would trigger sympathy for the suffering of underclass others, generating an emotional cathexis that would extend cultural identification, putting "ordinary people" (whites mostly) in the position of the oppressed and allowing them to "experience what we go through on a daily basis."

To produce such vicarious symbolic experience, the portrayal of protest in the news media was key. This constituted the second act of the Black Lives Matter performance. It began with journalists inter-preting the protests and filing stories that their news organizations projected outward via print, television, and Internet. The first circuit of the double movement – social media directives to a committed network that brought Black bodies into the streets – had produced the performance of the racial underclass as a new Black subject. The second performative circuit aimed to connect this protest with a much more distant audience. The new Black subject had to be recognized by influential white core groups, and in a sympathetic way.

In their massive study of 40.8 million movement-related tweets between June 1, 2014, and May 31, 2015, Freelon et al. (2016) recon-structed the network structure of BLM's digital communications. Two findings suggest precisely the kind of double movement I am propos-ing here. The first is that the digital network was decidedly loose, composed of weak rather than strong ties, among which there was relatively little exchange back and forth. Instead of a "dense network with many reciprocal ties – conducive to building trust between con-nections" – the kind which, according to Freelon and his colleagues, would be ideal for "circulat[ing] ideas for how to mobilize" – the researchers found an "extremely diffuse" network, one much more "clearly conducive to broadly distributing and circulating informa-tion" (ibid., 16).[5] The second finding concerned not the geography of the network, but the substantive identity of its nodes. By far the most frequently connected hubs were media organizations, not individuals or protest groups, and most of these media were mainstream.[6] "In the case of the Black Lives Matter Web network," Freelon and colleagues concluded, "what primarily gets produced and distributed is news, which is meant to be widely distributed" (ibid.).

This empirical information illuminates the neural structure of the double movement. Directives from protest organizers not only triggered street performances but also massive retweetings among activists, which were subsequently posted directly, or redirected, to interested journalists. Alerted, reporters then put themselves imme-diately on the scene, virtually in real time or bodily in real space. Initiating the second performative circuit, reporters posted contempo-raneous stories on media blogs. These were picked up by participants inside the demonstrations and, more or less simultaneously, by the tens, sometimes hundreds of thousands of potentially attentive watch-ers on the outside, many of whom re(re)tweeted to new nodes on the network in turn.

This two-part performative structure remained in place even as the protest movement's organization and tactics changed. In later 2015, the controversies concerning police killings seemed to abate.[7] "If the goal of Black Lives matter was [. . .] to convince more Americans that police brutality existed," the *New York Times* reported, then "it was successful." With that success, the *Times* observed, "the momentum began to shift and transform into something else," and "there were fewer protests than before" (Howard 2016). BLM's national organization broke into more than 30 relatively independent, locally based activist groups. While scattered street demonstrations continued, attention shifted to more targeted disruptions (Aron 2015; Ruffin 2016; Stockman 2016), especially of the Presidential primary competitions that were becoming increasingly visible (cf. Eligon 2016). #BLM demonstrators took control of a "Netroots Nation forum featuring [Bernie] Sanders and Martin O'Malley in Phoenix and began chanting slogans" (Helsel 2015). At a Sanders rally in Seattle, two female #BLM activists took over the microphone, demanding the candidate extend his calls for radical reform from class to race. In Atlanta, #BLM interrupted a speech by Hillary Clinton on criminal justice and race. At a rally in Philadelphia, her husband, former President Bill Clinton, tried facing down chants from angry activists who linked his 1994 crime bill to the massive incarceration of Black men. "Black Activists Are Literally Stealing the Stage from 2016 Contenders – And It's Working," one liberal blog headlined (Moore 2015a).

It certainly appeared to be the case that, in response to the disruptive confrontations, Democratic "contenders . . . recalibrated their messages and tone" (Moore 2015b). O'Malley apologized for saying "all lives matter" (ibid.). Sanders added "racial justice" and penal reform to his list of political priorities (ibid.). Hillary Clinton began a "Mothers of the Movement" campaign, encouraging the mourning mothers of Trayvon Martin, Eric Garner, Michael Brown, Tamir Rice, and Sandra Bland "to organize and travel the country with her campaign" and paying their expenses so they could attend the Democratic presidential debates (Chozick 2016a). Describing the impact of this dramatic tactic, the *New York Times* noted how it bolstered the authenticity of Hillary Clinton's character and the vitality and verisimilitude of her campaign's performance.

> Having these women by her side has provided Mrs. Clinton with powerful and deeply sympathetic character witnesses as she makes her case to African American voters. And they have given her campaign, an often cautious and poll-tested operation, a raw, human, and sometimes gut-wrenching feeling. (Chozick 2016a)

Mr. Clinton, too, felt compelled to be publicly responsive, the *New York Times* headlining: "Bill Clinton Says He Regrets Showdown With Black Lives Matters Protesters" (Chozick 2016b).

BLM's newly disruptive tactics were also directed at Republican candidates, but, rather than eliciting supportive responses, these protests appeared to be aimed at highlighting what activists regarded as the uncaring whiteness of the conservative movement. During the primary period, this tactic seemed particularly effective *vis-à-vis* the candidacy of Donald Trump. The violent responses of his white supporters to BLM's provocations provoked Republican anxieties about the anti-civil, "over the line" character of the New York real estate developer's campaign.[8]

While the *New York Times* described the sequence of iterative demonstrations analyzed in this section as "the most formidable American protest movement of the 21st century to date" (Kang 2015), BLM's performative power remained relatively constricted in comparison with what had been generated by its mid-twentieth-century predecessor. Critical elements of social performance were infelicitously prepared, or even completely missing. There were problems, for example, with BLM's script. The persuasive reach of "disruptive indignation" is limited. More powerful myth would have laid out a redemptive pathway from suffering to salvation, from underclass to social justice, perhaps underscoring "American exceptionalism" or the idea of America as God's chosen people. The secular tone of BLM seemed to preclude a fecund connection with American civil religion (Bellah 1970b).

The lack of larger-than-life characters proved another major obstacle. Protagonists must be embodied in order to become heroic; collective subjects, online discourses, and digital images are not enough. DeRay Mckesson may have been the only distinguishable persona to have emerged from a protest movement that remained remarkably anonymous, but his 2016 Baltimore mayoral campaign still floundered for want of "name recognition" (Howard 2016). In late December 2015, CNN claimed Mckesson "drives the conversation" (Sidner 2015). Four months later, the *New York Times Magazine* reported Mckesson "was on Fortune's World's Greatest Leaders list last year" and "has been to the White House so many times that he says he doesn't get nervous anymore" (Howard 2016). Such claims of charismatic authority were vastly overstated. Mckesson registered on the American radar screen, but he didn't penetrate its sacred center. He did not become a collective representation of Black suffering and hope, either for the racial underclass or the protest drama's multicultural and multiclass audience on the outside. Mckesson did not embody, in the words he spoke, the tone of his voice, or the lines of his face, contemporary African American aspirations for justice. An effective organizer who became a recognizable face, Mckesson was more a celebrity, famous for being famous, than a genuine hero.[9]

Despite the protests of generations of Black and white intellectuals and legal reformers, the masses of African Americans suffered mostly in silence for decades after the gutting of post-slavery Reconstruction in 1877. It was the performative genius of Martin Luther King and his supporting staff that finally gave them voice. The drama they forged projected a redemptive narrative that riveted key segments of the Northern white audience, gained significant political power, and made major repairs in the rent racial garment of American life. Fifty years later, even as social scientists laid out the structural forces encircling the new Black underclass, Black Lives Matter forged anew an active Black subject. Deploying the newly digital means of symbolic production, its organizers projected compelling narratives, slogans, and gestures, triggering massive African American protest and, fusing with sympathetic journalists, brought the racially affirmative demand that Black lives matter as much as white lives into the heart of the nation.

While the explosive protests faded in the whiplash polarization of the 2016 presidential campaign, BLM's afterlife was extraordinary and extended, boring deeply into the racial configurations that, from the very origins of America's civil sphere, had distorted its promises for freedom, equity, and solidarity. "Systemic racism" became a central topic of conversation among white Americans, and dozens of states adopted policies aimed at "decarceration." Critical Race Theory became a mandated topic for teaching in many white-majority schools. Professional associations and private corporations created new anti-racist programs and training courses for their colleagues and employees. "DEI" protocols for upgrading diversity, equity, and inclusion permeated organizational life. How-to books instructing whites on becoming less racist, like Ibram X. Kendi's *How to Be an Anti-Racist*, became bestsellers. In 2020, *Time* reported that "the demand for books about race and antiracism . . . has soared" (Haynes 2020). "We've seen a tremendous increase, and I think it really is stemming from white people," remarked the owner of Mahogany Books, a Washington DC bookstore specializing in African diasporic literature. "In light of recent events," she explained, "a lot of people are now feeling a very visceral response in how they show up this world, and how they see it from our lens" (ibid.).

— 5 —

OBAMA–TAHRIR–OCCUPY
UTOPIAS OF CIVIL LIBERATION

The utopian ideal of civil solidarity sits uneasily in a world of social inequality and individual restriction. Dissatisfaction with existing social arrangements is chronic. Civil society becomes restless. Episodes of liminality and demands for civil repair are the periodic result.

The utopian idea of a solidary community composed of autonomous yet mutually responsible citizens has been at the heart of Western modernity since the City States of the Renaissance. In the seventeenth and eighteenth-century revolutions in England, America, and France, the civil imaginary was crystallized in democratic revolutions that made constitutionally regulated and self-governing communities of citizens the new rulers of their respective states. With the rise of industrial capitalism in the mid nineteenth century, the program for political democracy came to be gradually displaced by the "social question," a focus on class inequality that pushed for socialism rather than democracy. Efforts to control the ravages of industrial capitalism and imperialism demanded the creation of enormous state bureaucracies. In the crush of these newly insistent interests, the civil society imperative was often pushed aside. Revolutionary strategy shifted from wide public mobilization to clandestine militancy, and violent political organizations became *de rigueur* on the left and right.

One of the most remarkable political developments over the late twentieth and early twenty-first centuries was the withering of state-centrism and Jacobin ideals. Democracy re-emerged as a radical idea and civil society as a revolutionary movement. In 1981, to the astonishment of liberal, radical, and conservative pundits alike, the "Solidarity" movement emerged in Poland. It was repressed the year

126

after, but the decade that followed enshrined its idea of democratic civil society as a radical, revolution-inspiring goal. The blossoming of newly democratic Spain defied predictions that Franco's passing would trigger a bloody civil war. The "flower power" of the Philippine "People's Revolution" compelled Ferdinand Marcos to flee and the military to accede power to the million protesters in Manila's public square. Throughout the Southern Cone of Latin America, civilian governments pushed military juntas aside.

That first arc of global civil society movements culminated in the magical year of "1989," when one communist dictatorship after another fell before non-violent velvet revolutions. In June 1989, the communist state in China nearly met its match in Tiananmen Square. In 1990, pressure from global civil society compelled a peaceful transition to multicultural democracy in South Africa.

The 1980s created a new script for revolutionary social upheaval, one that left the utopia of socialism and the repertoire of violent militancy behind. Shifting from the proletariat to cross-class coalitions, from vanguard to mass participation, and from violence to nonviolence, the series of utopian uprisings made civil society seem radical. This story of liberation was narratively constructed in familiar binary manner, as a movement of purity from danger, of light breaking through darkness, of enslaved peoples breaking their chains. But the characters who enacted this narrative had now changed. They took global politics in a new direction, back from 1917 and 1933 to 1789 and 1776. In the 1980s and 1990s, a new sort of "world revolution" was being born (Sobral 2011).

In this chapter I describe three social upheavals that, two decades later, continued this long arc of civil liberation, "global civil society social movement[s]" (Khosrokhavar 2012) that disrupted world routines and inspired the global collective imaginary – the first Obama presidential campaign, the Egyptian uprising, and Occupy Wall Street. These movements, I suggest, should be seen not simply politically, as struggles for state power, but as symbolic upheavals in the spiritual hearts of their own nations that resonated in the hearts of audiences in other societies around the globe. Emotionally laden eruptions of utopian possibility, these performances wildly inspired their immediate participants even as they projected "tableaux" beyond the scene, to tens of millions in the national and global citizen audiences who fused with the performances from outside.

"O-ba-MA"

One can explain the two-year campaign that Obama waged for the American presidency as a struggle for political power, filled with strategy and money and ending with a resounding, if still relatively narrow, majority of votes. One can also understand these pre-presidential Obama years as a utopian social movement. Obama's rise inspired tens of millions of Americans to hope and believe – in the unifying, egalitarian, and individually liberating possibilities of the civil sphere (Alexander 2010). The delirium of Obama's rallies marked liminal interruptions of public space, civil rituals that resounded with democratic effervescence. Obama's person became an iconic symbol radiating an aura of fundamental social change. His triumphal progress signaled inclusion over exclusion, hope over fear, civil solidarity over fragmentation, the victory of democratic justice over cynical resignation to the abuses of power. "O-ba-MA, O-ba-MA, O-ba-MA" was the call of a people's movement, of the civil sacred challenging the anti-civil profane, of purity winning out against danger, of the street beating the establishment, of grassroots organizing defeating money and institutions.

The difficulties encountered by Obama-in-office should hardly be surprising. The utopian hopes his campaign stirred and embodied could never be satisfied by the mundane machinery of government. Indeed, Obama himself seemed the victim of his own utopian aspirations. The President seemed to believe that his political enemies would help him restore civil solidarity. Humiliated by political catastrophe, Republicans were prepared to do no such thing. Obama's dream of civil repair was defeated by a felicitous counter-performance of adamant Republican partisanship, which made a farce of his utopian aspirations.

Tahrir

It was only weeks after Republicans handed Obama his head on a platter – in the November 2010 Congressional elections – that the restless arc of civil social movement stretched to North Africa and the Middle East. Like the rise of Obama, the Arab Spring was utterly unexpected. It was experienced as a volcanic eruption of almost foolhardy aspiration, and few believed it could be sustained. Yet Tunisia's Jasmine Revolution triggered a whole series of volcanic uprisings, the

128

lava eventually flowing to Egypt, Libya, Yemen, Jordan, Morocco, Bahrain, and Syria. They drew from a quiet intellectual upheaval inside the Arab world, an internal political-cultural development that, pushing back against Occidentalism, socialism, and violent Islamism, tentatively embraced the tenets of liberal if not secular democracy.

Yet it was in Tahrir Square, in Cairo, that this unexpected outpouring of radical democratic sentiment symbolically peaked. In a nation in the heart of the Arab world, the Egyptian drama of democracy called the "January 25 revolution" played out over 18 days. There were many hundreds of deaths and thousands of injuries, but the millions of protestors remained nonviolent. Tahrir Square became a microcosm of civil utopia (Alexander 2011). The January movement didn't just protest and demand it, but performatively enacted it. The narratives of Tahrir projected by mainstream, alternative, and social media featured cross-class and cross-religious solidarities. Egypt seemed born again, rising like a Phoenix from the suffering and humiliation of the Mubarak regime.

Like "Obama" and the civil upheavals decades before, Tahrir projected meanings in public far beyond the boundaries of the Egyptian nation state. The revolution's English Facebook page cast its narrative of civil revolution around the globe, receiving tens of thousands of wildly supportive posts in response. "The People Want the End of the Regime," "The People Want the End of Military Trials," "The People Want the Rule of Law" – these chants from Tahrir Square reverberated not only across the Middle East and North Africa, but Europe and North America as well. Massive demonstrations broke out in Madrid, in London, in Tel Aviv, and Madison. In one part, these were pushbacks of civil against market society, protests against the restrictive demands of fiscal austerity in the wake of the Great Recession and the craven submission of democratic governments to failed corporate and financial elites. In some other part, these massive protests referenced the Arab Spring. Explicit references to "Tahrir" frequently appeared, not only in chants but in iconic displays, prominently among them Guy Fawkes, the grinning white-faced anti-hero of the 1605 British "Gunpowder Plot" who had metamorphized in the 1980s comic book *V for Vendetta* and, in 2006, commercially successful dystopic film of the same name (Sobral 2011).

The brutal repression that eventually punctured the liminal moment of Tahrir was not pre-ordained. Its utopian civil aspiration moved so explosively across classes and religions and into the depths of Egyptian life that President Mubarak was forced to step aside and the army feared for months to intervene. While the army fought a concerted backstage against Tahrir, in public it felt compelled to praise the people's revolution and support free elections, which allowed the Muslim Brotherhood, by far the best organized mass party, to come to political power. Its narrow outlook, shaped by Islamism and decades of repression, made its government as unstable as it was unpopular. The secular left tacitly supported the military's coup d'etat, naively agreeing what turned out to be a suicide pact that landed its leaders in prison alongside those of the Muslim Brotherhood. The utopia of Tahrir shattered, but the dream of cooperative democracy carried on for a decade in Tunisia, where the Jasmine Revolution had set off the Arab Spring, until Kais Saied suppressed the independence of the civil sphere's communicative and regulative institutions in July 2021.

Occupy

During the months that the arc of civil upheaval spread Westward and Eastward from Cairo, its most potent poetic transliteration came from New York in September 2011, when hundreds of protestors sat down on Wall Street chanting "We are the 99%." As a reporter for the *New York Times* put it: "The idea, according to some organizers, was to camp out for weeks or even months to replicate the kind, if not the scale, of protests that had erupted earlier in 2011 in places as varied as Egypt, Spain, and Israel" (Moynihan 2011).

"Occupy Wall Street" was stunning and unexpected, a random electric spark that started a hot brush fire. The American left had been prostrate, the far-right Tea Party in command, and the Obama revolution seemingly in full retreat. Initially derided, the scruffy gathering of a few hundred protestors in Zuccotti Park soon became a catalyzing social event. Powerful ideological statements are metaphors, creating new relations among previously disparate social elements. Propelled by felicitous performances, ideological metaphors can make meaning in public in new and surprisingly consequential ways.

Wall Street was occupied virtually, not literally, yet "Occupy" was as a brilliantly felicitous performance that thrust the critical, demanding, and egalitarian spirit of American democracy into the stultifying and musky chambers of elites. If its message and effect were symbolic, the performance itself was physically demanding. There were rain, tents, dirt, latrines, police attacks, and the angry gathering lasted more than 60 days. Efforts to repress Occupy triggered immediate and effusive outpourings of public sympathy, the gritty determination, nonviolence, and participatory democracy of the protestors – with their endless open meetings and "human microphone" – gradually garnering grudging admiration.

By sticking it out, and publicly sticking it to the financial and cor-porate elite, Occupy embodied the ongoing struggle between civil and market society. Occupy had little by way of policy demands, but that was the point. Experts inside and outside the beltway had been churning out policy proposals for years. It was the long-lasting performance of Occupy that was itself the achievement. Riveting citizen-audience attention well beyond the relatively narrow band-width of frustrated progressives, Occupy commanded the means of symbolic production – network and cable news, front pages of news-papers, and leading blog sites. It supplied its own facilities as well, live cam streams to cable TV, cell phone pictures leaping to websites around nation and world. Its gutsy, aggressive, yet determinedly civil performance of social justice earned Occupy a distinctive mystique, an aura of sacrality that provided protection against repressive moves from the state. The protests had the wind of public opinion at their back. If Mubarak's army was afraid to intervene in Tahrir, how much more reluctant were the police forces of a relatively democratic state?

Zuccotti Park did not change policy, elect new representatives, or lower the unemployment rate.[1] What it did was create a vastly more energetic and critical form of civil power. One way to understand this upgrade is how it energized the left. Iterations of Occupy sprang up in more than 150 cities: Occupy Oakland, Occupy Los Angeles, Occupy Chicago, even Occupy New Haven, Occupy Harvard and Yale. A coalition of seventy liberal organizations, the American Dream Movement," formed to provide material and support.

The impact of these liminal performances went beyond the audience on the left. It entered into the center of American collective conscious-ness. As a front-page article in the *New York Times* headlined: "The 99% Has Become an Ingrained Part of the Cultural Lexicon" (Stelter 2011). One percent and ninety-nine percent became magical numbers, culture structures that redistributed civil sacred and profane, morally re-weighting economic and political "realities." Long viewed as bun-gling but not venal, and certainly worth saving, the financial and corporate elite now became the vilified and polluted "One Percent." The masses of struggling Americans, formerly characterized as hapless objects – victims, shlepers, and pretty much schmucks – were trans-formed into the purified "Ninety-Nine Percent," a collective agent demanding justice, a maligned hero finally fighting back.

For a time, the movement dramatically changed the very meaning of the word occupation. In early September, "occupy" signaled

on-going military incursions. By the end of the two-month movement, it signified political protest. Rather than the force of military
power, it referenced standing up to injustice, inequality, and abuse of
power. Instead of occupying a space, the term now connoted transforming that space (Alim 2011). One month after the occupation of
Zuccotti Park, half of a national sample of Americans told pollsters
that Occupy reflected the views of most Americans, and two-thirds
of all those queried, including one-third of the Republicans, said the
distribution of wealth needed to be made more equal (Kohut 2011).
Three months later, a national survey reported that two-thirds of
Americans now believed there were "strong conflicts" between the
rich and poor, eclipsing divisions of race and immigration. Since
2009, there had been a 50 percent increase in this perception of class
conflict; the largest increases were reported among whites, middle-
income, and independent voters, the latter presenting the most
dramatic shift, from 23 to 68 percent (Tavernise 2012). As these
post-Occupy effects began to be felt, right-wing Republicans cam-
paigning for their party's Presidential nomination began eviscerating
their fellow contender Mitt Romney as a "vulture capitalist," for his
work with Bain Capital.

The arc of utopian civil movement once again reached outside the
United States. In October, the *New York Times* wrote that "demon-
strations in emulation of Occupy Wall Street were held in Europe,
Asia, and the Americas, drawing crowds in the hundreds and the thou-
sands" (Kristoff 2011). At the end of December, a radical leader of the
Russian democracy movement evoked Occupy from his hospital bed.
In a fiery speech projected on large screens outside on the Moscow
streets, he called the assembled protestors "the 99 percent" and said
Russia was led by a corrupt one percent of bureaucrats and oligarchs.
In an article entitled, "Occupy Wall Street Occupies Obama's 2012
Campaign," the *Washington Post*, reporting that "inequality . . . will
be the major theme in [Obama's] reelection campaign," pointed to
"Occupy Wall Street's success in turning the national conversation
towards inequality" (Klein 2011). Declaring "this country doesn't
succeed when only the rich get richer" (MacAskill 2012), Barack
Obama roundly defeated his Republican opponent Mitt Romney
in the 2012 Presidential campaign, portraying him as an economic
elitist who betrayed the solidarity bonds upon which the civil sphere
depends (Alexander and Jaworsky 2014).

132

— 6 —

FROM CIVIL WAR TO CIVIL PEACE
TRAUMA AND REPAIR

What are the conditions for civil comity and peaceful conflict inside of nation-states? To begin with, we might conceptualize peace simply as the absence of violence. Making the transition to peace means rejecting physical force as a legitimate means of conducting – expressing, mediating, and resolving – social and cultural conflicts and, more broadly, of struggling for power. This minimalist definition of peace requires the civil regulation of conflict, such that persuasion replaces coercion. The integrity of one's opponents must be recognized, however opposed their material and ideal interests appear to our own. They must be attributed sincerity in their motives and honesty in their relations. If their right to have rights (Arendt 1951) is so honored, then threatening one's opponents with physical force is out of bounds. Violence negates the other, defining an opponent as a thing that must be obliterated in order to be changed. For a society to be peaceful, persuasion must become the only legitimate mode for changing other minds. Armament replaced by argument.

Such a minimalist definition of peace is the empirical bottom line for a civil society to exist. Certainly, Max Weber (1946) was right to insist that monopolization of the means of violence by nation-states was a major civilizational advance. For Weber, modernity is a rational-legal order that provides more predictability and more fairness than the arbitrary power of patrimonial authority. If anybody other than representatives of the state has access to the means of violence, legal-rational legitimacy is destroyed, and laws cannot be carried out.

To say that peace is the absence of violence, however, is not to say peace is only that. There is much more to peace than simply the absence of extra-legal violence. Even if governments can succeed in

133

monopolizing violence, what would prevent violent struggle from soon breaking out once again? With this question, we reach the limits of Weberian sociology. Essaying the limits on violence exceeds the theory of modernity as a rationalized society. We need a more cultural sociology, one that can theorize feelings, symbols, morality, and meta-physical belief (Alexander, Jacobs, and Smith 2012). Violence is physical, but it has its roots in cultural processes of shaming, polluting, splitting, and objectifying. Peace requires moving in the other direction, toward a powerful vision of a social solidarity that can anchor and limit the state. And not the state alone: An independent civil sphere also sets limits on the economy, church, university, family, ethnic and racial communities, and voluntary associations.

The civil sphere (Alexander 2006) is an idealized utopian community that is partially, but never fully, institutionalized in such communicative organizations as journalism and civil associations and such regulative organizations as the law and voting. The civil sphere posits a society of self-regulating individuals, who see not only themselves but also others as honest, independent, open, cooperative, and rational, as fellow members of a horizontally organized community who merit their trust. Most of the persons inhabiting large territorial communities will never know one another face-to-face. We can encounter one another only via symbolic representations. Only insofar as we symbolize distant others in terms of shared civil qualities can we experience solidarity and expansive community. Others then become, in fact and not only in name, our fellow citizens. Kant (1999: 329) linked the conditions of peace to the expansion of hospitality, insisting that the "use of the right to the earth's surface belongs to the human race in common," declaring that this idea of common belonging would "bring the human race ever closer to a cosmopolitan constitution." Common belonging under a cosmopolitan canopy (Anderson 2011) is exactly what civil sphere theory has in mind.

But the cultural codes of the civil sphere are not only about belonging and hospitality. They are also, paradoxically, about exclusion, rudeness, and downright aggression. The discourse of civil society is binary. Not only in high philosophy but also in the everyday language of the street, we find idealized civil qualities emphatically contrasted with their opposites – rational with irrational, honesty with deceit, independence with dependence, open with secretive, cooperative with aggressive, trust with distrust. For every individual and group represented as possessing the sacred qualities that merit membership in the civil sphere, core groups represent others in terms of the polluted

134

qualities (Douglas 1966) that demand exclusion in order for the fragile stability of democratic civil societies to be maintained.

Path dependence and institutional structures create ideal and material interests that make it easier to code some individuals and groups in anti-civil terms. Colonialism treated Indigenous Peoples and their societies as means to imperial ends, representing native religions, social practices, and skin colors as the anti-civil quintessence – dependent, animalistic, deceitful, irrational, and aggressive. But interests are never dispositive. Relatively autonomous ideas – cultural systems (Geertz 1973) – powerfully affect the tracks along which ideal and material interests run. In the sixteenth century, some influential Spanish church leaders insisted that the conquered Indians were also human beings, urging Spanish occupiers to offer some hospitality to these strangely appearing other members of the human race, so that someday there could be, under God, a cosmopolitan constitution (Stamatov 2013). In the centuries that followed, more secular republican ideas from the European Renaissance (Skinner 1978a) infiltrated the institutional structures of the new world, creating community patterns that were anti-patrimonial, establishing relatively democratic conditions for domestic peace (Forment 2003).

When economic combined with racial power to create the Western slave system, religious and secular commitments to broader human obligation inspired abolitionist movements (Stamatov 2013) and, eventually, civil wars between enslavers and liberators, which after a century of struggle wiped economic slavery off the face of the earth. Western civil spheres expanded, and new possibilities for domestic peace emerged. A century later, the civil rights movement challenged the legacy of racism in the Southern United States. Martin Luther King evoked the dream of a more multiracial American creed and a less fragmented, more solidary American civil sphere. In post-colonial South Africa, where Black masses were dominated and exploited for Afrikaners' ideological and economic interests, it was not only the African National Congress but also white middle-class reformers connected with global secular and religious partners who launched the anti-Apartheid movement, which eventually succeeded in restructuring the South African civil sphere in a less racist, more multicultural, more solidary way (Thorn 2006).

In the early and mid twentieth century, social polarization produced barbaric political and ideological movements that spread worldwide. Fascist and Bolshevik dictatorships came to power, and the future of liberal democracy looked dim. But the utopian dream of an independent and inclusive civil sphere could never be entirely suppressed.

A world war was waged for freedom and dignity, the Holocaust was exposed, massive trials against war crimes were publicly staged, and a new global civil organization, the United Nations, issued the International Declaration of Human Rights. Democratic governments took root in Germany and Japan, and expansive foundations for civil peace were laid. In the 1970s, after the death of the fascist Generalissimo Franco, Spain undertook an extraordinary process of peaceful, if still deeply fraught, democratic transition (Edles 1998). Soon after, religious and secular idealism inspired the Solidarity movement that brought Poland's communist dictatorship to its knees. By the end of that decade, Bolshevik dictatorships advocating state violence were broadly displaced, and civil society movements challenged military dictatorships in Latin America's Southern Cone. Non-violent transitions to more democratic regulation of conflict unfolded in East Asia as well, in post-Chiang Kai-shek Taiwan, in post-UK Hong Kong, and, perhaps most spectacularly, in Korea, in the series of uprisings that stretched from the 1980 Gwangju Uprising to the June Democratic Uprising of 1987 (Alexander, Palmer, Park, and Ku 2019b). In region after region across the globe, democratic states, whose power was legitimated by discourses of civil society, established the cultural basis for domestic peace.

Domestic peace depends on taking violence out of politics, creating a state regulated by an independent judiciary and directed by civil sphere representatives elected to office after publicly agonistic struggles for state power. For such a conflictual public to be stabilized, to be agonistic rather than antagonistic (Mouffe 2000), the audience of citizens must experience themselves as members of a solidary community sharing mutual obligations.

When narrow and particularistic institutional structures undermine and restrict possibilities for expansive mutual obligation, massive reform movements and even civil and revolutionary wars may result. In such conditions of social polarization, establishing respect for the autonomy, honesty, and trustworthiness of fellow citizens is severely challenging (Alexander, Kivisto, and Sciortino 2021). How can counterveiling forces expand the signifying references of the sacred side of the binary discourse of civil society? How can groups that have been stigmatized and excluded – classes; Indigenous Peoples; ethnic, religious, and regional groups – be symbolized by core groups and third parties in more respectful, more sympathetic ways?

The agency of the dominated is crucial, and it can be triggered by stubbornly utopian visions of an alternative, more civil society. When social solidarity has broken down and social peace becomes merely a hegemonic slogan, social movements representing subaltern groups resort to violence. But they also can project civil performances to third-party audiences, whatever their material interests (Waghmore 2013). They can engage not only in a battle of arms, but also in what Gramsci called a battle of position.

Transitions to cosmopolitan peace depend on symbolic performances that lay the cultural foundations for expanded civil solidarity. If such social performances are successful, they connect the experience of structural deficits with dreams for civil repair (Kane 2019). If both sides of the social conflict are symbolically and emotionally engaged, performances weave cultural structures of intertextuality that expand the reach of civil signification. The circulation of distorting, anti-civil representation diminishes. Objectifying representations that divide citizens, framing not only excluded but core groups as fit subjects for violence and obliteration, are pushed further to the margins.

How can the civil sphere be repaired, its fissures sewn up in such a way that solidarity expands and sources of social suffering diminished? Painful social injuries must be lifted out of the symbolic frames that earlier had justified their imposition. New, more civil narratives must be created, stories that allow the weak and the powerful, the victims and their persecutors, to switch moral places. The groups and individuals who had triggered and justified traumatic injuries now become profaned and punished; those who earlier were represented in terms of the dark, anti-civil underside of social discourse can now be purified, re-signified in a manner connecting them with the civil sacred. When victims become humanized, they are transmogrified, from being degraded symbols of anti-civil objectification to being personified as shining figures of edifying civil identification (Tognato 2011). Once venerated heroes now become denigrated perpetrators, their identities soiled and their divisive ideologies and movements removed from the newly emerging social frame.

In the remainder of this chapter, I bring this theoretical argument down to earth, examining transitions to peace after wars between nations and within them. I will suggest that such transitions involve a cultural trauma process (Alexander, Eyerman, and Breese 2011) that allows the victims of violence to be re-signified and communities to be reconstructed in more civil ways.

Democracy had defeated fascist dictatorship during World War II, but the internal ideologies of the defeated nations did not automatically change. Only if they were transformed, however, would Germans and Japanese be allowed to rejoin the common territory of the human race. Those who had directed fascist dictatorships would have to be polluted as anti-civil, not only outside of Germany but within. Those who had organized fascist projections of violent power would have to be condemned as anti-patriotic, for undermining peace and endangering the nation-state. Not only fascist leaders but their followers would have to accept their re-signification as perpetrators, assuming moral responsibility and exhibiting sympathy for those they had oppressed (Eyerman 2019).

One step in such a trauma process is the personalization of victims (Alexander 2012b,c). In reflecting upon Germany's transition from war to peace, intellectual observers have often focused on such immediate postwar events as the postwar Nuremberg trials. These were powerful political performances of civil justice, and decades of trials, exposures, recantations, and reconciliations followed in their wake. But deeper cultural transformations were required for the German civil sphere to be expanded and repaired.

Throughout European history, Jews had been depicted as insidious, distrustful strangers to whom the gates of the civil sphere must be barred. The gates had only begun to swing open when Nazi Germany initiated its antisemitic mass murder campaign. Christian people who fought Germany did not do so on behalf of the Jews, a stigmatized and subordinated group for whom most Europeans and Americans felt scarce emotional identification and experienced little cultural connection. In the decade after the war, however, as the Jewish mass murder moved from its representation as a war-related "atrocity" to a *weltgeschichte* "Holocaust," this interpretive situation markedly changed. Rather than portraying murdered Jews as a bathetic and depersonalized mass, Western fictional and factual media began to portray them as individual human beings. The story of the life and death of Anne Frank, the German everygirl who had hidden from the Nazis with her family in an Amsterdam attic, became a heart-wrenching parable, a legend of tragic suffering, exemplary pluck, and extraordinary courage. Anne's *Diary* became required reading for millions of school children. Novels, movies, and television melodramas, thousands of them, followed in Anne Frank's wake. Holocaust fiction and testimonies became bestsellers inside Germany and outside of it as well.

For a trauma process to be successful, another step is necessary: The role of perpetrator must be generalized. In the early days after World War II, Germans conceived of responsibility for genocidal war narrowly, blaming Hitler and his loyal band of Nazi fanatics. Over the ensuing decades, however, as the war crime became transformed into Holocaust, the sense of moral responsibility for the mass murder broadened, to the millions of ordinary Germans who supported Hitler; to the German soldiers who fought for Nazi conquest; and to generations of Germans who were born after Hitler's death (Giesen 2004). Eventually, the perpetrator role extended well beyond Germany, to occupied nations who had secretly cooperated with Nazi extermination policies and even to the Allied nations, who had refrained from bombing death camps and who came to be accused, in their anticolonial wars in the 1950s and 1960s, of committing genocide themselves.

What postwar Germany accomplished – moving from violent state aggression to a more inclusive and tolerant civil sphere controlling the state – provided a pivotal reference point to measure the success and failure of other efforts. In her examination of the process that unfolded in postwar Japan, Akiko Hashimoto (2015) demonstrates the staying power of the militarist narrative that triggered Japan's 20-year-long Pacific war. Nationalistic leaders continued to see themselves as the putative victims of Western imperialism, glorifying their earlier military conquests as redemptive and refusing to extend sympathy to their Korean, Chinese, and American victims. This militarist postwar narrative is hardly hegemonic. As John Dower (1999) demonstrated in his remarkable revisionist history, the defeated Japanese "embraced defeat" and leaped to reject their fascist structures, institutionalizing party-democracy and adopting a pacifist constitution. Still, the unapologetic nationalist narrative retains great power. While it has been challenged by a powerful peace movement, even such an anti-militarist story represents Japan not as perpetrator but as passive victim, citing U.S. firebombing of major Japanese cities, the nuclear bombing of Hiroshima and Nagasaki, and Japan's military alliance with the U.S. today. Neither of the principal narratives that have emerged from Japan's postwar trauma process assumes the kind of moral responsibility for violence that is necessary to lay down cultural foundations for peace (Wang 2019).

Post-Franco Spain provides a striking contrast. Civil wars may end bitterly, with violence abated while polarization continues beneath a thin veneer of peace. How such a dangerous, and temporary, denouement can be avoided is explained by Laura Edles in *Symbol and Ritual in the New Spain* (Edles 1998). Certainly, institutional changes were significant in Spain's peaceful transition from dictatorship to democracy (Edles 1998: 32–33). It had been a poor, agricultural country before the Civil War, and Franco's postwar policies of economic autarchy and protectionism drastically undermined per capita income. Beginning in the 1950s, however, Spain entered UNESCO

139

and the International Labor Organization, instituted technocratic market capitalism, and opened up the country to foreign investment and tourism, policies that allowed the nation to participate in the massive economic boom of the 1960s. Similar openings were initiated inside Spain's religious and political institutions. Still, when Franco died in 1975, nothing was guaranteed. To the contrary, pessimistic predictions about continuing authoritarianism were the order of the day.

These expectations were upended by a series of public performances, some carefully coordinated, others spontaneous, that broadcast unprecedented appeals for national solidarity and articulated new respect for once vilified others. Franco's death, Edles suggests, "evoked a transcendent understanding of temporal separation" that created a symbolic space for moving from the past to the future, for a more civil narrative to be put into place. Both regime and opposition elites shared in fervent incantations about a sacred "new beginning," evoking not only the right to vote but a utopian spirit the Spanish called "*convivencia*," a term that denotes living together with others but connotes, as well, tolerance and peace (Edles 1998: 43). When the communist poet and electoral candidate Rafael Alberti returned from exile, he avowed, "I left with my fist closed because it was a time of war, and I return with my hand open for fraternity" (ibid.). A right-wing Catalan coalition named itself "*convivencia Catala.*" Such rhetorical performances of a newly embracing solidarity implied, as well, the purifying re-signification of polluted others. The influential philosopher Julian Marias declared, "Spain is being returned to herself, she moves with considerable liberty, [we] are erasing the differences between two Spanish classes, and many of us are beginning to feel that we are not going to be alien to our collective life" (Edles 1998: 45). Contemporary social actors, whose forebears had been implacable enemies fighting a violent civil war, "came to define democracy as their most important goal" and "violence as an inappropriate means to achieve it" (Edles 1998: 15). In the face of national strikes, organized performances of worker-capital solidarity offered grand financial bargains. When fascist violence did erupt, it triggered mass marches against extremism. When coup plotters occupied parliament in the name of the King, Juan Carlos publicly rebuffed them; calling for "serenity and prudence" (Edles 1998: 145), the King became a hero in the performance of democracy. Rather than maximizing ideal and material interests in a zero-sum manner, groups created self-binding rules that allowed compromise.

Twenty years later, when South Africa made the same transition from civil war to democratic peace, public performances were once again central, providing a liminal space in which a more inclusive solidarity could be performed and imagined before it had become operational in any institutional way. A major organizational innovation in this transition was the *Truth and Reconciliation Commission.* Reconstructing this symbolizing project in her study *Staging Solidarity*, Tanya Goodman (2015: 27) shows how the years long, nationally publicized inquiry created a powerful *mis-en-scène* that dramatized testimonies offering "examples of the evils of the past" while juxtaposing them "with the ideal of an imagined community, coded as the new South Africa." As the new South Africa was symbolized, the meaning of national belonging was reconstructed. The TRC performed "the new contours of a basic moral universe" (Goodman 2015: 27–28), the post-Apartheid "rainbow nation" envisioned by Bishop Desmond Tutu, who chaired the TRC.

"To move between the past and future," Goodman observes, "required a change in the way in which people viewed each other and a reconstitution of the boundaries of who belonged" (Goodman 2015: 16). In a manner that echoed the civil reconstruction of the Holocaust, individual testimonies of tragedy personalized Apartheid's once nameless Black victims. Instead of a "depersonalized other," victims become "individuals with faces, families, [and] feelings ... with whom others could identify across class and color lines" (Goodman 2015: 16). In April 1996, the TRC heard testimony from Nomonde Alata, the widow of a Black activist who had been brutally murdered by state security officers in 1984. A commissioner who participated in the hearing described the scene:

> In the middle of her evidence, she broke down, and the primeval and spontaneous wail from the depths of her soul was carried live on radio and television. [It] caught up in a single howl all the darkness and horror of the apartheid years. It was as if she enshrined in the throwing back of her body and letting out the cry the collective horror of the thousands of people who had been trapped in racism and oppression for so long. (Goodman 2015: 46)

The sympathetic chords struck by such performances were palpable. As third-party observers experienced such expressions of human suffering, solidary feelings were extended.

> Witnesses, onlookers, commission gophers, [and] journalists all broke down at one time or another as the widows and mothers of apartheid activists laid bare their personal pain and loss to the world ...

Sometimes the tears seemed to be contagious. A witness would sob and then a member of the audience would begin to cry. Soon the tears would spread like a bush fire . . . One foreign observer was overhead to remark: "This country is so traumatized. If one person is hurt then so is everybody."   (Goodman 2015: 48).

In this solidarity-expanding performance, the positions of victims and their torturers were reversed. Representing Black victims as heroes, TRC interlocutors framed "stories that told of suffering [as] an honorable sacrifice in anticipation of freedom from oppression" (Goodman 2015: 16). A mother whose son had been murdered by security forces implored the TRC to find his bones and make sure that "the world knew he was a hero" (Goodman 2015: 50). Those who had once been proud and disdainful torturers accepted the shaming status of perpetrator, humbly asking forgiveness. Facing his former victim, an Apartheid agent notorious for cruel techniques of torture and assassination offered apology, explaining "[we] lived in a different era, we were enemies then." But no longer: "My motivation [was] patriotic in the *then* South Africa of the day, as much as I *now* realize that you gentlemen must have been just as patriotic to your country of birth" (Goodman 2015: 60, original italics). Facing the family of another victim, the same Army captain tried to make amends "for the death of their son and brother," extending mutual identification: "Once again, I apologize to the family for his death and thank God that I, who also have children . . . was not the person who was killed on that day" (61).

Trauma processes can deepen the transition to peace, extending cultural meaning and emotional identification among groups whose earlier enmity triggered violence, among nations and within them. Between dominator and subjugated, perpetrator and victim there exist none of the brotherly and sisterly feelings that bind people together in peaceful ways. To create such a structure of feeling in modern societies, face-to-face interactions are insufficient. Powerful symbols must be projected and dramas of civil integration performed. The discourse of civil society provides the cultural foundations for peaceful repair. Speaking this language allows democratic recognition, transforming aggression into agonism, and providing opportunities for signification that can transform enemies into friends.

Learning to speak the language of civil solidarity after intense periods of social strife and polarization requires much more than engaging in speech acts. It depends on deeply emotional and highly symbolic social performances of reconciliation. Only via such cultural performances can experiences of collective trauma become occasions for reconstructing collective identity, one in which antipathy gives way to mutual identification. If a new structure of feeling is constructed, then civil comity can lay the basis for a cosmopolitan constitution.

— 7 —

THE CRISIS OF JOURNALISM AND CREATIVE (RECON)STRUCTION

For most members of the civil sphere, and even for members of its institutional elites, the news is the only source of firsthand experience they will ever have about the vast majority of their fellow citizens, about their motives for acting the way they do, the kinds of relationships they form, and the nature of the institutions they create. Journalistic judgments, thus, possess an outsized power to affect the shape-shifting currents of contemporary social life, from people's movements to legal investigations, foreign policy, public opinion, and affairs of state. The reputation of news media – their ability to represent the public to itself – depends on the belief by their audiences that they are truly reporting on the social world, not making stuff up, that they are describing news factually rather than representing it aesthetically or morally.[1]

Conceptualizing news media in this manner provides a dramatically different perspective on the contemporary "crisis in journalism." Most social commentators, and journalists themselves, understand this crisis in economic and technological terms – as the challenge to the economic viability of newspapers triggered by the digital revolution in publishing and news distribution. Many leading journalistic institutions in the West have experienced great economic upheaval, cutting staff and undergoing deep, often radical, reorganization – in efforts to meet the digital challenge. Rather than seeing technological and economic changes as the primary causes of current anxieties, however, I wish to draw attention to the role played by the cultural commitments of journalism itself. Linking these professional ethics to the democratic aspirations of the broader societies in which journalists ply their craft, I will suggest that the new technologies can be, and are being, shaped to sustain value commitments, not only undermine them.

144

Recent technological change and the economic upheaval it has produced are coded by social meanings. It is this cultural framework that has transformed material innovation into social crisis – for the profession, the market, and for society at large. But cultural codes not only trigger sharp anxiety about technological and economic changes; they also provide pathways to control them, so that the democratic practices of independent journalism, rather than being destroyed, can be sustained in new forms.

The Fragility of Autonomy

Democratic societies depend on the interpretive independence of mass media. Situated between hierarchical powers and citizen-audiences, journalism can speak truth to power. Supplying cultural codes and narrative frameworks that make contingent events meaningful, news reports create a mediated distance that allows readers to engage society more critically. The ability to sustain mediation depends on professional independence. To some significant degree, journalists regulate themselves, via formal and informal professional organizations that have autonomy *vis-à-vis* state and market. Organizing their own work conditions and their own criteria for creating and projecting news, journalists evoke such professional ethics as transparency, independence, responsibility, balance, and accuracy.

These professional ethics significantly overlap with the broader discourse of democracy, the set of beliefs that sustain an independent civil sphere (Alexander 2006). Journalism is a critical element of the institutional-cum-cultural world of elections, parliaments, laws, social movements, and publicity that creates the conditions for democracy. Just as the independence of the civil public sphere is continuously threatened by incursions of markets, states, and ethnic and religious organization, so is the autonomy of journalism itself. Journalistic boundaries are often fraught and always permeable. The interpretive independence of journalism is never assured. An ongoing accomplishment, partial and incomplete, the profession and its social supporters must engage in continuous struggle for it to be sustained.

Authoritarian leaders go to great lengths to prevent the interpretive independence of journalists (Arango 2014; Buckley and Mullany 2014; Forsythe and Buckley 2014; Mullany 2014; Shear 2014). What is less widely understood is that such independence is also highly fraught inside democratic societies themselves (Schudson 1978; Alexander 1981). Efforts to sustain professional autonomy in the

145

democratic societies of the West and East have often been markedly successful. Yet such efforts also cause journalists to experience their institutional independence as fragile and threatened. Even as they successfully defend their professional ethics, journalists experience them as vulnerable to subversion in the face of technological and economic change. Independent journalists and the social groups who support them often feel as if they are losing the struggle for autonomy.

Because social change is endemic in modern societies, it is hardly surprising that the history of journalism has been marked by continuous eruptions of crisis. Just as current anxieties have been triggered by computerization and digital news, so were earlier crises of journalism linked to technological shifts that demanded new forms of economic organization (Breese 2016). Radio and television were feared as objective threats that would undermine print journalism's capacity for independence and critical evaluation. Neither actually did so. Neither did the transition from network to cable news in the United States, nor the transformation of the public service TV model in Europe that created overwhelming anxiety about privatization in the 1980s (Luengo and Sanz 2012; Larsen 2016a,b).

Examining the upheavals created by television and cable reveals how the deep meaning structures of journalism construed new technology and economic organization as dire threats to journalistic integrity, anxieties that, paradoxically, actually helped maintain the independence of journalism in new organizational forms. Case studies of contemporary newspapers in crisis – from the New Orleans *Times-Picayune* (Luengo 2016) and other metropolitan American dailies to papers in Norway (Steen-Johnson et al. 2016; Larsen 2016b), Germany (Revers 2016), Spain (Luengo 2014), France (Oputo 2014), and Britain (Schlesinger and Doyle 2015) – illuminate how the same combustible combination of enduring cultural structures and rapidly shifting technological and economic change is at work today, and how new platforms of journalistic work are being forged and engaged. Critical jeremiads against the profane, putatively anti-democratic effects of technology and economy should be seen less as accurate depictions than as spirited rallying cries to protect the sacred, and still robust, ethics of independent journalism.

While European newspapers do not always share American journalism's ethic of liberal neutrality, journalists on both sides of the Atlantic emphatically embrace a professional identity of interpretive and institutional independence (n. 1, above.) The digital-cum-economic challenge to these values has triggered crises in both European and American journalism, creating extraordinary organizational upheaval and economic strain. Tens of thousands of individual careers have been disrupted, and the profession's most venerable institutions are being severely tested (Minder and Carvajal 2014; Ramirez 2014). But this economic crisis needs to be understood not only in terms of Schumpeterian creative destruction but also as the culturally informed reconstruction of new organizational forms. What are institutional arrangements that, under the conditions of digital reproduction, can allow the cultural commitments of democratic journalism to be sustained? If networked news productions are making efforts to adapt professional journalism to the digital age, while maintaining journalistic civil values, are there parallel adaptations from the digital side? Is the anti-professional ideology of "citizen journalism" also being reconsidered, shifting the balance between news blogs and professional news writing in the new world of journalism emerging today?

I begin by reconsidering the theoretical underpinnings of scholarly writings about digital technology and journalism. Against reductionism, I argue for journalism's independent cultural power. This theoretical corrective allows empirical studies to be framed differently, the causes and consequences of the contemporary crisis to be approached with more clarity, and the ongoing, if often submerged, processes of institutional repair to receive the attention they deserve.

The Problem of Reduction

In an essay in the *Times Literary Review*, Nicholas Lemann (2013) wrote the "situation in journalism is changing so rapidly that it is difficult to get a sure sense of what is going on," adding, "while there is an endless series of panel discussions and blog posts where there are plenty of confident assumptions," there is "not much reliable data." In the last ten years, an enormous amount of scholarship has been devoted to the crisis in journalism, a profusion of empirical studies about its causes, current condition, near term consequences, and long-term effects. The problem isn't a dearth of data but its reliability. Empirical investigators have produced drastically divergent findings. It is the striking incommensurability among this plethora of studies that prevents observers from being able to get any sure sense about the crisis of journalism today.

The problem with current scholarship is theoretical. Empirical analysis rests upon theoretical presuppositions about how societies work, about what motivates social action, what institutions are most important, how they interact, and why (Alexander 1982). Theoretical rather than methodological logic determines the possibilities for getting empirical social science right. In studying the crisis of journalism, theoretical guidance has often been misleading, and sometimes downright wrong. The crisis of journalism can be reconsidered only if we get the theory right. Efforts to empirically assess the nature, causes, and effects of the crisis have been perniciously affected by technological and economic determinism. This reductionism needs to be challenged and corrected for understanding of the current crisis to move ahead.

It is obvious, for example, that the Internet has been centrally involved in creating the problems of contemporary journalism. What is not obvious at all, however, is that the social effects of this invention can be treated in a purely technological way. Like every major practical scientific discovery of the modern era (Alexander 2003b), the Internet has exerted its force not only as technology but also as narrative, as a culture structure inspiring faith as an "agent of change" (Negroponte 1995a; cf. Sanz 2014; Couldry 2014). From the moment of its emergence, the Internet was wrapped up inside a radically utopian social narrative, promising to "flatten organizations, globalize society, decentralize control, and help harmonize people," as one of its most influential early proponents, MIT professor Nicholas Negroponte (1995b: 182), predicted two decades ago: "It is creating a totally new, global social fabric . . . drawing people into greater world harmony . . . It is here. It is now" (Negroponte 1995a: 183, 230–223; cf. Van Dijck 2005; Benkler 2006; Jarvis 2011). The Internet was introduced as a material technique that would make us cooperative and free. Its effect on the mass media was portrayed as wonderful and immense, liberating us from the stifling effect of an anti-democratic, professional elite. "From now on," promised Clay Shirky (2008: 64), Professor of New Media at NYU, "news can break into public consciousness without the traditional press weighing in."[2] Exclaiming "nothing like this has ever been remotely possible before," Dan Gillmore, nationally syndicated columnist from the San Jose *Mercury News* and blogger for Silicon.Valley.com, explained:

> Big media . . . treated the news as a lecture. We told you what the news was . . . It was a world that bred complacency and arrogance on our part. Tomorrow's news reporting and production will be more of a conversation. The lines will blur between producers and consumers . . . The communication network itself will be a medium for everyone's voice, not just the few who can afford to buy multimillion-dollar printing presses, launch satellites, or win the government's permission to squat on the public's airwaves. (Gillmore 2004: xii–xiii)

It was, in other words, as salvationary techno-culture that the Internet's economic effects on journalism were far-reaching. "Technology has given us a communications toolkit that allows anyone to become a journalist at little cost," Gillmore explains (2004: xii). "What happens when the costs of reproduction and distribution go away? What happens when there is nothing about publishing anymore because users can do it for themselves?" asks Shirky (2008: 60–61): "Our social tools remove older obstacles to public expression, and thus remove the bottlenecks that characterized mass media. The result is the mass amateurization of efforts previously reserved for media professionals" (ibid.). With such utopian expectations, attaching a fee to liberation seemed not only conservative but downright profane. Even as public opinion compelled newspapers to make their products available online, the utopian expectations framing Internet culture prevented online access from being contingent on fees.[3] Efforts to erect paywalls – filters requiring payment for Internet access – were broadly stigmatized. "Paywalls," Shirky (2010) predicted, "don't expand revenue from the existing audience, they contract the audience to that subset willing to pay." And, indeed, when paywalls were initially introduced, they encountered such critical and financial headwind that they were quickly shut down (Perez-Pena 2007). Meanwhile, the breathless spirit of freedom that energized Internet expansion allowed blogs to aggregate the fruits of journalism – "news" – without paying for the labor that created it.[4] "As career journalists and managers," wrote newspaper mogul and new technology advocate John Paton, "we have entered a new era where what we know and what we traditionally do has finally found its value in the marketplace, and that value is about zero" (in Mutter 2011).

The social effects of the cultural mantra "information will be free"[5] – not the materiality of the Internet strictly considered – forged the economic vise within which journalism finds itself squeezed today. Newspapers were compelled – for cultural reasons – to forgo compensation for the labor power that created their complex product. Only then did it become economically impossible to compensate newspapers for declining advertising.[6] At the same time, fierce market competition emerged from new business forms – news-aggregating blogs – that could commoditize journalism without paying production costs. No wonder newspaper expenses began to far exceed revenues. The vise forged by techno-culture began to tighten its grip. The bottom lines of newspapers caved in.

If Internet technology were simply material, and the current crisis purely economic, then the direction of the unfolding crisis would be a one-way street and its social consequences impossible to deter. Journalism would become Exhibit A of capitalist "creative destruction," the process Joseph Schumpeter believed "incessantly revolutionizes the economic structure from within, incessantly destroying the old one, incessantly creating a new one" (Schumpeter 1975 [1942]: 83, original italics). In the face of more efficient technology, such economic logic holds, more profitable forms of business organization must replace newspapers. The economic foundations of journalism will be destroyed so that information can be distributed in a more efficient way.

It is such reductionist logic that compelled *The New Republic* (2009) to headline "The End of the Press" and Philip Meyer (2009) to speak of the "vanishing newspaper"; that moved Alex Jones (2009: 51) to claim "the nation's traditional news organizations are being transformed into tabloid news organizations," and Marcel Broersma (2013: 29) to announce journalism "has entered a state of progressive degeneration," one that "will not be curable"; and that led Robert McChesney and Victor Pickard (2011) to ask, "will last reporter please turn off the lights."

Journalism as Sacred Profession

Because the theoretical presuppositions of these arguments are misleading, their empirical predictions have not come to pass. Instead of being pushed over, journalism has pushed back. It is a profession, not only a market-responsive business.[7] Organized by a deeply entrenched cultural code, the twentieth century profession erected a virtual "wall" (Revers 2013: 37) between news reporting and profitmaking, a cultural division perceived as protecting the sacred from the profane. Business managers devote themselves to trying every which way to commercialize the products of journalism, but crafts persons, not owners and managers, create the news. The culture that regulates investigating, writing, and editing news is so revered it long ago acquired a quasi-religious status. In 1920, complaining that "the news of the day as it reaches the newspaper office is an incredible medley of fact, propaganda, rumor, suspicion, clues, hopes, and fears," Walter Lippmann (1920: 47) declared "the task of selecting and ordering that news" to be "one of the truly sacred and priestly offices in a democracy." For Lippmann, the newspaper was "the bible of democracy, the book out of which a people determines its conduct" (ibid.). A few years earlier, Walter Williams, University of Missouri's first journalism Dean, published what he called the Journalists' Creed, inscribing "clear thinking, clear statement, accuracy, and fairness" at the ethical core of the profession (in Farrar 1998). Contemporary practitioners sometimes refer to Bill Kovach and Tom Rosenstiel's *Elements of Journalism* as the "bible" and Kovach as journalism's "high priest" (Ryfe 2012: 51). The book asserts that "journalism's first obligation is to the truth" because "its first loyalty is to citizens," not to the powers that be. If journalists are to "serve as an independent monitor of power," then they "must maintain an independence from those they cover" and "exercise their personal conscience." If these moral obligations are met, this professional bible assures its readers, journalism can "provide a forum" not only for "public criticisms" but also for "compromise" (Kovach and Rosenstiel 2007 [2001]: 5–6).

In *The Communist Manifesto*, Karl Marx and Friedrich Engels (1962 [1848]: 36) proclaimed that, with the coming of capitalism, "all that is holy is profaned," that there can be no "religious fervor," that there survives neither "honor" nor "reverent awe" for any professional occupation. But this was their reductionism speaking.[8] In the century and a half since those predictions were made, journalism continued to inspire reverence, its professional ethics seeming sacred and holy, its moral obligations honored not only in the breach but in daily acts.[9] Matthias Revers (2013: 46) has documented how "symbols, myths, and narratives of triumph and failure" are "ingrained" in the occupation of journalism. The profession's culture is organized not only around mundane practices but sagas of courageous heroes (Carlson 2016; Revers 2013) who sacrifice, and sometimes even die, to uphold the values of autonomy, fairness, and critique, struggling against corrupt villains from the worlds of politics, money, ethnicity, religion, and state, who are motivated by greed and wanton disregard, acting in ways to undermine journalistic ideals.

Theoretical reductionism depicts the products of journalism as merely informational. If journalism is only about information, then it is indeed simply a technology, one bound to be superseded by the super-efficient, high speed, user-friendly information-processing capacities of the Internet Age.[10] In a biting critique, Dean Starkman links such Internet rhetoric to the vision of a "network-driven system of journalism in which news organizations will play a decreasingly important role."

News won't be collected and delivered in the traditional sense. It will be assembled, shared, and to an increasing degree, even gathered by a sophisticated readership, one that is so active that the word "readership" will no longer apply. This is an interconnected world in which boundaries between storyteller and audience dissolve [into] the transformative power of networks [and] faith in the wisdom of crowds and citizen journalism, in volunteerism over professionalism [and] in "iterative" journalism – reporting on the fly, fixing mistakes along the way – versus traditional methods of story organization, fact-checking, and copyediting.   (Starkman 2011)

Such reduction of news to information lends support to the fatalistic picture of journalism's displacement. Via a mechanical series of ineluctable facts, the all-powerful forces of capitalism's creative destruction will have sway. But if journalism is craft and profession, its product must be much more than the mechanical recording and transmission of information (Kreiss 2016). Michael Schudson documents how journalism, once not so very different than stenography, gradually became a source of "fundamental translation and interpretation," projecting the "meaning of events" to "a public ill-equipped to sort [this] out for itself" (Schudson 1982: 99). Anthony Smith (1978: 168) describes news reporting as "the art of structuring reality, rather than recording it." Donald Matheson shows how, between 1890 and 1930, journalism became transformed from "raw information" into a nuanced, thickly construed, and esoteric kind of discourse, a "textual apparatus of interviewing, summarizing, quoting and editing that would allow it to be able to claim to represent reality" (Matheson 2000: 563) in a manner that was more objective, and thus authoritative, than other claims.

Journalism as Civil Institution

Kovach and Rosenstiel describe the elements of journalism as "principles that have helped . . . people in self-governing systems to adjust to the demands of an ever more complex world," helping people "to be free" (2007 [2001]: 5). Journalism is not only about professional ethics but civic morals (Durkheim 1950). The neutrality, the perspective, the distance, the reflexivity, the narrating of the social as understood in this time and this place – all this points beyond the details of craft and the ethics of profession to the broad moral organization of democratic life. Even as the sacred codes of professional journalism reach downward into the practical production of daily, hourly, and minute-by-minute news, they reach upward into the more ethereal world of civic morals. When journalists make meaning out of events, transforming randomness into pattern, they do so in terms of the broader discourse of civil society (Alexander 2006: 75–85). Fairness to both sides is not just a narrowly professional obligation but a fundamental principle of citizenship, one that requires divided interests to play by the rules, to imagine themselves in place of the other even as they fight for interests of their own. Exercising individual conscience, being independent of one's sources, conducting interviews that allow sources to speak, providing neutral information that makes compromise possible – these professional mandates not only create news but contribute to the moral discourse that makes civil solidarity possible. As journalist and political scientist Jim Sleeper has put it, "journalism is a civic art."[11] Believing that a disinterested, more impersonal truth is possible allows demos to criticize cosmos and moral universalism to seem not just a cheap trick, a camouflage for self-aggrandizement, but a morality whose ideals have the power to reign.[12]

Evoking the sacrality that binds journalism to democracy, James Carey once described "public" as the "god term of journalism" – "its totem and talisman, and an object of ritual homage" (1987: 5, in Ryfe 2012). Conceptualizing journalism in public sphere terms, however, can create theoretical blinders that prevent the current crisis from being properly understood. Drawing upon an idealized view of the Greek polis, Hannah Arendt and Jürgen Habermas tie democracy to publicness, to openness and transparency, to making assertions that everybody can hear and see. In other words, the exchange of information is key. Hardly surprising, then, for public sphere theorists to have heralded the Internet as a great democratic invention, as deepening transparency and widening the circle of participation (Cohen and Arato 1992; Bohman 2004; cf. Shirky 2011).[13] Their enthusiasm is shared by such social theorists as Manuel Castells (1996), who view society as nodes of communication writ large (cf. Jarvis 2011).

> The development of interactive, horizontal networks of communication has induced the rise of a new form of communication, mass self-communication, over the Internet and wireless communication networks ... It is self-generated in content, self-directed in emission, and self-selected in reception by many that communicate with many [*sic*]. We are indeed in a new communication realm, and ultimately in a new medium, whose backbone is made of computer networks, whose language is digital, and whose senders and the largely autonomous origin of most of the communication flows that construct, and reconstruct every second, the global and local production of meaning in the public mind. (Castells 2007: 238, 248)

153

While divergent in various ways, public sphere and network theory can be dangerously reductionist, viewing communication technology as sui generis and new forms of social understanding as emanating directly therefrom.

From the perspective of a more cultural sociology, by contrast, the public sphere is less normative highpoint than performative stage, one that offers bigoted demagoguery a chance to succeed alongside the more civil forces of democratic life. Blogs can narrow networks, not only widen them, allowing likeminded people to huddle together in the virtual public sphere, creating nodes of communication that empower particularism in dangerous ways. Synthesizing recent research about "how people exercise their newfound freedom online," Ryfe finds that people "tend to congregate in 'small worlds'" (2012: 7).

> A small world is a network structure characterized by dense clusters of individuals linked together via bridges or connectors. Within these dense clusters, individuals go on with their virtual lives much as they do in their real ones: they interact with people who are familiar, or with whom they share a common interest. Indeed, one way of thinking about the Internet is that it amplifies people's social tendency to interact with others like them, and brings this tendency to scale. (ibid.)[14]

The professional ethics and civic morals of journalism can counter such narrowing, but public and network theorists are indifferent to the culture that sustains it.[15] The fate of professional journalism has been of little concern to theorists of the public and the information age.

Journalism is much more than the publicizing and networking of information. It is about interpreting information in a broader, often more universalizing manner, "wrest[ing] meaning from the torrent of events rather acting as mere transmission belts" (Grant in Barnhurst and Mutz 1997: 47), providing the "context of social problems, inter-pretations, and themes" (Barnhurst and Mutz 1997: 28). Neither journalism nor democracy is about letting more people say what they want, more rapidly, in increasingly public ways. Yes, journalism does provide information, but it is knowledge filtered through stringent, often acerbic standards of moral judgment – "reporting that is aggres-sive and reliable enough to instill fear of public embarrassment, loss of employment, economic sanctions, or even criminal prosecution in those with political and economic power" (Downey and Schudson 2009). News not only observes but judges, stigmatizing violations of civil morality and dramatizing heroic struggles against injustice. Journalism is not simply about the public but also about the civil sphere (Jacobs 1996a, b).[16]

154

Such an enlarged understanding of journalism and its environment helps us understand why, despite a decade of economic hardship and mushrooming moral panic, journalism has not finally been pushed aside. In fact, "in many countries, after a phase of depression, pessimism has receded," the Director of Oxford's Reuters Institute for the Study of Journalism, David Levy, recently told *Le Monde*. "Moving away from the idea of internet killing journalism to a more balanced perception," according to Levy, has allowed "actors to focus on what they can do to improve the situation" (Levy 2013).

Pushback: Journalism Defends Independence

This pushback has come from inside and outside the profession. *Vis-à-vis* demands to transform themselves into bloggers, journalists have put up a furious resistance, adamantly refusing to subordinate their sacred professional ethics and idealistic civic morals to what they see as the profane, polluting logic of market and technology. When they have remained employees, journalists have not allowed news reporting to be transformed into information collection. When they have been fired, journalists have continued to ploy their craft in professionally inflected news blogs – at last report, as many as 10 percent of those who have lost regular newspaper jobs (Schudson quoted in Levy and Nielson 2010: 17). Pushback against economic and technological "desecration" has also emerged from the broader civil sphere within which journalism nests. The last decade has witnessed a chorus of *cris de coeur* from public intellectuals, academics, columnists, religious authorities, public figures, and even politicians.

In May, 2012, Newhouse Publications, the corporate owners of the New Orleans *Times-Picayune*, announced plans to reduce publication of the once daily newspaper to just three times a week, while pouring money into news reporting on its 24/7 website. What followed was an explosion of protest and heated self-defense, "mobilizations across urban social networks in New Orleans, public demonstrations on behalf of the newspaper, and a statement signed by the newly formed '*Times-Picayune* Citizens Group' of influential citizens" (Luengo 2014). Each side evoked civil discourse, one to trigger critical reactions among journalists and the wider public, the other to justify management changes. Examining local and national news coverage, Maria Luengo found that while "these articles reported changes as facts," the events reported "were actually coded facts" – "thickened with a selective factual reporting that reveals civil and anti-civil codes

155

in narrative and analytical levels" (Luengo 2014).The previous, daily newspaper was represented nostalgically, as a crusading, corruption-fighting, public-serving, ultra-professional democratic medium. One church pastor from a poor neighborhood, for example, urged his congregation to pray for the *Times-Picayune* and the reporters who were losing their jobs. Describing the newspaper as a "tonic," the religious leader lamented that many in his flock would be shut out by the changes (Luengo 2014: 5). Even the city's mayor, himself a frequent *Times-Picayune* target, felt compelled to testify: "The dedication of journalists and their professionalism have made our civil, business and education institutions stronger, more transparent and honest" (ibid.). Looking forward rather than back, the new digitally oriented managers at the *Times-Picayune* framed their changes as necessary to preserve professional ethics and civic morals. Organizational forms for producing print news were no longer appropriate, they argued, if journalistic standards were going to be sustained in the "new digital space."

> Reporters do not have assigned desks and this was a source of great consternation when we announced the move, given that reporters are by nature hoarders and nesters. But in our model we wanted reporters to be out in the communities where the news is happening and not sitting at their desk hiding behind piles of documents. We want them talking to people and we have given them the tools and the infrastructure to be able to report their stories wherever they are. They do not have to come back to the newsroom to plug into a network and edit the story. So we have shared workstations, people come in, plug in their computers, do their work, unplug, and leave the space for the next person.
>
> (Luengo 2016)

Luengo concludes that the upheaval had the paradoxical effect of pushing institutions to explore new and better ways of defending journalism in New Orleans. News organizations do not seem to be declining, nor is local journalism dying in New Orleans. Years ago relatively few news media organizations were operating in the city. Now there is a proliferation of news media outlets: *The Times-Picayune*, *The Advocate*, New Orleans CBS-affiliated WWL-TV, Fox 8, the nonprofit *The Lens*, and a wide range of online and offline media outlets. After the critical coding of the *Times-Picayune*'s print reduction, layoffs, and expansion of the website, some reporters were re-hired by the new company, Nola.com, while other journalists joined *The Advocate*, a new home-delivered daily newspaper that had partnered with the WWL TV station to reinvigorate investigation. Meanwhile, *Times-Picayune* editors made fervent public declarations about maintaining professional standards with serious investigative reporting. A series of investigative stories on campaign finance entitled "Louisiana Purchased" was launched, and distribution of a tabloid version of the paper, *TPStreet*, started on digital-only days. Yet the *Times-Picayune* and its website remain the largest news organization in the region.

Cultural Power and Hybridity

The discourse that triggers the crisis of journalism is sharply binary, filled with ominous claims and counter-claims about purity and danger, the sacred and profane. Yet the practices taking shape on ground-zero of journalism have proved increasingly hybrid (Revers 2014, 2015). Of course, many scholars continue to make breathless observations about blogs and Twitter ushering in "ambient" (Hermida 2010a, b) new worlds of "immersion" (Ahmad 2010) that will tear down the walls between news and information, writing and marketing, and journalist and audience, creating a seamless new world of empowered citizens reporting to and about themselves. Certainly, when political repression (Papacharissi and Oliveira 2012; Zeyunep and Wilson 2012; Hermida, Lewis, and Zamith 2012; Alexander 2012a) and extreme natural disaster (Ostertag 2013) make independent journalism impossible, social media can provide crucial alternatives. Aside from these situations, however, web technology has rarely been successfully deployed in a manner that severs the link between reporting information and professional journalistic norms.

As Pablo Boczkowski (2004: 102–103) first suggested in his foundational study of the *New York Times*, new technology has "repurposed" the print process into "online newsrooms"; digital media has displayed familiar forms of "print storytelling"; and "online journalists" have exhibited an "occupational identity that resembled the one of their print counterparts, as defined partly by a traditional gate-keeping function and a disregard for user-authored content" (103). These findings were confirmed in Jane Singer's more methodologically controlled study of journalist-bloggers. While affirming that "political j-bloggers use links extensively" in a "highly interactive and participatory format," she insists these are "mostly to other mainstream media sites," that "although expressions of opinion are common, most journalists are seeking to remain gatekeepers" (2005: 173). Singer concludes that journalists "are 'normalizing' the blog as a component, and in some ways an enhancement, of traditional journalistic norms and practices" (ibid.). Investigations of more contemporary web technology also have discovered a normalizing process. Dominic Lasorsa and colleagues (2012: 19) demonstrated that journalist-Tweeters strongly resist the partisanship of blog culture. Although non-elite journalists sometimes do "act more like other non-journalist Twitter users – by posting their opinions on Twitter," only one in seven J-Tweeters actually engages in "major opining" (Lasorsa et al. 2012: 228–30). In an ethnography of political reporters in Albany, New York, Revers (2014) observes "journalism has embraced Twitter" as a welcome "augmentation of news production space," but warns that "the idea of replacement of one by the other is absurd." Concerns about professionalism are a "constant subject of discussion" among even the youngest, most twittering reporters, who justify their tweeting of ongoing events by expanding, not inverting, such traditional norms as speed, accuracy, responsiveness, and transparency (ibid.; cf. Steen-Johnson et al 2016).

Recent studies of small, less institutionalized community news websites also have discovered an emerging hybridity. While Nikki Usher (2011: 266) believes the new technology can allow "what counts as a public concern . . . to be defined by citizens themselves" – rather than relying "on traditional news organizations for the dissemination of content" – she finds that, on the ground, "reality is not that simple."

> The Web 2.0 world, in fact, has only accelerated the extent to which a commercial and professional impulse from news outlets permeates citizen content. News organizations can take advantage of the ease and speed that citizens have in sharing their content in a way that is timely and relevant.　　　　　　　　　　　　　　　　　　　(ibid.)

Reporting on a study of 100 start-up news websites on the West coast of the United States, David Ryfe (2013) writes that while entrepreneurs were "initially inclined to do something different with their sites," they are pushed by sources, readers, and even advertisers to employ the new technology in a manner that conforms more closely to journalistic models of news.

> Imagine for a moment that you are a news entrepreneur . . . You have never worked in a newsroom or covered a daily news beat. You do have some technical skills. Maybe you worked for a technology startup in the past. After several months of work setting up your site, you are ready to launch [but] you need access to information. You need to figure out how are you going to make money. And you need credibility. You quickly find that these problems are interrelated. For instance, one of the first things you do is attend a city council meeting. Before the meeting, you want to

ask a few questions of the city councilmen [sic]. When you approach, one of them naturally asks, who are you? Who do you work for? You explain that you have just started a new community news site. This response elicits the question: you aren't one of those bloggers, are you? The next day, in an attempt to attract advertising to your site, you visit a neighborhood bookstore and ask to talk to the owner ... She asks if you work for the small neighborhood newspaper that has existed in the community for years. You shake your head no. She narrows her eyes just a bit and asks: Then who do you work for? Are you a blogger? ... Gaining access to information and advertising is directly tied to credibility. Sources will be less willing to talk with you if you are not a journalist, and business owners will be less likely to place an advertisement on your site. Even audiences will be less likely to visit ... The accusation of being a blogger rather than a journalist was not merely a blow to the ego of these entrepreneurs. Potentially, it could harm their business.   (ibid.)

Ryfe's conclusion about new Internet-based websites – that their "alignment with core elements of journalism's culture is obvious" (cf. Ryfe 2012) – confirms the broader argument I am making here.

This new hybridity is underscored, as well, by whistleblowers choosing to filter their exposés through the web of journalism instead of simply dumping bucketsful of incriminating digital material directly on the Web. WikiLeaks began as merely a website "providing a universal way for the revealing of suppressed and censored injustices" (Wikileaks n.d., in Bieber 2013: 322), but that soon changed: "Having learned from the minor impact on public discussion of its earlier leaking activity, WikiLeaks.org (in the person of Julian Assange) established connections to globally known media actors in order to secure worldwide attention to the information to be distributed" (Bieber 2013: 323). Only the independent cultural power of professional journalism could secure for these anti-establishment leaks the legitimacy – the aura of balance and truthfulness – that citizen-audiences demand. When Edward Snowden secreted his digital revelations about the NSA, he turned them over to Glenn Greenwald, a *Guardian* columnist expert in national security issues, and Barton Gellman, a *Washington Post* journalist with Pulitzer prizes for reporting on the war on terror. Snowden's reasoning cut to the heart of journalism as craft and ethics: "I selected these documents based on what's in the public's interest [and] I'm relying on you to use your journalistic judgment to only publish those documents that the public should see" (Halpern 2014: 16). As Greenwald recounted, Snowden "stressed that it was vital to publish the documents journalistically – meaning working with the media and writing articles that provided the context for the materials, rather than just publishing them in bulk." Snowden explained, "if I wanted the documents just put on the Internet en masse, I could have done that myself" (ibid.). When the revelations were first reported, Gellman told C-Span that Snowden "does not try to direct, suggest, hint at what should be written," but instead asks journalists "to look at it carefully . . . and consider what the balance ought to be" (Halpern 2014: 18).

Pathways of Reconstruction

Journalism is not facing the creative destruction that Schumpeter, focused on the entrepreneurs of technology and markets, proclaimed as capitalism's fate. The prophesized transition from news journalism to infosphere – the brave new world of every-citizen-a-reporter – is not on offer. Money-making machines of Internet technology – Google, Facebook, Amazon, and such aggregating engines as the *Huffington Post* – are compelled to directly or indirectly support journalistic modes of news gathering and reporting; otherwise, there would not be any news to sell, to aggregate, to advertise, to analyze or satirize. Google created a $74 million fund to help French publishers with their digital operations (Scott 2014). Facebook has entered into serious conversation with the *New York Times*, among other media companies, to host journalism directly instead of merely providing its users an external link, and to pay handsomely for the privilege (Somaiya, Isaac, and Goel 2015).[17] The emerging symbiotic relationship also goes the other way: Search engines direct millions of readers daily to newspapers' websites.

> After Germany passed rules that permitted publishers to charge aggregating sites when their articles appeared online, Google removed many German organizations from its sites, which led to a drastic fall in online traffic to some newspapers' sites. Axel Springer . . . experienced a 40 percent decline in traffic coming from Google's search results and an 80 percent drop in traffic from Google News. [Their] chief executive said that Axel Springer would have "shot ourselves out of the market" if the company had continued demanding that news aggregating sites pay a licensing fee for its content. (ibid.)

The pathways of journalism's creative reconstruction are not set in concrete. Whether on-the-ground hybridity will allow private companies to generate enough profit to finance journalism is not a question that can be definitively answered at the present time. In the United States, some of the private enterprises marketing journalism nationally appear increasingly resilient. The *New York Times'* second effort to erect a paywall succeeded in 2011, and America's preeminent news platform now has 750,000 digital-only subscriptions to its website, the most visited worldwide.[18] The newspaper's financial free fall having been broken, the Sulzberger family owners of the *Times* are not going anywhere soon (Nagourney 2023). *The Wall Street Journal* installed its own paywall in 1997 and currently has one million online subscribers. Purchasing the family-owned company in 2007, Rupert Murdoch so expanded the breadth and depth of its national coverage that the once primarily business-oriented daily now puts a full court press on the *Times* (Pew Journalism Research Project 2011). The *Washington Post* presents yet a different pathway to sustaining profitability on the national scene. After purchasing the company from the Grahams in 2013, Amazon founder Jeff Bezos began upgrading, significantly increasing staff and infrastructure.[19] Does this move mark the beginning of new political-economy for journalism, its autonomy underwritten by those who control the post-industrial means of production? Will Internet billionaires displace old-time industrial money, plowing their surplus into the creation of hybrid journalism? At least on the national level, Downey and Schudson (2009) are right to observe "consumers of news have more fresh reporting at their fingertips . . . than ever before."

While paywalls are also being built around local newspapers,[20] their economic conditions are significantly less sanguine. Hundreds of small-town papers are disappearing, and larger city and regional papers have significantly contracted (Downey and Schudson 2009). Competition from Internet advertising is one major economic factor, as classified ads move to specialized blogs and local marketing shifts online (Starr 2009). But other issues are also at play. There are self-inflicted wounds: local papers have sometimes resisted the transition to hybridity until it proved financially too late (Anderson 2013; Ryfe 2012). Institutional processes having nothing to do with digitalization are also at work. From the 1950s onward, there has been a shrinking appetite for long-form, non-tabloid news reporting of the local scene (Lemann 2013). Most of the nation's major metropolitan areas became one-newspaper towns decades before the appearance of the Internet. Meanwhile, national news chains began buying up small-town papers, displacing serious reporting with the tabloid approach to news so glaringly evident in local television reporting. Cultural homogenization may also be a factor, diluting the distinctive differences that generate interest in locality while creating conditions for the emergence of national newspapers at the same time. Finally, there is the political economy of family capitalism, with family properties founded in the industrial period cashing out for more generalized media of exchange. The Chandlers sold the *Los Angeles Times* to the Tribune Company, the Bancrofts relinquished *The Wall Street Journal*, and the McCormicks gave up control of the *Chicago Tribune*. With so much path-dependency, broad causal claims become difficult. Linking the weakness of local newspapers exclusively to the rise of the Internet is another reduction-driven mistake.

Whatever the causes, the business form that sustained journalism on the local and regional level is no longer in good health. In response to the crisis of local newspapers, however, online news-gathering sites have emerged with the aim of taking their place. In the Seattle metropolitan region, for example, Ryfe (2012: 159ff) recently counted more than a hundred such new sites. Many, if not most, of these small, often ultra-local, efforts will not survive (Ryfe 2013), but others will undoubtedly appear. Is there enough profit to finance more efficient, better networked, and more creatively managed online news sites – to balance the decrease in local newspapers? If not, some local and regional platforms for American journalism may have to be removed from the commodity chain. Just as contemporary capitalist societies have made art, education, and sometimes television and radio programming into public goods, so might decisions be made to decommodify (Kopytoff 1986) segments of the journalistic field. In the United States, such decommodification efforts have come principally from philanthropists and nonprofit foundations, with $128 million invested in financing online platforms in the five years from 2005 to 2009.[21] While contemporary American politics makes any sweeping effort to extend government subsidies unlikely (Pickard 2011), more indirect support via changes in tax laws is possible (Downey and Schudson 2009). Outside the United States, it is more likely that local, regional, and national governments will step in.

The Performativity of Journalism

How many well-financed platforms for serious news are necessary for the professional ethics and civic morals of journalism to be sustained? In order to answer this question, one last theoretical revision need be made. Just as news must be reconceived as discourse rather than information, so must the idea of an informed reader give way to interpreting audience. The civic impact of journalistic judgment has always involved performativity, as much telling as showing (Austin

1957; Alexander 2011). The cultural effect of a news story is mostly achieved by the very act of publishing it. If an audience of critical and influential citizens is presumed to be in place, then authoritative publication of critical news judgments becomes a self-fulfilling prophecy.[22] Members of the citizen-audience envision one another to be reading and deciphering the same journalistic judgment, and those in positions of social power are compelled to make the same assumption at the same time.[23] "News becomes a theatre," Schudson (2010) observes, "regardless of whether the public audience is large or small."

> Journalism can perform its institutional role as a watchdog even if nobody in the provinces is following the news. All that matters is that people in government *believe* they are following the news. If an inner circle of attentive citizens is watchful, this is sufficient to produce in the leaders a fear of public embarrassment, public controversy, legal prosecution, or fear of losing an election.   (ibid., italics added)

Whether hundreds, thousands, or millions of readers in the networked audience actually do access the alerts becomes less important than the act of signaling itself (Spence 1973).[24]

As the Internet instantaneously spreads news far and wide, the spatial and temporal projection of news discourse has dramatically increased. When contemporary actions and events seem threatening to civil ideals, as reported by an authoritative forum, the "news" is accessible much more quickly, and to an exponentially larger audience, than in pre-Internet days. As Philip Meyer (2009: 213) suggests, "not all readers demand such information, but ... the educated, opinion-leading, news-junkie core of the audience always will." Asking "won't democracy be endangered if the newspaper audience shrinks down to this hard core," Meyer answers "not at all" (ibid.)

> The Paul Lazarsfeld et al. (1948) two-step flow effect can only be enhanced by the Internet. It is being converted to a many step flow. The problem is not distributing the information. The problem is maintaining a strong and trusted agency to originate it. Newspapers have that position of trust in the minds of the public. That trust – or influence – is their core product. If the product is directed at the hard-core news junkies and opinion leaders in the community, circulation will shrink, and that's not a bad thing ... Those readers are the most valuable – not just for their consuming habits but for their influence on others.   (ibid.)

Even as the platforms for projecting news are becoming fewer, the readership for serious news diminishing to a smaller circle of committed readers, the cultural and institutional vitality of journalism is being sustained. Such voraciously interpreting citizens constitute an ample audience. The Internet allows news judgments to be projected in widening spirals that compel responses from other institutions, shaping public opinion and shaking up the powers that be.

Only by piercing the fog of technotopian discourse does it become apparent that the Internet and journalism have been changing from agonistic binaries into friends. Theoretical reduction created false hopes and false fears. Neither technology nor economics exercises their social effects in isolation. They are mediated by the professional ethics of journalism and the civic morals that anchor them. Like every major technological invention over the last two centuries, the social and economic upheavals triggered by the Internet are real and often destructive. But predictions of the Internet's transformative consequences for social life, for better and for worse, have been greatly exaggerated. Culture is the dark matter of the social universe, invisible but exercising extraordinary power. The meanings of journalism are fervently formed and fiercely delineated, and the cultural power of the profession resists technological and economic determinism. Cultural power generates individual and collective agency: the resourcefulness that allows journalists, and supportive communities and institutions not only to resist desecration but also to engage in civil repair.

Certainly, the preservation of any professional craft is never guaranteed. The more central a profession to a society's core beliefs and institutions, however, the more its existential struggles generate defense and support. The professional ethics of journalism are deeply intertwined with the civic morals of democratic practices and institutions, and have been for centuries. Only if we comprehend this centrality can we understand why a crisis of journalism exists. Only by clarifying the cultural roots of this crisis can we comprehend how it can be reconsidered and repaired.

NOTES

1 Giambattista Vico, translated by Bergin, T. G. and Fisch, M. H. 2016. Paragraph 331, p. 96 in *The New Science of Giambattista Vico: Unabridged Translation of the Third Edition (1744) with the addition of "Practice of the New Science."* Cornell University Press.

INTRODUCTION: CIVIL REPAIR AND SOCIAL THEORY

1 One must acknowledge a small handful of notable exceptions, most significantly among them Tocqueville, Arendt, and Parsons. While in the first volume of *Democracy in America*, Tocqueville wrote incisively, if unsystematically, about the culture and institutions sustaining early American democracy, and in the second volume wrote critically about democracy's defaults, the impact of his thinking on modern social theory has been limited because it was focused on pre-industrial society. Parsons theorized variously about institutions and meanings in modern democratic societies, in a manner implicitly republican, but his defensively conservative liberalism and self-satisfied evolutionism made his later theorizing as one-sidedly optimistic as critical theory is despairing. Arendt elegized "the political" as an aesthetic breakthrough of freedom and possibility, but she under-theorized democracy, limiting it to episodes of face-to-face deliberation that could not be sustained in the face of mass society and the shrinking of the public sphere.

2 Which meant that Weber also had little to say about the prospects of democracy outside the West. The effort to reconstruct the Weberian project in the framework of an "Axial" breakthrough that spanned not only Western but also "Eastern" religion (Bellah 2011; Eisenstadt 1982) avoids the orientalism that marred Weber's understandings of China and India, but does not redress his failure to trace the thread of democratic thought and institutions. Perhaps it was in response to this aporia that Bellah devoted a chapter in his final work, *Religion and Human Revolution*, to Ancient Greece. While making the case that Greek secular philosophy can be conceived as a parallel Axial

165

breakthrough, Bellah does not try to think through the relationship between secular and religious versions of Axiality, much less evaluate secular Greek Axiality in terms of its ability to create the civic republican discourse that laid down tracks not only for Roman institutions but for the late medieval revival of democratic forms. That in recent decades relatively independent civil spheres have emerged in some East and South Asian nations (Alexander et al. 2019b) testifies to synergy between between Axial religion and secular democratic culture and institutions, the latter the product of thick interchange with Western life.

3 Walzer's early *The Revolution of the Saints* (1965) and his later *Exodus and Revolution* (1986) marked extraordinary exceptions not only to the Weberian failure to consider the cultural foundations of modern democracy but also to its failure to link Axial and post-Axial religiosity to secular political traditions. In an obscure and singular consideration of early American democracy, Weber adumbrated Walzer's work, linking its possibility to sectarian Protestantism (Alexander and Loder 1985), even as he continued to ignore the long institutional and cultural history of "secular" republicanism and liberalism. In the wake of Germany's humiliating defeat in World War I, Weber (1978) entertained the notion of democracy as an effective oversight mechanism to prevent political authorities – like the German Kaiser and generals – from escaping political realities. Notably, even here, Weber polluted modern mass democracy as a "Ceasarism" that depended upon anti-rational charismatic leadership and mere plebiscitarianism (Mommsen 1984).

1 THE LONG AND WINDING ROAD: CIVIL REPAIR OF INTIMATE INJUSTICE

1 The neologism m/otherhood is my own.
2 Kerber notes the blocking quality of the motherhood trope explicitly:

> Republican motherhood was one of a series of conservative choices that Americans made in the postwar years as they avoided the full implications of their Revolutionary radicalism. In America responsibility for maintaining public virtue was channeled into domestic life. By these decisions Americans may well have been spared the agony of the French cycle of revolution and counterrevolution. Nevertheless the impact of this choice was to delay the resolution of matters. When the war was over, Judith Sargent Murray predicted a "new era in female history." That new era remained to be created [b]ut it could not be created until the inherent paradox of Republican Motherhood was resolved, until the world was not separated into a woman's realm of domesticity and nurture and a man's world of politics and intellect. The promises of the republic had yet to be fulfilled. (*Women's America* 1995: 95)

3 Rabinovitch's essay is conspicuously marked by such blurring, continuously moving back and forth between the contemporary multicultural rhetoric of difference, which rings with a powerful authenticity, and nineteenth-century difference talk, whose essentializing view of gender would create powerful negative reactions if it were clearly seen.
4 In his most recent effort, Habermas (1996) has subtly but nonetheless fundamentally altered his understanding of public, rejecting face-to-face encounters for public opinion formation. Yet he seeks to maintain his early

166

liberal understanding of civil society as consisting primarily of voluntary associations. I use the word "seeks" because at many points Habermas adds that these are "civil" voluntary associations only if they are enmeshed in a "liberal political culture." With this addition, he gets into the morass of ad hoc reasoning that Rawls (1993) encounters in his efforts to flee from neo-Kantianism in *Political Liberalism*. For a sustained and revealing argument against overlapping and overburdened meanings of the term "public," see Weintraub (1997).

5 The theoretical resources I draw upon here range from Kenneth Burke and Erving Goffman, to Victor Turner's decade of seminal theoretical break-throughs, to the explorations of public dramaturgy and narration by Robin Wagner-Pacifici (1986, 1994, 2000) and recent discussions of performance theory. See also the range of empirical and theoretical studies of ritual and public-discursive behavior cited by me in note 2, above.

6 "The requirement that needs and their interpretations become the focus of discursive argumentation has the consequence that those traditions and prac-tices, the semantic content of which defines the good life and happiness, are thematized. In practical discourses, a certain conception of justice is revealed to rest on a certain understanding of our needs, the cultural traditions which justify them, and the socialization patterns which shape them . . . If the subject matter of discourses is not artificially restricted, if the process of self-reflection reaches these presuppositions, then issues of justice and the good life flow into one another . . . It is ultimately the process of discourse . . . that establishes the truth and falsehood of our needs . . . A genuinely fluid and unrepressed relation to inner nature consists in the capacity for constant criti-cal reevaluation and reconsideration of our most cherished needs" (Benhabib 1986: 36, 38).

2 FEMINISM, PUBLIC OPINION, AND PRESIDENTIAL POWER (WITH WILLA SACHS)

1 This holds not only for the "contentious politics" approach of PPT but for more culturally oriented approaches to social movements as well. The latter examine how frames mobilize particular "target" groups such as elite allies or potential recruits, as Bloemraad, Silva, and Voss (2016: 1651) note, rather than how public opinion, crystallized by frames, continuously affects state decision-making (cf. Ghaziani, Taylor, and Stone 2016; Bernstein and Taylor 2013). Theorists of "new social movements," for their part, have examined public opinion as an outcome of so-called identity-movements, an emphasis that precludes analyses of state responsiveness to movements and opinion (for a review, see Earl 2004).

2 In response to challenges from more culturally oriented theories, PPT theo-rists tried to wedge open their model (e.g., Kriesi 2004; McAdam, Tarrow, and Tilly 2001; McAdam, McCarthy, and Zald 1996). The revised model, however, largely retains its original structuralist bent. Tilly, for instance, describes public claims-making as a pragmatic action drawn from a "reper-toire of contention" (2002), rather than as a discursive construction drawn from a shared pattern of meanings (as Emirbayer argues 2010: 413).

3 Law is another powerful regulative institution of the civil sphere, and it, too, is deeply influenced by public opinion (see, e.g., Friedman 2009). "Office" is

another vital regulatory institution, obligating the exercise of power in ways that refract public opinion (Alexander 2006: 132–192).
4 One survey, for instance, revealed that in 1972, 70% of respondents would vote for a qualified female presidential candidate, a jump from 55% in just 1969 (Ferree and Hess 1995: 87).

3 #METOO AS SOCIETALIZATION

1 I use the adjectives "hypothetical" and "putatively" and the verbs "appears" and "imagined" because I wish to emphasize, vis-à-vis functionalist and conflict theorizing about inter-sphere boundary relations, that steady state does not refer to a condition of objective equilibrium but, rather, to institutional insulation – a condition in which significant conflicts inside spheres are not experienced as threatening to the society at large. This distinction marks the difference between a mechanistic model of inter-sphere relations and the cultural-sociological approach I employ here. In Keynes' critique of classical economic theory, he makes a similar point. While classical predictions about economic equilibrium assumed stable rates of capital investment, Keynes argues that the latter actually depends on the propensity to invest, which he equates with subjective estimations of probability. Because optimistic or pessimistic predictions about future interest rates cannot be proved objectively, Keynes argued, equilibrium depends on social conventions and collective states of mind (Keynes [1936] 1964: 141–153).
2 "The foundation of democracy is faith in the capacities of human nature; faith in human intelligence and in the power of pooled and cooperative experience. It is not belief that these things are complete but that if given a show they will grow and be able to generate progressively the knowledge and wisdom needed to guide collective action" (Dewey 1937).
3 Symbolic interactionist theorists concentrate on agency in theorizing the construction of social problems as scandals, for example, Becker's (1963) "moral entrepreneurs" and Fine's (1997) "reputational entrepreneurs." Such pragmatist approaches, however, tend to reduce agency to the cynical pursuit of self-interest. For example, while Cohen (1972: 112 [italics added]) rightly warns that "the presence alone [of] values does not guarantee successful . . . social problem definition," arguing "there must also be enterprise," it does not follow that "someone [who] takes the initiative" does so simply "on the basis of interest" and instrumentally "uses publicity techniques to gain" support.
4 The exploits of civil heroes are recounted in bestselling books and award-winning movies. The tenacious idealism of Boston Globe investigators into Church pedophilia was cinematized in Spotlight (2015), which won the Academy Award for best picture. Bob Woodward and Carl Bernstein, the intrepid reporters who code shifted the Watergate scandal, were the principal protagonists of All the President's Men (1976), the legendary 1970s film that won four Academy Awards. Four decades later, two of Watergate's other civil heroes, Ben Bradlee and Katharine Graham, were cinematized in The Post (2017), which received a best picture nomination from the Academy Awards and was named best film of 2017 by the National Board of Review.

5 In 1905, the legendary muckraker Upton Sinclair first published chapters of *The Jungle*, his societalizing call-out of the meat-packing industry, in an influential popular magazine aptly titled *Appeal to Reason*.

6 Blumer (1971: 302) once observed that "the pages of history are replete with dire conditions unnoticed and unattended to." The theory of societalization presented here allows this constructionist insight to be explained in a macro-sociological way.

7 In 1979, the radical feminist legal theorist Catharine A. MacKinnon wrote: "Sexual assault as experienced during sexual harassment seems less like an ordinary act of sexual desire directed toward the wrong person than an expression of dominance laced with personal contempt, the habit of getting what one wants, and the perception (usually accurate) that the situation can be safely exploited in this way – all expressed sexually. It is dominance eroticized" (MacKinnon 1979: 162). This pioneering work by MacKinnon – *Sexual Harassment of Working Women: A Case Study of Sex Discrimination* – opened the pathway toward what eventually became the legal thicket of sexual harassment law.

8 "The term 'sexual harassment' itself grew out of a consciousness-raising session Lin Farley held in 1974 as part of a Cornell University course on women and work" (Siegel 2003).

9 "A Pew survey conducted in November and December 2017 found that 69 percent of Republican women thought recent allegations of harassment and assault reflected widespread problems in society, compared with 74 percent of Democratic women" (VOX 2018).

10 These data were filtered by "ProQuest for Wire Feeds, Blogs, Podcast, Websites, Newspapers, Trade Journals, and Other Sources featuring the Harvey Weinstein Scandal" on October 5, 2017. The following are ordered alphabetically by news source:

1. "El magnate Harvey Weinstein, acusado de acoso sexual toma licencia." *AFP International Text Wire in Spanish.*
2. "Magnata Harvey Weinstein se desculpa após alegações de assédio sexual." *AFP International Text Wire in Portuguese.*
3. "Harvey Weinstein to take leave amid sexual harassment report." *AP Financial.*
4. "Film Mogul Weinstein Takes Leave Amid Harassment Allegations." *Bloomberg Wire Service.*
5. National Audio. *The Canadian Press.*
6. "Harvey Weinstein Apologizes." *CTV National News.*
7. "Harvey Weinstein Takes Leave from Studio After Harassment Allegations." *Dow Jones Institutional News.*
8. "New York Times destapa historial de sepuesto acoso sexual de Harvey Weinstein: HOLLYWOOD ABUSOS." *EFE News Service, Miami.*
9. "Harvey Weinstein Apologizes for Sexual Harassment." *Finance Wire.*
10. "Daily briefing." *FT.com; London.*
11. "Trafficked Premiere Has Elizabeth Rohm But Not Judd." *Inner City Press; Bronx.*
12. "Harvey Weinstein Apologizes for Sexual Harassment." *International Wire.*

13. "Harvey Weinstein's Hollywood future is in question after sexual harassment allegations." *Los Angeles Times* (online).
14. "Harvey Weinstein unloads Connecticut home for $1.65 million." *Los Angeles Times* (online).
15. "Lena Dunham, Rose McGowan add voices to Harvey Weinstein scandal." *Los Angeles Times* (online).
16. "Harvey Weinstein to take a leave of absence amid sexual harassment claims, threatens lawsuit over report." *Los Angeles Times* (online).
17. "Hollywood exec Harvey Weinstein to take leave following sexual harassment report." The National – *CBC Television*; Toronto.
18. "Las Vegas, Harvey Weinstein, Spain: Your Thursday Evening Briefing." *New York Times* (online).
19. "Actresses Respond to Harvey Weinstein's Accusers: 'I Believe You'." *New York Times* (online).
20. "Mediaite: Turns Out Harvey Weinstein is Backing His Feminist Attorney Lisa Bloom's New Show Too." *Newstex Trade & Industry Blogs.*
21. "Mediaite: BOMBSHELL: NYT Report Accuses Film Mogul Harvey Weinstein of Being Serial Sex Predator." *Newstex Trade & Industry Blogs.*
22. "Mediaite: TBT: Harvey Weinstein Once Wrote an Op-Ed Defending Child Rapist Roman Polanski." *Newstex Trade & Industry Blogs.*
23. "Mediaite: Film Mogul Harvey Weinstein Reportedly Lawyers Up Ahead of Explosive Stories About His Behavior." *Newstex Trade & Industry Blogs.*
24. "Mediaite: Democratic Senators Are Reportedly Giving Harvey Weinstein's Campaign Donations to Charity." *Newstex Trade & Industry Blogs.*
25. "Mediaite: What Exactly Does NY Times Mean By Saying Harvey Weinstein 'Initiated' a Massage 'Himself.'" *Newstex Trade & Industry Blogs.*
26. "Second Opinion." *PE HUB.*
27. "Canadian Press Budget for Thursday, October 5, 2017." *The Canadian Press*; Montreal.
28. "Harvey Weinstein to take leave of absence after NYT exposé." *Screen International*; London.
29. "Amid Harassment Reports, Harvey Weinstein Takes Leave of Absence." The Two-Way [BLOG], Washington: *NPR*.
30. "Harvey Weinstein Takes Leave from Studio After Harassment Allegations; Media report details several instances of sexual harassment by producer; Weinstein says he will 'deal with this head on.'" *The Wall Street Journal* (online).
31. "Harvey Weinstein is accused of sexual harassment in explosive story, takes leave of absence." *Washington Post – Blogs* (online).
32. "Report Women accuse Harvey Weinstein of sexual harassment." *Washington Post – Blogs* (online).
33. "Harvey Weinstein and Democrats' deals with Hollywood's devils: Harvey Weinstein is reminder that Hollywood's relationship with liberalism is mired in contradiction and failures of ideals." *Washington Post – Blogs* (online)

One may assume ProQuest was unable to pick up all media reports featuring the October 5 *Times* story. This selection does not reflect, for example, U.S. television and radio coverage of the story. What this list does demonstrate is the immediate uptake of the story, translation into international markets, and elaborations. In terms of elaborations, these represent strategies to extend the original reporting, so as not to make the pick-up redundant, e.g., finding fresh angles. The latter include: editorials expounding on the hypocrisy of liberalism; Democrats placing immediate distance between Weinstein and themselves by giving his campaign donations to charity; actresses and actors showing immediate approval and support for the accusations.

11 These include:

> *Boston Globe*
> *Chicago Tribune*
> *Hartford Courant*
> *TCA Regional News*
> *USA Today*
> *Dow Jones Institutional News*
> *Gulf News*
> *Inner City Press*
> *Los Angeles Times*
> *National Post*
> *New Statesman*
> *New York Times*
> *Newsweek*
> *Philadelphia Tribune*
> *Economic Times*
> *Economist*
> *Village Voice*
> *Washington Post*
> *Toronto Star*
> *Variety*
> *Wall Street Journal*
> *Washington Post*

12 In the midst of this social media effervescence, it was discovered that "MeToo" had actually been introduced as a hashtag a decade earlier by Tarana Burke, an African-American activist, as a means of making more visible the sexual exploitation of women of color.

13 These graphs were created by Crimson Hexagon/George Washington University.

14 This is not to suggest that other national newspapers are not also influential. Such newspapers as the *Washington Post* and the *Wall Street Journal* also break stories that drive the news cycle as, less often, do such important regional papers as the *Boston Globe* and the *Los Angeles Times*.

15 In this reconstruction, I am not myself making the argument that newly appointed women would actually make institutional power more civil but, rather, that these were the arguments made by communicative institutions as they simultaneously represented and crystallized public opinion. My point is that, in the context of societalization, men were *constructed* as anti-civil, women increasingly as civil.

16 Here is a rough survey of the most notable accusations by job and apology/
no apology between October 5, 2017, and May 23, 2018.

Apology
1. *Oct. 5:* Harvey Weinstein (Apology)
2. *Oct. 10:* Ben Affleck (Apology)
3. *Oct. 17:* Chris Savino – Nickelodeon producer (Apology)
4. *Oct. 19:* Lockhart Steele – Editorial director, Vox Media (Apology)
5. *Oct. 21:* John Besh – Celebrity chef, chief executive of Besh Restaurant Group (Apology)
6. *Oct. 24:* Leon Wieseltier – New Republic editor (Apology
7. *Oct. 25:* Knight Landesman – Artforum publisher (Apology)
8. *Oct. 26:* Ken Baker – E! News correspondent (Apology)
9. *Oct 26:* Mark Halperin – MSNBC political analyst, co-author of "Game Change" (Apology)
10. *Oct. 29:* Kevin Spacey – Actor (Apology)
11. *Oct. 30:* Hamilton Fish – New Republic president and publisher (Apology)
12. *Oct. 31:* Michael Oreskes – NPR chief editor (Apology)
13. *Nov. 1:* Dustin Hoffman – Actor (Apology)
14. *Nov. 1:* Jeff Hoover – Kentucky House Speaker (Apology)
15. *Nov. 9:* Louis C.K. – Comedian (Apology)
16. *Nov. 16:* Al Franken – U.S. Senator (D-Minn.) (Apology)
17. *Nov. 20:* Charlie Rose – PBS and CBS host (Apology)
18. *Nov. 20:* Glenn Thrush – New York Times White House reporter (Apology)
19. *Nov. 21:* John Lasseter – Pixar and Disney Animation chief (Apology).
20. *Nov. 29:* Matt Lauer – NBC "Today" show morning host (Apology)
21. *Dec. 1:* Ruben Kihuen – U.S. House of Representatives (D-Nev.) (Apology)
22. *Dec. 11:* Mario Batali – TV star, renowned chef (Apology)
23. *Dec. 13:* Morgan Spurlock – Hollywood director (Apology)
24. *Dec. 18:* Alex Kozinski – California federal court judge (Apology)
25. *Jan. 2:* Dan Harmon – Creator of "Community" and "Rick and Morty" (Apology)
26. *Jan 5:* Ben Vereen – Tony Award-winning actor (Apology)
27. *Jan. 11:* James Franco – Actor (Apology)
28. *Feb. 21:* Daniel Handler – Author known as Lemony Snicket (Apology)
29. *March 5:* Sherman Alexie – Native American author (Apology)
30. *March 29:* John Kricfalusi – Creator of "The Ren & Stimpy Show" (Apology)
31. *May 4:* Junot Díaz – Author, MIT creative writing professor (Apology)

No Apology
1. *Oct. 12:* Roy Price – Amazon executive (No Apology)
2. *Oct. 22:* James Toback – Writer-director (No Apology)
3. *Oct. 23:* Terry Richardson – Fashion photographer (No Apology)
4. *Oct. 30:* Jeremy Piven – Actor (No Apology)
5. *Oct. 31:* Andy Dick – Comedian (No Apology)

6. *Nov. 1:* Brett Ratner – Filmmaker (No Apology)
7. *Nov. 3:* David Guillod – Primary Wave Entertainment co-CEO (No Apology)
8. *Nov. 7:* Ed Westwick – Actor known for "Gossip Girl" (No Apology)
9. *Nov. 8:* Jeffrey Tambor – Actor (No Apology)
10. *Nov. 9:* Roy Moore – Alabama judge and politician, U.S. Senate candidate (R.-Ala.) (No Apology)
11. *Nov. 9:* Matthew Weiner – "Mad Men" creator (No Apology).
12. *Nov. 16:* Gary Goddard – CEO of The Goddard Group, behind the creation of theme park attractions including the Georgia Aquarium and the Monster Plantation ride at Six Flags Over Georgia (No Apology)
13. *Nov. 16:* Eddie Berganza – Editor of DC Comics (No Apology)
14. *Nov. 16:* Andrew Kreisberg – Executive producer of "Arrow," "Supergirl," "The Flash" (No Apology)
15. *Nov. 20:* John Conyers – U.S. Senator (D-Mich.) (No Apology)
16. *Nov. 22:* Nick Carter – Backstreet Boys member (No Apology)
17. *Nov. 29:* Garrison Keillor – Creator and former host of "A Prairie Home Companion" (No Apology)
18. *Nov. 30:* Russell Simmons – Entrepreneur, co-founder of Def Jam Recordings (No Apology)
19. *Dec. 6:* Warren Moon – NFL Hall of Fame quarterback, co-founder and president of Sports 1 Marketing (No Apology)
20. *Dec. 11:* Ryan Lizza – The New Yorker Magazine's Washington correspondent (No Apology)
21. *Dec. 11:* President Donald Trump (No Apology)
22. *Dec. 15:* Gene Simmons – Bassist for band KISS (No Apology)
23. *Jan. 5:* Paul Haggis – Oscar-winning director and screenwriter (No Apology)
24. *Jan. 9:* Stan Lee – Former editor-in-chief, publisher, chairman of Marvel Comics (No Apology)
25. *Jan. 13:* Aziz Ansari – Actor, comedian (No Apology)
26. *Jan 13:* Mario Testino – Photographer (No Apology)
27. *Jan 14:* Bruce Weber – Photographer (No Apology)
28. *Jan 16:* Seal – Singer (No Apology)
29. *Jan. 18:* Michael Douglas – Actor (No Apology)
30. *Jan. 25:* David Copperfield – Magician (No Apology)
31. *Jan. 27:* Scott Baio – Actor (No Apology)
32. *Feb. 1:* Paul Marciano – GUESS co-founder (No Apology)
33. *Feb. 2:* Vincent Cirrincione – Talent manager (Apology)
34. *Feb. 16:* Patrick Demarchelier – Photographer (No Apology)
35. *Feb 16:* Greg Kadel – Photographer (No Apology)
36. *Feb 16:* Andre Passos – Photographer (No Apology)
37. *Feb 16:* Seth Sabal – Photographer (No Apology)
38. *Feb 16:* David Bellemere – Photographer (No Apology)
39. *Feb. 22:* Philip Berk – Former president of Hollywood Foreign Press Association (No Apology)
40. *Feb. 28:* Jeff Franklin – Former "Fuller House" showrunner (No Apology)

41. *April 4:* Nicholas Nixon – Former photographer, professor at Massachusetts College of Art and Design (No Apology)
42. *May 7:* Eric Schneiderman – New York Attorney General (No Apology)
43. *May 23:* Morgan Freeman – Actor (No Apology)
Apologies = 30/73 or 41.1%
No Apology = 43/73 or 58.9%

4 FROM CIVIL RIGHTS TO BLACK LIVES MATTER

1 I draw here from Alexander (2006), *The Civil Sphere*, Chapter 5.
2 I am grateful to Anne-Marie Champagne for the research assistance she provided for this section.
3 "Clearly there is some degree of overlap between #Blacklivesmatter and Black Lives Matter: organization members (along with many others) use the hashtag, which in turn almost certainly leads prospective members to the organization. At the same time, the two terms are sometimes used to refer to a third idea: the sum of all organizations, individuals, protests, and digital spaces dedicated to raising awareness about and ultimately ending police brutality against Black people" (Freelon et al. 2016: 9).
4 Fusion and de-fusion describe different ideal-typical reponses of audiences to social performance, the former receptive and embracing, the latter unresponsive and rejecting.
5 "With a graph density of .003 . . . only a tiny fraction of all the links that could exist within the network actually exist. As a comparison, a random network with the same number of nodes has a density of .02, meaning that the network contains two percent of all possible ties. There is little reciprocity between sites (in 97% of cases, sites linking out to another site don't receive a link in from the latter site). Whether unidirectional or reciprocal, few sites have multiple links to any one site (the average tie weight – the number of times any two sites link to each other – is one, and only 30% of ties have a weight greater than one)" (Freelon et al. 2016: 16).
6 "59% of the entire Black Lives Matter network are news sites [and] more than 75% of sites with direct connections to BlackLivesMatter.com are news sites. [W]e've pointed out that as a whole, the network is very sparse. However, connections among news sites in the network are extremely dense, meaning that they primarily connect to one another, and much less so to non-news sites" (Freelon et al. 2016: 17).
7 Not the police killings themselves, however. In a 12-month Pulitzer Prize winning investigation, the *Washington Post* discovered there had been 990 fatal police shootings in 2015 (Kindy et al. 2015) and 250 in the first 3 months of 2016 (Sullivan et al. 2016). Those killed in 2015 were disproportionally minorities, 258 African Americans and 172 Hispanics, for a total of 430 as compared with 494 whites. One-third of the victims were aged 18–29.
8 Note that this reaction of traditional Republican leaders shifted in the wake of Trump's nomination, even as the backlash against BLM – "Blue Lives Matter," "All Lives Matter" – began to cost Hillary Clinton votes among moderate voters in swing states (Ostertag 2019).
9 It is revealing that, while recounting Mckesson's many accomplishments,

174

the *Times* observed that "he collects celebrity 'friends' (Azealia Banks, Jesse Williams, Susans Wojcicki and Sarandon, Rashida Jones, Tracee Ellis Ross)[and] refers to them solely by their first names," explaining this was "because, over the last year and a half, he has been the best known face of the Black Lives Matter movement, traveling the country to protest police violence" (Howard 2016).

5 OBAMA–TAHRIR–OCCUPY: UTOPIAS OF CIVIL LIBERATION

1 See, for example, the complaint by columnist Nicholas Kristof, *New York Times*, October 1, 2011.

7 THE CRISIS OF JOURNALISM AND CREATIVE (RECON)STRUCTION

1 Whether journalistic news platforms are more or less differentiated – independent – from political parties and their ideologies, or for that matter from religious, ethnic, economic, or racial groups, is an empirical question that has been intensely debated over the course of three decades of historical and comparative sociology (Schudson 1978; Alexander 1981; Chalaby 1996; Hallin and Mancini 2004, 2012; Jones 2013; Mancini 2013). What has gone relatively unnoticed in this debate, however, and what actually is crucial for any sociological understanding of the institution of journalism, is the factual *self*-presentation of journalists as independent, whatever the actual nature of their boundary connections. Such putative autonomy allows news media to present themselves as third-party alternatives *vis-à-vis* partisan struggles between openly ideological parties and their depictions of social reality. For example, in a 2013 editorial the *New York Times* (2013) weighed in on the controversy surrounding the murder of America's ambassador to Libya. Conservatives alleged that a Hillary Clinton–led conspiracy had occluded public understanding of the "Benghazi affair." Headlined "The Facts About Benghazi," the *Times* claimed its own investigation had disproved such conspiracy claims: "An exhaustive investigation by The *Times* goes a long way toward resolving any nagging doubts about what precipitated the attack on the United States mission in Benghazi, Libya, last year that killed Ambassador J. Christopher Stevens and three other Americans." As grounds for confidence that its journalists had discovered "the facts," the *Times*' editorial referenced its reporter's marshaling of evidence, his logic, his commitment to reasonable standards of proof, and the probing quality of his interviews, implicitly linking these fact-finding methods to the integrity of paper and reporters:

> The report, by David Kirkpatrick, The *Times*' Cairo bureau chief, and his team turned up no evidence that Al Qaeda or another international terrorist group had any role in the assault, as Republicans have insisted without proof for more than a year. [Republican Representative Mike] Rogers, the chairman of the House Intelligence Committee who has called Benghazi a 'preplanned, organized terrorist event,' said his panel's findings [were] based on an examination of 4,000 classified cables. If Mr. Rogers has evidence of a direct Al Qaeda role, he should make it public. Otherwise, the *Times*' investigation, including extensive

interviews with Libyans in Benghazi who had direct knowledge of the attack, stands as the authoritative narrative.

2 In 2011, the *Economist* hailed Shirky as "one of the preeminent public intellectuals of the internet" (Ottawa 2011).
3 "Newspapers from the start were caught in a frustrating dilemma. Overwhelmingly, the culture of the Web is that content is free. If newspapers put the content of the newspaper online for free, they would encourage subscribers to drop their subscriptions and undermine the circulation of their print version. If they charged for content, the prospective audience would avoid them and go instead to other sites where content was free" (Jones 2009: 186).
4 "Search engines and Web portrayals such as Google and Yahoo and AOL are all major providers of news, but very little of it's originated by them. They are 'free riders,' who get the benefit of offering their audience a range of reported news that has been generated by newspapers and other traditional media ... Google, in other words, makes money from the news article while the newspaper does the work. The 'free rider' syndrome is also at the heart of the portion of the burgeoning blogosphere devoted to news and public affairs, because all of their commentary is based on the traditional media's reporting" (Jones 2009: 187).
5 This iconic phrase, which has assumed an almost folkloric status, is attributed to a presentation that Stewart Brand made at the first Hackers Conference in 1984. Brand was the creator of the *Whole Earth Catalogue*.
6 The economic consequences of the cultural equation of the Internet with freedom extend even into media systems that are not nearly as market-braced as the United States. Steen-Johnsen et al. (2016) show that, while the Norwegian state generously subsidizes print media, it has refused such support to online newspapers, despite the fact that "it is precisely free access that has been blamed for the crisis in the industry."
7 While in modern sociology Parsons (1954 [1939]) was the first to conceptualize professions as horizontal organizations resisting the instrumental forces of the market and the hierarchical pressures of bureaucracy, the idea of professions as buffers was already deeply institutionalized in early twentieth-century social theory and society (e.g. Tawney 1920: 94).
8 Shirky's predictions that the Internet will destroy journalism are based upon the reductionist equation of professional form with economic production: "The definition of journalist, seemingly a robust and stable profession, turns out to be tied to particular forms of production" (Shirky 2008: 70). In 2011, Anderson challenged Shirky's understanding of professions:

> In the web era, we have usually told a particular story about institutions and the professions they house, one summed up nicely in Clay Shirky's [argument that] professions are monopolistic guilds designed to raise barriers to entry in order to maintain professional privilege at the expense of the public good ... It is a story I've told myself. But it's not the only side to the tale. *The other side to institutions and professions*, a side long recognized by even the harshest critics of professional power, is that *they create non-material cultures that insulate workers from the ravages of the free market*. Professions create an alternative reward system in which status and pay are determined not simply though the workings of the market, but through *alternate hierarchies of worth*.   (2011, original italics)

176

9 That sacrality can powerfully structure social organization even in modern times is conceptualized in Durkheim's late work, *The Elementary Forms of Religious Life* (1995 [1912]), and the premise has been foundational to the emergence of the cultural turn in contemporary sociology (Alexander and Smith 2003; Lynch 2014).

10 "We are undoubtedly in an information age . . . The information superhighway is about the global movement of weightless bits at the speed of light. As one industry after another looks at itself in the mirror and asks about its future in a digital world, that future is driven almost 100 percent by the ability of that company's product or services to be rendered in digital form . . . Media will become digitally driven by the combined forces of convenience, economic imperative, and deregulation. And it will happen fast" (Negroponte 1995a: 11–13).

11 Yale University seminar, January 28, 2014.

12 Bourdieu theorizes disinterest as just this sort of camouflage, complexly constructed but still a cheap trick. He can do so because he ignores the relative independence of cultural power, viewing group struggles within and between fields merely as efforts to increase symbolic capital (Alexander 1995a). But if journalism has significant autonomy as an independent field (Benson and Neveu 2005), it has secured this cultural capital because of the cultural power of professional ethics and their connections to their civic morals of the civil sphere in which journalism plays a central part. In his comparative study of the coverage of immigration in French and American journalism, Benson makes precisely this same critique of Bourdieu:

> In both countries, a hybrid space exists in which the seemingly opposed civic and market logics are brought together. In the United States, civic ends have been financed by profit-driven news companies whose owners, nevertheless, retain a public service orientation. In France, some subsidized, public service-oriented newspapers have worked hard to expand their audiences and revenues. It is generally in this hybrid space that we find the forms of professional practice richest in the symbolic capital of prestige: in the United States, investigative and other types of long-form daily journalism; in France, elegantly written, in-depth analysis and evaluation of ideas and social issues. Contra Bourdieu, this 'autonomous' journalism is not strictly opposed to the market but rather represents a variety of fragile, ongoing attempts to balance market and civic demands. (Benson 2013: 37)

13 Thus Jarvis, in his paean to net-based journalism:

> Publicness is an emblem of epochal change. It is profoundly disruptive. Publicness threatens institutions whose power is invested in the control of information and audiences . . . Publicness is a sign of our empowerment at their expense. Dictators and politicians, media moguls and marketers try to tell us what to think and say. But now, in a truly public society, they must listen to what we say . . . We can now wield as groups – as publics. (Jarvis 2011)

14 In his empirical study of the *Guardian* online, Ahmad (2010: 151) observed "the levels of bilious and abusive comments under any given article," suggesting that the "bitterly negative" tone often seemed to undermine journalism's civil code and solidaristic aspirations.

15 Authoritarian societies are often highly wired, their citizens digitally networked and continuously communicative – even as the communicative and regulative institutions of their civil spheres remain tightly controlled by the

state. Narrowly focusing on technology, networks, and public-ness, for example, has misled analysts about the effects of web technology in China. In their study of Sina Weibo, Huang and Sun (2014) suggest "microblogging services might have long-term effects on collective action by fostering issue networks among civil society organizations or activists in different provinces," but King et al. (2013) have demonstrated the contrary. Online communication is subject to massive pre-review and post-posting censorship, and keyword searches and massive human surveillance continuously sever the connection between communication and collective action (cf. Sullivan 2014 and Hassid 2014).

16 Some of the most stigmatizing news reports emerge from journalistic self-judgments, stories polluting the departures from professional-cum-democratic practices of news media themselves. Such self-criticism was markedly evident, for example, in January, 2015, when *NBC Evening News* anchor Brian Williams was condemned for exaggerating his personal participation in critical news events. The scandal provided an occasion for reaffirming the binaries of truth/deception and modesty/egoism that are key constituents of professional journalism's moral code (e.g. Noonan 2015). Western journalists also extensively report on violations of professional standards by media in authoritarian regimes, prominently featuring confessions of guilt and shame: "A nation's TV station is the face for the entire nation," said Wang Qinglei, a former producer who worked at CCTV from 2003 until he was fired in 2013 for publicly denouncing propaganda on the network. "Now this face is dirty and full of mud. There should be a cleansing process to wash it, so that the entire nation can be proud again" ... "It is shocking how corrupt the Chinese media is," Zhan Jiang, a professor of journalism and media studies at Beijing Foreign Studies University, said in a recent online discussion. "It is the most corrupt in the world. To put it bluntly, it is the shame of our country" ... "Recently I spoke to another director of programming at CCTV, who is leaving," Mr. Wang said. "This person told me, 'Each day I spend at CCTV is another day I'm spending in shame'" (Wong 2015).

> The same day, in a story headlined "A Russian TV Insider Describes a Modern Propaganda Machine," the *Times* highlighted the binary truth/fiction:

>> "Normally a boisterous sort, Peter Pomerantsev says he kept quiet when he found himself, at the age of 24, in a Moscow meeting room listening to 20 of the country's top media executives discussing the news agenda for the week. Not what the news was, but what they could make it ... He listened in amazement, he says, as a prominent news anchor reviewed the coming events as if they were part of a film script, musing on how best to entertain the audience and questioning who that week's enemy should be. 'It was shocking,' said Mr. Pomerantsev ... 'They really saw ... news as a movie.'"

> (Castle 2015)

17 "With 1.4 billion users, the social media site has become a vital source of traffic for publishers looking to reach an increasingly fragmented audience glued to smartphones ... Facebook has discussed ways for publishers to make money from advertising that would run alongside the content [saying] publicly that it wants to make the experience of consuming content online

more seamless. News articles on Facebook are currently linked to the publisher's own website, and open in a web browser, typically taking about eight seconds to load. Facebook thinks that this is too much time, especially on a mobile device, and that when it comes to catching the roving eyeballs of readers, milliseconds matter ... Even marginal increases in the speed of a site ... mean big increases in user satisfaction and traffic ... Facebook has not historically done any kind of revenue-sharing with content publishers. Essentially, its position has been 'Put your content on Facebook and we'll send you traffic'. But lately Facebook has been experimenting with revenue-sharing options" (Somaiya, Isaac, and Goel 2015).

18 "The pile of paywall money is still growing and for the first time, the Times Company has broken out how big it is: More than $150 million a year ... To put that $150 million in new revenue in perspective, consider that the Times Company as a whole will take in roughly $210 million in digital ads this year. And that $150 million doesn't capture the paywall's positive impact on print circulation revenue. Altogether, the company has roughly $360 million in digital revenue" (Chittum 2013). By the end of 2013, *NYT.com* had 30 million unique visits monthly within the United States, 45 million worldwide, and an additional 20 million visitors from mobile devices and tablets. On all platforms combined, the paper had 1,926,800 daily paid subscribers and 2,409,000 Sunday (*The New York Times Company Annual Report* 2013). When it called off its first paywall experiment in 2007, the *Times*' circulation from all platforms totaled only 787,000, including 227,000 online, its website generating just 13 million unique visitors monthly (Perez-Pena 2007). By the end of 2023, digital subscriptions to the Times had risen to nearly 10 million.

19 "In his first conspicuous move as the new owner of *The Washington Post*, Jeff Bezos has approved a budget hike this year that will enable the paper to boost staffing after years of cutback ... Several blogs and print sections will get more resources and staff additions throughout the year ... The Fix, a political blog, will get more reporters. The paper is also starting a new blog that will use data to explain public policies. 'Our staff of politics reporters will grow by five early this year,' [editor Marty] Baron said. They will work with an expanded staff of photo editors, data specialists and graphics and photo staffers, he said. The paper's website will be redesigned this year, which will require new hires. A new breaking-news desk will operate from 8 a.m. until midnight with the mission of posting stories more quickly online. Money will be spent on print products as well. The Sunday magazine will be given more pages and a new design. A new Sunday Style and Arts section will be introduced in the spring ... Adam Kushner, executive editor of the *National Journal*, was named recently to head a new digital team for online commentary and analysis. The paper is currently hiring for the team. Fred Barbash, who was running White House and congressional coverage for Reuters, is returning to the Post to oversee an overnight staff that will refresh news for morning readers" (Yu 2014). Steven Hills, *Washington Post* president told the *Financial Times*, "Bezos is focusing on developing a great digital audience 10 years from now, 20 years from now, rather than immediate profits" (Luckerson 2014). Bezos "hopes ... to develop a worldwide digital newspaper suitable for e-readers like the Kindle – a digital newspaper that might ultimately thrive on subscription revenue" (Coll 2014: 32).

20 The *New York Post, New York Daily News, Newsday, Newark Star-Ledger, Los Angeles Times,* and the *Denver Post* – local newspapers – each have over 100,000 digital subscribers (Schudson 2016).

21 The *New Haven Independent,* an online news site created by prize-winning local journalist Paul Bass, receives 150,000 unique visitors monthly. In an article reporting the *Independent*'s ten-year anniversary, the daily newspaper *Hartford Courant* told its readers:

> What makes the Independent unusual is that unlike most news organizations it doesn't use advertising to pay for the cost of hiring the editorial staff, which consists of four staffers and a flock of freelancers . . . Originally, 75 percent of the Independent's funding came from national foundations, but, Bass said recently in his third-floor Elm Street office, "that funding dries up after a few years." Now 75 percent of his newsroom budget comes from the New Haven area. Funding comes from a variety of philanthropic groups and citizens that have one thread in common – a love for New Haven and news about it.
>
> (Kramer 2015)

> Nonprofit financing of digital platforms for professional journalism in the U.S. has begun to play a significant role on the national level as well: "Bill Keller, a columnist at the *New York Times* and its former executive editor, will leave the paper to become editor in chief of The Marshall Project, a nonprofit journalism start-up focused on the American criminal justice system." "It's a chance to build something from scratch, which I've never done before," Mr. Keller said, "and to use all the tools that digital technology offers journalists in terms of ways to investigate and to present on a subject that really matters."
>
> (Somaiya 2014)

22 "It mattered little to us that most of the one quarter million people in our little corner of Brooklyn couldn't have understood our paper's exposés . . . A newspaper alters the communication loops of a community even if it's read by just a hundred people on the planning board and in rival organizations and establishments and by a few important people downtown" (Sleeper 1990).

23 On September 9, 2013, two traffic lanes were closed on the Fort Lee, New Jersey, side of the George Washington Bridge, bringing outgoing traffic from New York to a snail's pace. In their initial response to complaints, New Jersey officials claimed the closings were part of a traffic control study, but suspicions of a political vendetta by New Jersey Governor Chris Christie soon surfaced. When these were reported in a small-town weekly, the Bergen County *Record,* a scandal erupted that quickly engulfed the Republican governor, until then a leading Republican contender for President in 2016 (Kleinfeld 2014). The readership of the *Record* was minuscule, but its judgments affected the highest levels of state power.

24 Conceptualizing signaling as a means by which parties to an exchange overcome the problem of asymmetric information, economist Michael Spence (1973) built on the theorizing of Erving Goffman, who developed a micro approach to the performative dimensions of social life.

REFERENCES

Agnone, J. 2007. "Amplifying Public Opinion: The Policy Impact of the U.S. Environmental Movement." *Social Forces* 85(4): 1593–1620.

Ahmad, A. N. 2010. "Is Twitter a Useful Tool for Journalists?" *Journal of Media Practice* 11(2): 145–155.

Alexander, J. C. 1981. "The Mass News Media in Systemic, Historical, and Comparative Perspective." In Katz and Szecsko (1981), pp. 17–52.

Alexander, J. C. 1982. *Positivism, Presuppositions, and Current Controversies*, vol. 1 of Alexander, J. C., *Theoretical Logic in Sociology*. Berkeley: University of California Press.

Alexander, J. C., ed. 1988. *Durkheimian Sociology: Cultural Studies*. Cambridge, UK: Cambridge University Press.

Alexander, J. C. 1988a. "Culture and Political Crisis: Watergate and Durkheimian Sociology." In Alexander (1988), pp. 187–224.

Alexander, J. C. 1995. *Fin-de-Siecle Social Theory*. London: Verso.

Alexander, J. C. 1995a. "The Reality of Reduction: The Failed Synthesis of Pierre Bourdieu." In Alexander (1995), pp. 128–217.

Alexander, J. C. 2001. "The Long and Winding Road: Civil Repair of Intimate Injustice." *Sociological Theory* 19(3): 371–400.

Alexander, J. C. 2003. *The Meanings of Social Life: A Cultural Sociology*. New York: Oxford University Press.

Alexander, J. C. 2003a. "On the Social Construction of Moral Universals: The 'Holocaust' From War Crime to Trauma Drama." In Alexander (2003), pp. 27–83.

Alexander, J. C. 2003b. "The Sacred and Profane Information Machine." In Alexander (2003), pp. 179–192.

Alexander, J. C. 2006. *The Civil Sphere*. New York: Oxford University Press.

Alexander, J. C. 2010. *The Performance of Politics: Obama's Victory and the Democratic Struggle for Power*. New York: Oxford University Press.

Alexander, J. C. 2011. *Performance and Power*. Cambridge, UK: Polity.

Alexander, J. C. 2012. *Trauma: A Social Theory*. Cambridge, UK: Polity.

Alexander, J. C. 2012a. *Performative Revolution in Egypt*. London and New York: Bloomsbury Academic.

Alexander, J. C. 2012b, "Holocaust and Trauma: Moral Universalism in the West." In Alexander (2012), pp. 31–96.

Alexander, J. C. 2012c. "Partition and Trauma: Repairing India and Pakistan." In Alexander (2012), pp. 136–154.

Alexander, J. C. 2013. *The Dark Side of Modernity*. Cambridge, UK: Polity.

Alexander, J. C. 2018. "The Societalization of Social Problems: Church Pedophilia, Phone Hacking, and the Financial Crisis." *American Sociological Review* 83(6): 1049–1078.

Alexander, J. C. 2019a. "Frontlash/Backlash: The Crisis of Solidarity and the Threat to Civil Institutions." *Contemporary Sociology* 48(1): 5–11.

Alexander, J. C. 2019b. *What Makes a Social Crisis? The Societalization of Social Problems*. Cambridge, UK: Polity.

Alexander, J. C. 2021. "Introduction: The Populist Continuum from within the Civil Sphere to Outside It." In Alexander et al. (2021), pp. 1–17.

Alexander, J.C. 2023. "Office Obligation as Civil Virtue: The Crisis of American Democracy, November 2, 2020 to January 6, 2021, and After." *Society* 60: 651–669.

Alexander, J. C. and Adams, T. 2023. "The Return of Antisemitism? Waves of Societalization and What Conditions Them." *American Journal of Cultural Sociology* 11(6): 251–268.

Alexander, J. C. and Horgan, M., eds. 2024. *The Civil Sphere in Canada*. Vancouver: University of British Columbia Press.

Alexander, J. C. and Jaworsky, B. N. 2014. *Obama Power*. Malden, MA: Polity.

Alexander, J. C. and Loder, C. 1985. "Max Weber on Churches and Sects: An Alternative Path toward Rationalization." *Sociological Theory* 3(1): 1–6.

Alexander, J. C. and Smith, P. 2003. "The Strong Program in Cultural Sociology: Elements of a Structural Hermeneutics." In Alexander (2003a), pp. 11–26.

Alexander, J. C. and Tognato, C., eds. 2018. *The Civil Sphere in Latin America*. New York: Cambridge University Press.

Alexander, J. C., Giesen, B., and Mast, J., eds. 2006. *Social Performance: Symbolic Action, Cultural Pragmatics, and Ritual*. Cambridge, UK: Cambridge University Press.

Alexander, J. C., Eyerman, R., and Breese, E. B., eds. 2011. *Narrating Trauma: On the Impact of Collective Suffering*. New York: Routledge.

Alexander, J. C., Jacobs, R., and Smith, P., eds. 2012. *The Oxford Handbook of Cultural Sociology*. New York: Oxford University Press.

Alexander, J. C., Breeze, E. B., and Luengo, M., eds. 2016. *The Crisis of Journalism Reconsidered: Democratic Culture, Professional Codes, Digital Future*. Cambridge University Press.

Alexander, J. C., Lund, A., and Voyer, A., eds. 2019a. *The Nordic Civil Sphere*. New York: Cambridge University Press.

Alexander, J. C. et al., eds. 2019b. *The Civil Sphere in East Asia*. Cambridge, UK: Cambridge University Press.

Alexander, J. C., Stack, T., and Khosrokhavar, F., eds. 2019c. *Breaching the Civil Order: Radicalism and the Civil Sphere*. New York: Cambridge University Press.

Alexander, J. C., Kivisto, P., and Sciortino, G., eds. 2021. *Populism in the Civil Sphere*. Cambridge, UK: Polity.

Alexander, M. 2012. *The New Jim Crow: Mass Incarceration in the Age of Colorblindness*. New York: New Press.

REFERENCES

Alim, H. S. 2011. "What If We Occupied Language?" The Opinionator (online). *New York Times*, December 21.

Allen, H. 2007. "A Journalist for Whom There Were Not Enough Words." *Washington Post*, April 25 (http://www.washingtonpost.com/wp-dyn/content/article/2007/04/24/AR2007042402512.html).

Almeida, P. 2019. *Social Movements*. Oakland: University of California Press.

Amenta, E. et al. 2010. "The Political Consequences of Social Movements." *Annual Review of Sociology* 36: 287–307.

American Conservative, The. April 19, 2018. "Six Months in, #MeToo Has Become Infantilizing and Authoritarian." Williams, J.

Anderson, C. W. 2011. "The Jekyll and Hyde Problem: What Are Journalists, and their Institutions, For?" *Nieman Journalism Lab*. www.niemanlab.org/2011/11/the-jekyll-and-hyde-problem-what-are-journalists-and-their-institutions-for

Anderson, C. W. 2013. *Rebuilding the News: Metropolitan Journalism in the Digital Age*. Philadelphia: Temple University Press.

Anderson, E. 2011. *Cosmopolitan Canopy: Race and Civility in Everyday Life*. New York: W.W. Norton.

Anderson, E. et al., eds. 2012. *Bringing Fieldwork Back In: Contemporary Urban Ethnographic Research, The Annals of the American Academy of Political and Social Science*, vol. 642. Thousand Oaks: Sage Publications, Inc.

Anderson, E. 2012a. "The Iconic Ghetto." In Anderson et al. (2012), pp. 8–24.

Anderson, E. 2015. "The White Space." *Sociology of Race and Ethnicity* 1(1): 10–21.

Anderson, J. 1971. "President Nixon and the Women." *The Boston Globe*, October 31, p. F4.

Anthony, S. B. 1995 [1876]. "Declaration of Rights for Women by the National Woman Suffrage Association." In Kerber and de Hart (1995), pp. 223–325.

Appadurai, A., ed. 1986. *The Social Life of Things*. Cambridge and New York: Cambridge University Press.

Arango, T. 2014. "In Scandal, Turkey's Leaders May Be Losing Their Right Grip on News Media." *New York Times*, January 12: A11.

Arendt, H. 1951. *The Origins of Totalitarianism*. New York: Schocken Books.

Armstrong, E. A. and Bernstein, M. 2008. "Culture, Power, and Institutions: A Multi-Institutional Politics Approach to Social Movements." *Sociological Theory* 26(1): 74–99.

Aron, H. 2015. "These Savvy Women Have Made Black Lives Matter the Most Crucial Left-Wing Movement Today." *LA Weekly*, November 9, 2015. www.laweekly.com/news/these-savvy-women-have-made-black-lives-matter-the-most-crucial-left-wing-movement

Associated Press (AP). 2014. "Thousands Protest Nationally after Ferguson Grand Jury Decision, More Protests Planned." *Times Picayune*, November 25. www.nola.com/crime/index.ssf/2014/11/national_ferguson_protest_mike.html

Atlanta Journal Constitution. March 16, 2018. "#MeToo Slow in Coming – and Kept Mostly Out of View – at Georgia Capitol." Getz, J. https://politics.myajc.com/news/state--regional-govt--politics/metoo-slow-coming-and-kept-mostly-out-view-georgia-capitol/WpH2h8JbREv02Ev3JjAQaM/

Austin, J. L. 1957. *How to Do Things with Words*. Oxford: Clarendon Press.

Bailyn, B. 1967. *The Intellectual Origins of the American Revolution*. Cambridge: Harvard University Press.

Banaszak, L. A. and Ondercin, H. L. 2016. "Public Opinion as a Movement Outcome: The Case of the U.S. Women's Movement." *Mobilization* 21(3): 361–378.

Banaszak, L. A. 2010. *The Women's Movement Inside and Outside the State.* New York: Cambridge University Press.

Barnhurst, K. G. and Mutz, D. 1997. "American Journalism and the Decline in Event-Centered Reporting." *Journal of Communication* 47(4): 27–52.

Barron's. April 24, 2018. "When Your Team Members Mock #MeToo." Ragatz, Julie.

Barton, J., ed. 2016. *Oxford Research Encyclopedia of Religion.* New York: Oxford University Press.

Bashevkin, S. 1994. "Facing a Renewed Right: American Feminism and the Reagan/Bush Challenge." *Canadian Journal of Political Science* 27(4): 669–698.

Bauman, Z. 1998. "On the Postmodern Uses of Sex." *Theory, Culture, and Society* 15 (3–4).

Becker, H. S. 1963. *Outsiders: Studies in the Sociology of Deviance.* New York: Free Press.

Beeson, E. 2015. "Trial Ace: Keker and Van Nest's John Keker." *Law 360,* August 25. https://www.law360.com/articles/694295/trial-ace-keker-van-nest -s-john-keker

Bellah, R. N. 1970. *Beyond Belief: Essays on Religion in a Post-Traditional World.* New York: Harper and Row.

Bellah, R. N. 1970a. "The Sociology of Religion." In Bellah (1970), pp. 3–19.

Bellah, R. N. 1970b. "Religious Evolution." In Bellah (1970), pp. 20–51.

Bellah, R. N. 2011. *Religion in Human Evolution.* Cambridge: Harvard University Press.

Benhabib, S. 1986. *Critique, Norm, and Utopia: A Study of the Foundations of Critical Theory.* New York: Columbia University Press.

Benkler, Y. 2006. *The Wealth of Networks: How Social Production Transforms Markets and Freedom.* New Haven: Yale University Press.

Benson, R. 2013. *Shaping Immigration News: A French-American Comparison.* New York: Cambridge University Press.

Benson, R. and Neveu, E., eds. 2005. *Bourdieu and the Journalistic Field.* Cambridge, UK: Polity.

Ben-Veniste, R. 2009. *The Emperor's New Clothes: Exposing the Truth from Watergate to 9/11.* New York: St. Martin's.

Berezin, M., Sandusky, E., and Davidson, T. 2020. "Culture in Politics and Politics in Culture." In Janoski (2020), pp. 102–131.

Berlin, I. 1998. "The Pursuit of the Idea." In Berlin, *The Proper Study of Mankind: An Anthology of Essays.* New York: Farrar, Straus, Girous, pp. 1–16.

Bernstein, M. and Taylor, V., eds. 2013. *The Marrying Kind? Debating Same-Sex Marriage Within the Gay and Lesbian Movement.* Minneapolis: University of Minnesota Press.

Bessinger, M. R. 2015. "Contentious Collective Action and the Evolving Nation-State." In Della Porta and Diani (2015).

Bieber, C. 2013. "Lessons of the Leak: WikiLeaks, Julian Assange, and the Changing Landscape of Media and Politics." In Hartley et al. (2013), pp. 322–335.

BillTrack50. February 15, 2018. "#MeToo, Time's Up and the Legislation behind the Movement." Evelynn, S.

Bloemraad, I., Silva, F., and Voss, K. 2016. "Rights, Economics, or Family? Frame

Resonance, Political Ideology, and the Immigrant Rights Movement." *Social Forces* 94(4): 1647–1674.

Bloomberg/Business Week. December 20, 2017. "How to Make Better Men: The #MeToo Movement Is Slowly Eliciting Change in Cultural Institutions that Help Define Masculinity." Suddath, C.

Blumer, H. 1971. "Social Problems as Collective Behavior." *Social Problems* 18(3): 298–306.

Bock, G. and James, S., eds. 1992. *Beyond Equality and Difference: Citizenship, Feminist Politics and Female Subjectivity.* London: Routledge.

Boczkowski, P. J. 2004. *Digitizing the News: Innovation in Online Newspapers.* Cambridge, MA: The MIT Press.

Bohman, J. 2004. "Expanding Dialogue: The Internet, the Public Sphere and Prospects for Transnational Democracy." *The Sociological Review* 52(1): 131–155.

Boltanski, L. and Thevenot, L. 1990. *De la Justification.* Paris: PUF.

Bonk, K. 1988. "The Selling of the 'Gender Gap': The Role of Organized Feminism." In Mueller (1988), pp. 82–101.

Bourdieu, P. 1980. "L'Opinion Publique N'Existe Pas." In *Questions de Sociologie.* Paris: Editions de Minuit, pp. 222–235.

Boyce, G., Curran, J., and Wingate, P., eds. 1978. *Newspaper History from the Seventeenth Century to the Present Day.* London: Constable.

Boydston, J. 1995. "The Pastoralization of Housework." In Kerber and de Hart (1995), pp. 142–153.

Bradlee, B. 1991. "Talking with David Frost." Channel 13. New York Public Television, September 27.

Bradlee, B. 1995. *A Good Life: Newspapering and Other Adventures.* New York: Simon and Schuster.

Bradlee, B. Jr. 2002. "Introduction," in Investigative Staff of the *Boston Globe, Betrayal: The Crisis of the Catholic Church,* pp. ix–xiii. Boston, MA: Little, Brown, and Company.

Branch, Taylor. 1988. *Parting of the Waters: America in the King Years, 1954–63.* New York: Simon and Schuster.

Breese, E. B. 2016. "The Perpetual Crisis of Journalism: Cable and Digital Revolutions." In Alexander et al. (2016), pp. 31–42.

Breitbart News. February 14, 2018. "Cassie Jaye on #MeToo: 'Falsely Accused People Are Victims, Too," Kraychick, R.

Breitbart News. September 19, 2018. "Haven Monahan to Testify at Kavanaugh Hearings." Coulter, A. https://www.breitbart.com/politics/2018/09/19/ann-coulter-haven-monahan-to-testify-at-kavanaugh-hearings/

Broersma, M. 2013. "A Refractured Paradigm: Journalism, Hoaxes, and the Challenge of Trust." In Broersma and Peters (2013), pp. 28–44.

Broersma, M. and Peters, C., eds. 2013. *Rethinking Journalism: Trust and Participation in a Transformed News Landscape.* London: Routledge.

Brooks, P. 1976. *The Melodamatic Imagination: Balzac, Henry James, Melodrama, and the Mode of Excess.* Yale University Press, New Haven, CT.

Buckley, C. and Mullany, G. 2014. "Hong Kong Paper Ousts Top Editor, Stirring Concern." *New York Times,* January 31: A4.

Burstein, P. 1998. "Bringing the Public Back in: Should Sociologists Consider the Impact of Public Opinion on Public Policy?" *Social Forces* 77(1): 27–62.

Burstein, P. 2020. "The Influence of Public Opinion and Advocacy on Public Policy: Controversies and Conclusions." In Janoski (2020), pp. 738–760.

Calhoun, C. ed. 1992. *Habermas and the Public Sphere*. Cambridge: MIT Press.

Calhoun, C. 1995. "The Politics of Identity and Recognition." In *Critical Social Theory*. New York: Blackwell, pp. 193–230.

Carlson, M. 2016. "Telling the Crisis Story of Journalism: Narratives of Normative Reassurance in Page One." In Alexander et al. (2016), pp. 135–152.

Caro, R. A. 2012. *The Years of Lyndon Johnson: The Passage of Power*. New York: Knopf.

Castells, M. 1996. *The Rise of the Network Society*, vol. 1 of Castells, M., *The Information Age: Economy, Society and Culture*. Oxford: Blackwell.

Castells, M. 2007. "Communication, Power and Counter-Power in the Network Society." *International Journal of Communication* 1: 238–266.

Castle, S. 2015. "A Russian Insider Describes a Modern Propaganda Machine." *New York Times*, February 14: A6.

Chalaby, J. K. 1996. "Journalism as an Anglo-American Invention: A Comparison of the Development of French and Anglo-American Journalism, 1830s–1920s." *European Journal of Communication* 11: 303–326.

Challenger, Gray, and Christmas. 2018. Press Release: "#MeToo Survey Update: More Than Half of Companies Reviewed Sexual Harassment Policies." https://www.challengergray.com/press/press-releases/metoo-survey-update-more-half-companies-reviewed-sexual-harassment-policies

Chicago Sun Times. March 21, 2018. "Until Celebrities Said 'Me Too,' Nobody Listened to Blue-Collar Women About Assault." Altmayer, K.

Chittum, R. 2013. "The NYT's $150 Million-a-Year Paywall." *Columbia Journalism Review*, August 1: www.cjr.org/the_audit/the_nyts_150_million-a-year_pa.php

Chozick, A. 2016a. "Mothers of Black Victims Emerge as a Force for Hillary Clinton." *New York Times*, April 13. http://nyti.ms/1qoblen.

Chozick, A. 2016b. "Bill Clinton Says He Regrets Showdown with Black Lives Matters Protesters." *New York Times*, April 9, A12.

CNBC. May 31, 2018. "In the Wake of #MeToo, Companies Turn to Private Investigators." Leslie, P. and Taylor, H. https://www.cnbc.com/2018/05/31/companies-are-turning-to-private-investigators-to-identify-harassers.html

CNN. September 12, 2018. "Norm Macdonald Apologizes after #MeToo Comments." France, L. R. https://www.cnn.com/2018/09/12/entertainment/norm-macdonald-metoo-apology/index.html

Cobb, J. 2016. "The Matter of Black Lives." *The New Yorker*, March 14: 33–40.

Cohen, J. and Arato, A. 1992. *Civil Society and Political Theory*. Cambridge, MA: MIT Press.

Cohen, M. 2018. "The #MeToo Movement Findings from The PEORIA Project." *The Public Echoes of Rhetoric in America (PEORIA) Project*, George Washington University. https://gspm.gwu.edu/sites/g/files/zaxdzs2286/f/downloads/2018%20RD18%20MeToo%20Presentation.pdf

Cohen, S. 1972. *Folk Devils and Moral Panics: The Creation of the Mods and Rockers*. London: MacGibbon and Kee.

Coll, S. 2014. "Citizen Bezos." *New York Review of Books*. July 10: 28–32.

Colorado Springs Independent. November 8, 2017a, p. 13. "The Profound Prevalence." Simison, C. https://www.csindy.com/coloradosprings/the-profound-prevalence-of-the-metoo-movement/Content?oid=8467727

Colorado Springs Independent. November 8, 2017b. "#WhoHasn't." Eurich, L. https://www.csindy.com/coloradosprings/whohasnt/Content?oid=8467730

Comey, J. B. 2013. "Fidelity, Bravery, and Integrity: The Essence of the FBI." Speech at Installation as Director. October 23. https://www.fbi.gov/news/speeches/fidelity-bravery-and-integrity-the-essence-of-the-fbi

Costain, A. N. 1992. *Inviting Women's Rebellion.* Baltimore: Johns Hopkins University Press.

Costain, A. N. and Majstorovic, S. 1994. "Congress, Social Movements, and Public Opinion: Multiple Origins of Women's Rights Legislation." *Political Research Quarterly* 47(1): 111–135.

Costain, W. D. and Costain, A. N. 1992. "The Political Strategies of Social Movements: A Comparison of the Women's and Environmental Movements." *Congress and the Presidency* 19(1):1–27.

Coste, F. 2016. "'Women, Ladies, Girls, Gals': Ronald Reagan and the Evolution of Gender Roles in the United States." *Miranda* 12: 1–17.

Cott, N. F. 1987. *The Grounding of Modern Feminism.* New Haven, CT: Yale University Press.

Cott, N. F. 1995. "Equal Rights and Economic Roles: The Conflict over the Equal Rights Amendment in the 1920s." In Kerber and de Hart (1995), pp. 355–365.

Cottle, S. 2004. *The Racist Murder of Steven Lawrence: Media Performance and Public Transformation.* Westport, CT: Sage.

Couldry, N. 2014. "The Myth of 'U.S.': Digital Networks, Political Change and the Production of Collectivity." *Information, Communication & Society,* DOI: 10.1080/1369118X.2014.979216

Critchlow, D. T. 2005. *Phyllis Schlafly and Grassroots Conservatism.* Princeton: Princeton University Press.

Critchlow, D. T and Stacheki, C. L. 2008. "The Equal Rights Amendment Reconsidered: Politics, Policy, and Social Mobilization in a Democracy." *Journal of Policy History* 20(1): 157–176.

Cut, The. September 12, 2018. "Hockenberry Accusers Speak Out After Harper's Publishes Essay." Ryan, L.

Dahlerup, D., ed. 1986. *The New Women's Movement.* Beverly Hills, CA: Sage.

Dallas News. October 16, 2017. "#MeToo Brings Dallas Stories of Sexual Assault to Social Media." Jaramillo, C., Meyer, B., and Churnin, N. https://www.dallasnews.com/life/digital-life/2017/10/16/metoo-brings-dallas-stories-sexual-harassment-assault-social-media

Darrow, C. 1961. *Attorney for the Damned: Clarence Darrow in the Courtroom.* Chicago: University of Chicago Press.

De Hart, J. S. 1995. "The New Feminism and the Dynamics of Social Change." In Kerber and de Hart (1995), pp. 539–560.

de Tocqueville, A. 2004 [1835]. *Democracy in America,* vol. 1, part I. New York: Library of America.

Declaration of Sentiments. 1995 [1848]. Seneca Falls, New York.

Dees, M. 2011. *A Lawyer's Journey: The Morris Dees Story.* Chicago, Ill.: The American Bar Association.

Della Porta, D. and Diani, M., eds. 2015. *The Oxford Handbook of Social Movements.* New York: Oxford University Press.

Dewey, J. 1927. *The Public and its Problems.* New York: Holt.

Dewey, J. 1937. "On Democracy." Excerpted from Dewey, J., "Democracy and

Educational Administration," *School and Society* 45: 457–67. April 3. https://wolfweb.unr.edu/homepage/lafer/ dewey%20dewey.htm

Dietz, M. G. 1998. "Citizenship with a Feminist Face: The Problem with Maternal Thinking." In Landes (1998), pp. 45–64.

Digiday. February 5, 2018. "Agencies Rethink Their Dating Policies in the #MeToo era." Lffreing, I. https://digiday.com/marketing/agencies-rethink-dating-policies-metoo-era/

Domhoff, G. W. 2006. *Who Rules America?* 6th edn. New York: McGraw-Hill.

Douglas, M. 1966. *Purity and Danger: An Analysis of Concepts of Pollution and Taboo.* New York: Praeger.

Dower, J. W. 1999. *Embracing Defeat: Japan in the Wake of World War II.* New York: Norton.

Downey, L., Jr. and Schudson, M. 2009. "The Reconstruction of American Journalism." *Columbia Journalism Review*, October 19. www.cjr.org/reconstruction/the_reconstruction_of_american.php?page=all

Duneier, M. 2016. *Ghetto: The Invention of a Place, the History of an Idea.* New York: Farrar, Strauss, and Giroux.

Durkheim, E. 1950. *Professional Ethics and Civic Morals.* London: Routledge.

Durkheim, E. 1995 [1912]. *The Elementary Forms of Religious Life.* New York: Free Press.

Earl, J. 2004. "The Cultural Consequences of Social Movements." In Snow et al. (2004), pp. 508–530.

Edles, L. 1998. *Symbol and Ritual in the New Spain: The Transition to Democracy after Franco.* New York: Cambridge University Press.

Edwards, R. 1997. *Angels in the Machinery: Gender in American Party Politics from the Civil War to the Progressive Era.* New York and Oxford: Oxford University Press.

Eisenstadt, S. N. 1982. "The Axial Age: The Emergence of Transcendental Visions and the Rise of Clerics." *European Journal of Sociology* 23: 299–314.

Eisenstein, Z. 1987. "Liberalism, Feminism and the Reagan State: The Neoconservative Assault on (Sexual) Equality." *The Socialist Register* 23: 236–262.

Eligon, J. 2016. "Activists Move From Street to Ballot, Emboldened by Protests." *New York Times*, February 7: A1.

Emirbayer, M. 2010. "Tilly and Bourdieu." *The American Sociologist* 41(4): 400–422.

Equal Employment Opportunity Commission. n/d. "Sexual Harassment." https://www.eeoc.gov/laws/types/sexual_harassment.cfm

Esping-Andersen, G. 1990. *Three Worlds of Welfare Capitalism.* Princeton: Princeton University Press.

Evans, P., Rueschemeyer, D., and Skocpol, T., eds. 1985. *Bringing the State Back In.* New York: Cambridge University Press.

Eyerman, R. 2006. "Performing Opposition or, How Social Movements Move." In Alexander et al. (2006), pp. 193–217.

Eyerman, R. 2019. *Memory, Trauma, and Identity.* New York: Palgrave.

Eyerman, R. and Jamison, A. 1991. *Social Movements: A Cognitive Approach.* Cambridge, UK: Polity.

Farrar, R. T. 1998. *A Creed for My Profession: Walter Williams, Journalist to the World.* St. Louis, Missouri: University of Missouri Press.

Ferree, M. M. and Hess, B. 1995. *Controversy and Coalition*, 3rd edn. New York: Routledge.

Ferree, M. M. and Martin, P. Y., eds. 1995. *Feminist Organizations*. Philadelphia: Temple University Press.

Fine, G. A. 1997. "Scandal, Social Conditions, and the Creation of Public Attention: Fatty Arbuckle and the 'Problem of Hollywood'." *Social Problems* 44(3): 297–323.

Fink, G. M. and Graham, H. D., eds. 1998. *The Carter Presidency*. Lawrence, KS: University Press of Kansas.

Flippen J. B. 2011. *Jimmy Carter, the Politics of Family, and the Rise of the Religious Right*. Athens: University of Georgia Press.

Foner, E. 1988. *Reconstruction: America's Unfinished Revolution, 1863–1877*. New York: HarperCollins.

Forbes. September 17, 2018. "#MeToo After Moonves: What Should Companies Be Doing?" Levick, R.

Forment, C. 2003. *Democracy in Latin America, 1760–1900*. Chicago: University of Chicago Press.

Forsythe, M. and Buckley, C. 2014. "Thousands in Hong Kong Support Wounded Editor." *New York Times*, March 3: A6.

Fort Meyers News-Press, The. 1969. "Pat Says Women Don't Use their Equal Rights." May 8, p. 2–B.

Fortune. December 19, 2017. "Microsoft Changes Its Sexual Harassment Policies in the Wake." Morris, C.

Fortune. July 18, 2018. "Employers Are Clamping down on the Office Romance in the #MeToo Era." Zillman, C.

Fraser, N. 1992. "Rethinking the Public Sphere: A Contribution to the Critique of Actually Existing Democracy." In Calhoun (1992), pp. 109–142.

Frederickson, G. M. 1971. *The Black Image in the White Mind: The Debate on Afro-American Character and Destiny, 1817–1914*. New York: Harper and Row.

Frederickson, G. M. 1981. *White Supremacy: A Comparative Study in American and South African History*. New York: Oxford.

Freelon, D., McIlwain, C. D., and Clark, M. D. 2016. "Beyond the hashtags: #Ferguson, #Blacklivesmatter, and the online struggle for offline justice." *Center for Media and Social Impact*, February 29. -blacklivesmatter-online-struggle-offline-justice/ http://cmsimpact.org/resource/beyond-hashtags-ferguson

Freeman, J. 1975. *The Politics of Women's Liberation*. London: Longman.

Freeman, J. 2008. *We Will Be Heard*. Lanham, MD: Rowman & Littlefield.

Friedan, B. 1995 [1963]. "The Problem That Has No Name." In Kerber and de Hart (1995), pp. 519–523.

Friedland, R. and Alford, R. R. 1991. "Bringing Society Back In: Symbols, Practices, and Institutional Contradictions." In Powell and DiMaggio (1991), pp. 232–263.

Friedman, B. 2009. *The Will of the People*. New York: Farrar, Strauss, and Giroux.

Friend, T. 2015. "Dan and Bob." *The New Yorker*. November 2: 30–32.

Gamson, W. A. 1975. *The Strategy of Social Protest*. Homewood, IL: Dorsey Press.

Gamson, W. A. 2004. "Bystanders, Public Opinion, and the Media." In Snow et al. (2004), pp. 242–261.

Gerth H. and Mills, C. W., eds. 1946. *From Max Weber*. New York: Oxford University Press.

Geertz, C. 1973. "Ideology as a Culture System," pp. 193–233. *The Interpretation of Culture*. New York: Basic Books.

Ghaziani, A., Taylor, V., and Stone, A. 2016. "Cycles of Sameness and Difference in LGBT Social Movements." *Annual Review of Sociology* 42: 165–183.

Giesen, B. 2004. "The Trauma of Perpetrators: The Holocaust as the Traumatic Reference of German National Identity." In Alexander et al. (2006), pp. 113–143.

Gilligan, C. 1982. *In a Different Voice: Psychological Theory and Women's Development*. Cambridge, MA: Harvard University Press.

Gilligan, C. 1986. "Reply." *Signs* 11: 324–333.

Gillmore, D. 2004. *We the Media: Grassroots Journalism by the People, for the People*. Cambridge: O'Reilly.

Giugni, M. 2004. *Social Protest and Policy Change*. Boulder, CO: Rowman & Littlefield.

Glaser, V. 1969. "The Female Revolt: Women Demand Even Break in Our Male-Dominated Society." *Asbury Evening Press*, March 11.

Glennbeck.com. August 15, 2018. "#MeToo Is Coming After Its Own." https://www.glennbeck.com/glenn-beck/metoo-is-coming-after-its-own

Goodman, T. 2015. *Staging Solidarity: Truth and Reconciliation in a New South Africa*. New York: Routledge.

Graham, K. 1997. *Personal History*. New York: Vintage.

Greeno, C.G. and Maccoby, E. E. 1986. "How Different Is the 'Different Voice'?" *Signs* 11(2): 310–316.

Griffiths, R. 1991. *The Use of Abuse: The Polemics of the Dreyfus Affair and its Aftermath*. New York: Oxford University Press.

Gross, N. 2009. "A Pragmatist Theory of Social Mechanisms." *American Sociological Review* 74(3): 358–379.

Guardian. December 1, 2017. "Alyssa Milano on the #MeToo Movement: 'We're not going to stand for it anymore'." Sayej, N. https://www.theguardian.com/culture/2017/dec/01/alyssa-milano-mee-too-sexual-harassment-abuse

Guardian. September 18, 2018. "McDonald's Workers Walk Out in 10 U.S. Cities Over 'Sexual Harassment Epidemic'." Anonymous. https://www.theguardian.com/business/2018/sep/18/mcdonalds-walkout-workers-protest-sexual-harassment-epidemic

Guthrie, J. 2014. "John Keker Relishes the Fight in the Courtroom." *The Chronicle*. October 13. https://www.sfgate.com/bayarea/article/John-Keker-relishes-the-fight-in-the-courtroom-3622831.php

Habermas, J. 1989 [1963]. *The Structural Transformation of the Public Sphere*. Cambridge, MA: MIT Press.

Habermas, J. 1996. *Between Facts and Norms: Contributions to a Discourse Theory of Law and Democracy*. Cambridge, MA: MIT Press.

Hallin, D. C. and Mancini, P., eds. 2004. *Comparing Media Systems: Three Models of Media and Politics*. Cambridge: Cambridge University Press.

Hallin, D. C. and Mancini, P., eds. 2012. *Comparing Media Systems Beyond the Western World*. Cambridge: Cambridge University Press.

Hallock, S. M. 2010. *Reporters Who Made History: Great American Journalists on the Issues and Crises of the Late 20th Century*. Santa Barbara, CA: ABC-Clio.

Halpern, S. 2014. "Partial Disclosure." *New York Review of Books* LXI (12): 16–20.

Hannity. January 8, 2018. "Exposing Hollywood Hypocrisy Amid Oprah 2020 Rumors." Fox News. https://video.foxnews.com/v/5705538885001/?#sp=show-clips

Harrison, C. E. 1980. "A 'New Frontier' For Women: The Public Policy of the Kennedy Administration." *Journal of American History* 67(3): 630–646.

Hartford Courant, The. April 9, 1971. "Lawmakers Blasted for Abortion Stand." April 9.

Hartford Courant, The. December 25, 1972, p.40. "'72 Was a Good Year for Women."

Hartford Courant The. October 22, 2017. "#All of Us: Why #MeToo Is Taking Off." Tolland, L. M.

Hartley, J., Burgess, J., and Bruns, A., eds. 2013. *A Companion to New Media Dynamics.* London: Blackwell.

Hartmann, S. M. 1998. "Feminism, Public Policy, and the Carter Administration." In Fink and Graham (1998), pp. 224–243.

Hartmann, S. M. 2012. "Women's Issues." In Lerner (2012), pp. 149–162.

Hashimoto, A. 2015. *The Long Defeat: Cultural Trauma, Memory, and Identity in Japan.* New York: Oxford University Press.

Hassid, J. 2014. "The Politics of China's Emerging Micro-blogs: Something New or More of the Same?" Manuscript. China Research Centre, University of Technology Sydney.

Havill, A. 1993. *Deep Truth: The Lives of Bob Woodward and Carl Bernstein.* New York: Birch Lane Press.

Haynes, S. 2020. "Several Antiracist Books Are Selling Out. Here's What Else Black Booksellers and Publishers Say You Should Read." *Time.* June 2. https://time.com/5846732/books-to-read-anti-racism/

Healy, J., Stolberg, S. G., and Yee, V. 2015. "Ferguson Report Puts 'Hands Up' to Reality Test." *New York Times,* March 6: A1.

Helsel, P. 2015. "'Black Lives Matter' Activists Disrupt Bernie Sanders Speech." *NBC News,* August 9. www.nbcnews.com/politics/2016-election/black-lives-mattr-activists-disrupt-bernie-sanders-speech-n406546.

Henderson, J. 2016. "Ex-Greenberg Traurig Litigator Seeks Redemption for Sex Abuse Victims." *The American Lawyer,* January 8. https://www.law.com/americanlawyer/almID/1202746674729/ExGreenberg-Traurig-Litigator-Seeks-Redemption-for-Sex-Abuse-Victims/?slreturn=20180221132649

Hermida, A. 2010a. "Twittering the News: The Emergence of Ambient Journalism." *Journalism Practice* 4(3): 297–308.

Hermida, A. 2010b. "From TV to Twitter: How Ambient News Became Ambient Journalism." *M/C Journalism* 13(2). http://journal.media-culture.org.au/index.php/mcjournal/article/view/220.

Hermida, A., Lewis, S. C., and Zamith, R. 2012. "Sourcing the Arab Spring: A Case Study of Andy Carvin's Sources during the Tunisian and Egyptian Revolutions." Paper presented at the *International Symposium on Online Journalism.* Austin, Texas.

Hilgartner, S. and Bosk, C. L. 1988. "The Rise and Fall of Social Problems: A Public Arenas Model." *American Journal of Sociology* 94(1): 53–78. https://www.journals.uchicago.edu/doi/ abs/10.1086/228951

Hirsch, M. and Keller, E. F., eds. 1990. *Conflicts in Feminism.* New York and London: Routledge.

Honneth, Axel. 1995. *The Struggle for Recognition.* Cambridge, MA: MIT Press.

Hirschman, A. O. 1991. *The Rhetoric of Reaction: Perversity, Futility, Jeopardy.* Cambridge, MA: Harvard University Press.

Hofstadter, R. 1955. *The Age of Reform: From Bryan to FDR.* New York: Knopf.

Hollywood Reporter. May 3, 2018. "Roman Polanski, Bill Cosby Booted from Film Academy." Konerman, J. and Kiladay, G. https://www.hollywoodrepor ter.com/news/roman-polanski-bill-cosby-booted-academy-1108390

Howard, G. 2016. "DeRay Mckesson Won't Be Elected Mayor of Baltimore. So Why Is He Running?" *New York Times Magazine*, April 11. www.ny times.com/2016/04/11/magazine/deray-mckessonwont-be-elected-mayor-of-balti more-so-why-is-he-running.html?emc=eta1&_r=0

Huang, Rongghi and Xiaoyi Sun. 2014. "Weibo Network, Information Diffusion and Implications for Collective Action." *China Information, Communication & Society*: 17(1): 86–104, http://dx.doi.org/10.1080/1369118X.2013.853817

Huddy, L., Neely, F. K., and Lafay, M. R. 2000. "Trends: Support for the Women's Movement." *The Public Opinion Quarterly* 64(3): 309–350.

Huffington Post. April 7, 2011. "Sex Scandals in Science." Brooks, M. https:// www.huffingtonpost.co.uk/michael-brooks/sex-scandals-of-science_b_889755 .html?guccounter=1&guce_referrer_us=aHR0cHM6Ly93d3cuZ29vZ2xlLmNvb S8&guce_referrer_cs=8IXl18mKVypsWZLoiYR8FA

Huffington Post. September 12, 2018. "Norm Macdonald Thinks Me Too Will Lead to A Celebrity 'Sticking A Gun In His Head'." Wanshel, E. https://www .huffingtonpost.com/entry/norm-macdonald-me-too-movement_us_5b97fceee4b 0511db3e6b3de

Hunt, Sc. A., Benford, R. D., and Snow, D. A. 1994. "Identity Fields: Framing Processes and the Social Construction of Movement Identities." In Larana et al. (1994), pp. 185–208.

Is it Funny or Offensive.com. September 10, 2018. "Bill Maher Takes Heat for Indians Joke, Dismissing Michelle Goldberg In Al Franken Segment." https:// isitfunnyoroffensive.com/bill-maher-takes-heat-for-indians-joke-dismissing-mich elle-goldberg-in-al-franken-segment/

Jacksonville Free Press. December 7, 2017. "#ChurchToo: Women Share Stories of Sexual Abuse Involving the Church." Anonymous.

Jacobs, R. N. 1996a "Civil Society and Crisis: Culture, Discourse, and the Rodney King Beating." *American Journal of Sociology* 101 (5): 1238–1272.

Jacobs, R. N. 1996b. "Producing the News, Producing the Crisis: Narrativity, Television, and News Work." *Media Culture Society* 18(3): 373–397.

Jacobs, R. N. 2000. *Race, Media, and the Crisis of Civil Society: From Watts to Rodney King.* Cambridge, UK: Cambridge University Press.

James, S. 1992. "The Good Enough Citizen." In Bock and James, (1992), pp. 48–65.

Janoski, T. et al., eds. 2020. *The New Handbook of Political Sociology.* New York: Cambridge University Press.

Jarvis, J. 2011. *Public Parts.* New York: Simon and Schuster.

Jenkins, J. C. 1983. "Resource Mobilization Theory and the Study of Social Movements." *Annual Review of Sociology* 9: 527–553.

Jenkins, P. 1996. *Pedophiles and Priests: Anatomy of a Contemporary Crisis.* New York: Oxford University Press.

Jones, A. 2009. *Losing the News: The Future of the News That Feeds Democracy.* New York: Oxford University Press.

Jones, P. K. 2013. "Introducing Paolo Mancini and 'Media System'." *Theory: The Newsletter of the Research Committee on Sociological Theory International Sociological Association.* Autumn/Winter: 5–8.

Kane, A. 2019. "The Civil Sphere and Revolutionary Violence: The Irish Republican Movement, 1969–1998." In Alexander et al. (2019c), pp. 170–209.

192

Kane, A. 2022. "The Northern Ireland Republican Movement and Counterpublic Construction 1969–1976." In Reinisch and Kane (2022), pp. 24–52.

Kang, J. C. 2015. "'Our Demand Is Simple: Stop Killing Us.'" *New York Times Magazine*, May 4. www.nytimes.com/2015/05/10/magazine/our-demand-is-simple-stop-killing-us.html

Kant, I. 1999. "Toward Perpetual Peace." *Cambridge Edition of the Works of Immanuel Kant*. Cambridge, UK: Cambridge University Press.

Katz, E. and T. Szecsko, T., eds. 1981. *Mass Media and Social Change*. London: Sage.

Keane, J., ed. 1988. *Civil Society and the State*. London: Verso.

Keane, J. 1988a. "Introduction." In Keane, J. (1988), pp. 1–31.

Kerber, L. K. 1986. "Some Cautionary Words for Historians." *Signs* 11: 304–310.

Kerber, L. K. 1991. "The Republican Mother." In Kerber and de Hart (1991), pp. 87–95.

Kerber, L. K. 1995. "The Republican Mother." In Kerber and de Hart (1995), pp. 89–95.

Kerber, L. K. and de Hart, J. S., eds. 1991. *Women's America: Refocusing the Past*, 3rd edn. Oxford: Oxford University Press.

Kerber, L. K. and de Hart, J. S., eds. 1995. *Women's America: Refocusing the Past*, 4th edn. Oxford: Oxford University Press.

Keynes, J. M. 1964 [1936]. *The General Theory of Employment, Interest, and Money*. New York: Harcourt Brace Jovanovich.

Khosrokhavar, F. 2012. *The New Arab Revolutions that Shook the World*. Boulder, CO: Paradigm.

KHOU11. October 17, 2017. "Houston Women Join #MeToo Movement." Bludau, J. https://www.khou.com/article/news/local/houston-women-join-me too-movement/484065817

Kindy, K. et al. 2015. "A Year of Reckoning: Police Fatally Shoot Nearly 1000." *Washington Post*, December 26. www.washingtonpost.com/sf/investigative/2015/12/26/a-year-of-reckoning-police-fatally-shoot-nearly-1000/

King, G., Pan, J., and Roberts, M. E. 2013. "How Censorship in China Allows Government Criticism but Silences Collective Expression." *American Political Science Review* 107: 1–18. http://j.mp/LdVXqN

Kivisto, P. and Sciortino, G., eds. 2015. *Solidarity, Justice, and Incorporation: Thinking through The Civil Sphere*. New York: Oxford University Press.

Klandermans, B., Kriesi, H., and Tarrow, S., eds. 1988. *International Social Movement Research*, vol. 1, JAI Press.

Klatch, R. 1987. *Women of the New Right*. Philadelphia: Temple University Press.

Klein E. 1984. *Gender Politics*. Cambridge, MA: Harvard University Press.

Klein, E. 2011. "Wonkbook: Occupy Wall Street Occupies Obama's 2012 Campaign." *Washington Post*, December 7.

Kleinfeld, N. R. 2014. "A Bridge to Scandal: Behind the Fort Lee Ruse." *New York Times*, January 12. http://www.nytimes.com/2014/01/13/nyregion/a-bridge-to-scandal-behind-the-fort-lee-ruse.html

Kohut, A. 2011. "The 'Haves' and the 'Have-Nots'." *New York Times*, October 18, Opinion page.

Koopmans, R. 1993. "The Dynamics of Protest Waves: West Germany, 1965 to 1989." *American Sociological Review* 58(5): 637–658.

Kopytoff, I. 1986. "The Cultural Biography of Things: Commoditization as Process." In Appadurai (1986), 64–91.

Kotlowski, D. J. 2001. *Nixon's Civil Rights*. Cambridge, MA: Harvard University Press.

Kovach, B. and Rosenstiel, T. 2007 [2001]. *The Elements of Journalism: What People Should Know and the Public Should Expect*. New York: Random House.

Kramer, J. 2015. "New Haven Journalist Paul Bass, Still Reporting in the Independent." *Hartford Courant*, February 23.

Kreiss, D. 2016. "Beyond Administrative Journalism: Civic Skepticism and the Crisis in Journalism." In Alexander et al. (2016), pp. 59–76.

Kriesi, H. 2004. "Political Context and Opportunity." In Snow et al. (2004), pp. 67–90.

Kristoff, N. 2011. "The Bankers and the Revolutionaries." *New York Times*, October 1, SR 11.

Ku, A. 1998. "Boundary Politics in the Public Sphere: Openness, Secrecy, and Leak," *Sociological Theory* 16(2): 172–192.

Kudla, D. and Stokes, A. 2024. "The Societalization of Sexual Misconduct in Canada: From the Ghomeshi Scandal to State Reforms." In Alexander and Horgan (2024).

Kuttner, P. 2015. "Black Symbols Matter." *Cultural Organizing*, August 10. http://culturalorganizing.org/black-symbols-matter/

Landes, J. B. 1998. *Women and the Public Sphere in the Age of the French Revolution*. Ithaca, N.Y.: Cornell University Press.

Landry, B. 1988. *The New Black Middle Class*. Berkeley: University of California Press.

Larana, E., Johnston, H., and Gusfield, J., eds. 1994. *New Social Movements*. Philadelphia, PA: Temple University Press.

Larsen, H. 2016a. "The Crisis of Public Service Broadcasting Reconsidered: Commercialization and Digitalization in Scandinavia." In Alexander et al. (2016), pp. 43–58.

Larsen, H. 2016b. *Performing Legitimacy: Studies in High Culture and the Public Sphere*. New York: Palgrave.

Lasorsa, D. L., Lewis, S. C., and Holton, A. E. 2012. "Normalizing Twitter: Journalism Practice in an Emerging Communication Space." *Journalism Studies* 13(1): 19–36.

Lazarsfeld, P. F., Berelson, B., and Gaudet, H. 1948. *The People's Choice: How the Voter Makes up His Mind in a Presidential Campaign*. New York: Columbia University Press.

Lee, H. 2019. "Boundary Tension and Reconstruction: Credit Information Crises and the Civil Sphere in Korea." In Alexander (2019b), pp. 60–83.

Lemann, N. 2013. "On Borrowed Time." *Times Literary Review*, December 20.

Lerner, M. B., ed. 2012. *A Companion to Lyndon B. Johnson*. Malden, M.A.: Blackwell.

Levy, D. 2013. "Chaque media doit se demand dans quel domaine il peut propose une offer unique." *Le Monde*, December 26. http://www.lemonde.fr/recherche/?keywords=David+Levy+Reuters+&qt=recherche_globale

Levy, D. and Nielsen, R. K., eds. 2010. *The Changing Business of Journalism and Its Impact on Democracy*. Oxford, UK: Reuters Institute for the Study of Journalism.

Lippmann, W. 1920. *Liberty and the News*. New York: Harcourt, Brace and Howe.

Lippmann, W. 1925. *The Phantom Public*. New York: Harcourt, Brace and Company.

Los Angeles Times. October 7, 2017. "The Problem of Sexual Harassment is much Bigger than Hollywood's Vile 'Casting Couch' Culture." The Los Angeles Times Editorial Board. http://www.latimes.com/opinion/editorials/la-ed-weinstein-harassment-20171007-story.html

Los Angeles Times. October 11, 2017, p. A12. "Enabling Harvey Weinstein." Times Editorial Board.

Los Angeles Times. September 17, 2018. "A Generation after Clarence Thomas, the Senate Heads for Another Battle Over Judging Allegations of Sexual Misconduct." Lauter, D. http://www.latimes.com/politics/la-na-pol-kavanaugh-debate-20180917-story.html

Luckerson, V. 2014. "Jeff Bezos Makes His First Major Move at the Washington Post." *Time*, March 19: http://time.com/30243/jeff-bezos-makes-his-first-major-move-at-the-washington-post/

Luengo, M. 2014. "Constructing the Crisis of Journalism: Towards a Cultural Understanding of the Economic Collapse of Newspapers during the Digital Revolution." *Journalism Studies* 15. DOI: 10.1080/1461670X.2014.891858

Luengo, M. 2016. "When Codes Collide: Journalists Push Back against Digital Desecration." In Alexander et al. (2016), pp. 119–134.

Luengo, M. 2018. "Shaping Civil Solidarity in Argentina: The Power of the Civil Sphere in Repairing Violence against Women." In Alexander and Tognato (2018), pp. 39–65.

Luengo, M. and Sanz, S. 2012. "Public, Commercial and Civil Television in Europe's New Media Landscape." Paper presented at the 2012 ICA Regional Conference in Europe. Lille, France, March 7–9.

Luria, Z. 1986. "A Methodological Critique." *Signs* 11: 316–321.

Lynch, G. 2014. *The Sacred in the Modern World: A Cultural Sociological Approach*. Oxford, UK: Oxford University Press.

MacAskill, E. 2012. "Obama Campaign Launches Fresh Attack on Mitt Romney/s 47% Comments." *Guardian*. September 27.

MacKinnon, C. A. 1979. *Sexual Harassment of Working Women: A Case Study of Sex Discrimination*. New Haven: Yale University Press.

MacKinnon, C. A. and Siegel, R. B., eds. 2003. *Directions in Sexual Harassment Law*. New Haven: Yale University Press.

Mancini, P. 2013. "What Scholars Can Learn from the Crisis of Journalism." *International Journal of Communication* 7: 127–136.

Mann, M. 1993. *The Sources of Social Power,* vol. 2. New York: Cambridge University Press.

Mansbridge, J. 1986. *Why We Lost the ERA*. Chicago: University of Chicago Press.

Manza, J. and Brooks, C. 2012. "How Sociology Lost Public Opinion: A Genealogy of a Missing Concept in the Study of the Political." *Sociological Theory* 30(2): 89–113.

Market Watch. February 16, 2018. "What Shareholders Should Know About Their Investments and #MeToo." Lamagna, M.

Market Watch. July 14, 2018. "In the Wake of #MeToo, More U.S. Companies Reviewed their Sexual Harassment Policies." Buchwald, E.

Marrus, M. R. and Paxton, R. O. 1981. *Vichy France and the Jews*. Stanford: Stanford University Press.

Marshall, T. H. 1965. *Class, Citizenship, and Social Development*. New York: Free Press.

Martin, J. M. 2003. *The Presidency and Women*. College Station, TX: Texas A&M University Press.

Marx, K. and Engels, F. 1962 [1848]. "Manifesto of the Communist Party." In *Marx and Engels: Selected Works*. Moscow: International Publishers.

Massey, D. S. and Denton, N. A. 1993. *American Apartheid: Segregation and the Making of the Underclass*. Cambridge, MA: Harvard University Press.

Mast, J. L. 2006. "The Cultural Pragmatics of Event-ness: The Clinton/Lewinsky Affair." In Alexander et al. (2006), pp. 115–145 .

Mast, J. L. 2012. *The Performative Presidency: Crisis and Resurrection during the Clinton Years*. Cambridge: Cambridge University Press.

Mast, J. L. 2016. "Action in Culture: Act I of the Presidential Primary Campaign in the U.S., April to December, 2015." *American Journal of Cultural Sociology* 4(48): 241–88.

Matheson, D. 2000. "The Birth of News Discourse: Changes in News Language in British Newspapers, 1880–1930." *Media, Culture, and Society* 22 (5): 557–573.

Mattingly, D. J. 2015. "The Limited Power of Female Appointments: Abortion and Domestic Violence Policy in the Carter Administration." *Feminist Studies* 41(3): 538–565.

Maxwell, A. and Shields, T, eds. 2018. *I'm With Her*. Cham, Switzerland: Palgrave Macmillan.

McAdam, D. 1982. *Political Process and the Development of Black Insurgency, 1930–1970*. Chicago: University of Chicago Press.

McAdam, D. 1996. "The Framing Function of Movement Tactics: Strategic Dramaturgy in the American Civil Rights Movement." In McAdam et al. (1996), pp. 338–355.

McAdam, D. and Su, Y. 2002. "The War at Home: Antiwar Protests and Congressional Voting, 1965 to 1973." *American Sociological Review* 67(5): 696–721.

McAdam, D., McCarthy, J. D., and Zald, M., eds. 1996. *Comparative Perspectives on Social Movements*. New York: Cambridge University Press.

McAdam, D., Tarrow, S., and Tilly, C. 2001. *Dynamics of Contention*. New York: Cambridge University Press.

McCammom, H. J. et al., eds. 2017. *The Oxford Handbook of U.S. Women's Social Movement Activism*.

McChesney, R. W. and Pickard, V. 2011. *Will the Last Reporter Please Turn Out the Lights: The Collapse of Journalism and What Can Be Done to Fix It*. New York: The New Press.

McLaughlin, M. 2016. "The Dynamic History of #BlackLivesMatter Explained: This is How a Hashtag Transformed into a Movement." *The Huffington Post*, February 29. www.huffingtonpost.com/entry/history-black-lives-matter_us_56 d0a3b0e4b0871f60eb4af5

McVicar, M. J. 2016. "The Religious Right in America." In Barton (2016).

Meacham, A. 2011. "Pulitzer-Winning Former St. Petersburg Times Reporter Bette Orsini Dies at 85." *St. Petersburg Times*, March 29. https://www.cultedu cation.com/group/1284-scientology/25269-pulitzer-winning-former-st-petersb urg-times-reporter-bette-orsini-dies-at-85.html

Meeks, C. 2001. "Civil Society and the Sexual Politics of Difference." *Sociological Theory* 19(3): 325–343.

Meyer, P. 2009. *The Vanishing Newspaper: Saving Journalism in the Information Age*, 2nd edn. Columbia: University of Missouri Press.

Miami Times. November 19, 2017, p. 2A. "#MeToo – A Hashtag for Change." Anonymous.

Milkis, S. M. and Tichenor, D. J. 2019. *Rivalry and Reform: Presidents, Social Movements, and the Transformation of American Politics*. Chicago: University of Chicago Press.

Milkis, S. M., Tichenor, D. J., and Blessing, L. 2013. "'Rallying Force': The Modern Presidency, Social Movements, and the Transformation of American Politics." *Presidential Studies Quarterly* 43(3): 641–670.

Milkman, R. 1995. "Gender at Work: The Sexual Division of Labor during World War II." In Kerber and de Hart (1995), pp. 446–456.

Miller, J. T. 2012. "'Million Hoodie March' in New York Rallies Support for Trayvon Martin." *Time*, March 22. http://newsfeed.time.com/2012/03/22/million-hoodie-march-in-new-york-rallies-support-for-trayvon-martin/

Mills, C. W. 1956. *The Power Elite*. New York: Oxford University Press.

Minder, R. and Carvajal, D. 2014. "Third Spanish Paper Ousts Editor Amid Financial Woes." *New York Times*, February 19: A5.

Moe, H. G. 1969. "Urges Equal Rights for Women." *Hartford Courant*, September 8.

Mommsen, Wolfgang J. 1984 [1959]. *Max Weber and German Politics 1890–1920*. Chicago: University of Chicago Press.

Monterey County Weekly. October 26, 2017. "Speaking Up." Dunn, M.

Moore, D. L. 2015a. "Black Activists Are Literally Stealing the Stage from 2016 Contenders – And It's Working." *Identities.Mic.*, August 13. http://mic.com/articles/123796/black-activists-called-out-bernie-sanders-jeb-bush-hillary-clinton-and-martin-omalley#.8ktXIiucn

Moore, D. L. 2015b. "Two Years Later, Black Lives Matter Faces Critiques, but it Won't Be Stopped." *Identities.Mic.*, August 10. http://mic.com/articles/123666/two-years-later-black-lives-matter-faces-critiques-but-it-won-t-be-stopped#.kE68fRkeH

Morgan, K. J. and Orloff, A. S., eds. 2017. *The Many Hands of the State*. New York: Cambridge University Press.

Morgenstern, J. 2015. "'Spotlight' Review: Blazingly Bright, Fearlessly Focused." *Wall Street Journal*, November 5. https:// www.wsj.com/articles/spotlight-review-blazingly-bright-fearlessly-focused-1446750534

Morris, A. 1984. *The Origins of the Civil Rights Movement: Black Communities Organizing for Change*. Free Press, New York.

Morris, A. 2007. "Naked Power and The Civil Sphere." *The Sociological Quarterly* 48: 4, 629–640.

Mouffe, C. 2000. *The Democratic Paradox*. London: Verso.

Moynihan, C. 2011. "Wall Steet Protest Begins, with Demonstrators Blocked." *New York Times*. September 17. https://archive.nytimes.com/cityroom.globs.nytimes.-com/2011/0917/wall-street-protest-begins

Mueller, C. M. ed. 1988.*The Politics of the Gender Gap*. Sage: Newbury Park, CA.

Mueller, C. M. 1988a. "The Empowerment of Women: Polling and the Women's Voting Bloc." In Mueller (1988), pp. 16–36.

Mullany, G. 2014. "Attacker Slashes Hong Kong Editor Who Was Ousted." *New York Times*, February 25: http://sinosphere.blogs.nytimes.com/2014/02/25/hong-kong-editor-whose-ouster-stirred-protests-is-reported-stabbed/?_r=1

Mutter, A. D. 2011. "The Value of Journalism, Sir, Is not 'Zero'. *Reflections of*

a Newsosaur, June 13. http://newsosaur.blogspot.com/2011/06/value-of-journa
lism-sir-is-not-zero.html

Nagourney, A. 2023. *The Times: How the Newspaper of Record Survived Scandal, Scorn, and the Transformation of Journalism.* New York: Crown.

National Commission on the Observance of International Women's Year. 1976. "'To Form a More Perfect Union' . . . Justice for American Women: Report of the National Commission on the Observance of International Women's Year." Washington, DC: Dept. of State.

National Conference of State Legislatures. June 6, 2018. "2018 Legislation on Sexual Harassment in The Legislature." http://www.ncsl.org/research/about-st ate-legislatures/2018-legislative-sexual-harassment-legislation.aspx

National Public Radio. October 3, 2018. "Poll: More Believe Ford Than Kavanaugh, A Cultural Shift From 1991." Montanaro, D.

NBC News. October 7, 2016. "Trump on Hot Mic: 'When You're a Star . . . You Can Do Anything' to Women." Timm, J. C. https://www.nbcnews.com/poli tics/2016-election/trump-hot-mic-when-you-re-star-you-can-do-n662116

Negroponte, N. 1995a. *Being Digital.* New York: Knopf.

Negroponte, N. 1995b. "Being Digital, A Book (P) Review," *Wired.com* (1995). http://archive.wired.com/wired/archive/3.02/negroponte.html

New Jersey Jewish News. October 19, 2017. "Weinstein Scandal's 'Big Bang' in Orthodox Community." Dreyfus, H.

New Republic. 2009. "The End of the Press." March 4: Cover.

New York Review of Books. October 11, 2018. "Reflections on a Hashtag." Ghomeshi, J.

New York Review of Books. October 25, 2018, pp. 54–58. "Responses to 'Reflections on a Hashtag'." O. J. et al.

New York Times Company Annual Report. 2013. http://investors.nytco.com/ files/doc_financials/annual/2013/2013%20Annual%20Report.pdf

New York Times. December 31, 2013, A20. "The Facts about Benghazi."

New York Times. April 1, 2017. "Bill O'Reilly Thrives at Fox News, Even as Harassment Settlements Add Up." Steel, E. and Schmidt, M. S. https://www.ny times.com/by/emily-steel

New York Times. October 5, 2017. "Harvey Weinstein Paid Off Sexual Harassment Accusers for Decades." Kantor, J. and Twohey, M. https://www.ny times.com/2017/10/05/us/harvey-weinstein-harassment-allegations.html

New York Times. October 7, 2017. "The Pigs of Liberalism." Douthat, R. https:// www.nytimes.com/2017/10/07/opinion/sunday/harvey-weinstein-harassment-lib erals.html

New York Times. October 10, 2017. "Gretchen Carlson: How to Encourage More Women to Report Sexual Harassment." Carlson, G. https://www.nyt imes.com/2017/10/10/opinion/women-reporting-sexual-harassment.html

New York Times. October 15, 2017. "How to Break a Sexual Harassment Story." Symonds, A.

New York Times. October 17, 2017, p. A23. "The Myth of the Progressive Prosecutor." Rice, J.D.

New York Times. October 23, 2017. "After Weinstein Scandal, a Plan to Protect Models." Friedman, V. https://www.nytimes.com/2017/10/23/fashion/sexual -harassment-law-models-new-york-state-harvey-weinstein.html

New York Times. November 5, 2017, p. A25. "A Conspiracy of Inaction on Sexual Abuse." Leonhardt, D.

New York Times. December 14, 2017. "The Politics of Him Too." Edsell, T. B. https://www.nytimes.com/2017/12/14/opinion/democratic-party-sexual-misconduct.html

New York Times. January 9, 2018. "Catherine Deneuve and Others Denounce the #MeToo Movement." Safronova, V. https://www.nytimes.com/2018/01/09/movies/catherine-deneuve-and-others-denounce-the-metoo-movement.html

New York Times. March 23, 2018. "#MeToo Called for an Overhaul. Are Workplaces Really Changing?" Kantor, J.

New York Times. March 24, 2018, A1. "#MeToo Inspires, but Change Won't Come Easy." Kantor, J.

New York Times. April 4, 2018. "#MeToo Has Done What the Law Could Not." MacKinnon, C. A. https://www.nytimes.com/2018/02/04/opinion/metoo-law-legal-system.html

New York Times. April 16, 2018. "New York Times and New Yorker Share Pulitzer for Public Service." Grynbaum, M. M. https://www.nytimes.com/by/michael-m-grynbaum

New York Times. June 28, 2018. "After #MeToo, the Ripple Effect." Bennett, J.

New York Times. September 13, 2018, A1. "Revelation of Moonves's Deceit Was Last Straw for CBS Board." Stewart, J.

New York Times. September 13, 2018, B1. "Another Executive's Head Rolls at Besieged CBS." Koblin, J. and Brynbaum, M. M.

New York Times. September 16, 2018, SR9. "The Shame of the MeToo Men." Goldberg, M.

New York Times. September 19, 2018. "New York Review of Books Editor Is Out Amid Uproar Over #MeToo Essay." Buckley, C.

New York Times. September 23, 2018, SR1. "The Patriarchy Will Always Have Its Revenge." Weiner, J.

New York Times. September 27, 2018. "On Politics with Lisa Lerer: He Litigated, She Persuaded." Lerer, L. https://www.nytimes.com/2018/09/27/us/politics/on-politics-kavanaugh-blasey-ford-testimony.html

New York Times. September 29, 2018. "Kavanaugh Could Help G.O.P. in Senate Midterms. But Not in House Races." Martin, J. and Burns, A. https://www.nytimes.com/2018/09/29/us/politics/kavanaugh-republicans-midterms.html

New York Times. September 30, 2018, A1a. "Fight over Kavanaugh Shows the Power, and Limits, of #MeToo." Zernike, K. and Steel, E.

New York Times. September 30, 2018, A1b. "For Nominee, G.O.P. Takes A Big Gamble." Martin, J. and Burns, A.

New York Times. September 30, 2018, A23. "Court Pick Steals a Page from Trump's Playbook on White Male Anger." Peters, J. W. and Chira, S.

New York Times. September 30, 2018, SR8. "What America Owes Women." Gay, M.

New York Times. October 23, 2018. "#MeToo Brought Down 201 Powerful Men. Nearly Half of Their Replacements Are Women." Carlsen, A. et al.

New York Times. October 24, 2018. "In 'A Star Is Born,' Equality Is Deadly." Dargis, M.

New York Times. October 31, 2018, C1. "Louis C.K. Performs, And It's No Secret." Sopan, D.

New York Times. November 7, 2018, A29. "'It Was All Fake,' Trump Says in Kavanaugh Ploy." Baker, P.

New York Times. November 9, 2018. "Facebook to Stop Forced Arbitration Cases." Wakabayashi, D. and Silver-Greenberg, J. https://www.nytimes.com /2018/11/09/technology/facebook-arbitration-harassment.html

New York Times. November 26, 2018. "'Kavanaugh's Revenge' Fell Short Against Democrats in the Midterms." Hulse, C. https://www.nytimes.com/20 18/11/25/us/politics/kavanaugh-midterm-elections.html

New Yorker. October 10, 2017. "From Aggressive Overtures to Sexual Assault: Harvey Weinstein's Accusers Tell Their Stories." Farrow, R.

Newsweek. August 21, 1972. "The Administration: Help Wanted (Female)."

Newsweek. November 17, 2017. "A Senior Fox News Analyst Thinks a Man Can't Be Alone with a Woman without Sexually Assaulting Her." Solis, M. https://www.newsweek.com/senior-fox-news-analyst-thinks-man-cant-be-alone-woman-without-sexually-714920

Ngai, P. and Ng, K. T. F. 2019. "Attempting Civil Repair in China: SACOM's Campaigns and the Challenge to Digital Capitalism." In Alexander (2019b), pp. 148–166.

Noonan, P. 2015. "An Honest Reporter, and His Antithesis." *The Wall Street Journal*, February 14–15: A13.

Norton, M. 2014a. "Mechanisms and Meaning Structures." *Sociological Theory* 32(2): 162–187.

Norton, M. 2014b. "Classification and Coercion: The Destruction of Piracy in the English Maritime System." *American Journal of Sociology* 119(6): 1573–1575.

Numéro. April 12, 2018. "'All the Other Designers Hate Me . . .' Karl Lagerfeld gets ready to tell all." Utz, P. https://www.numero.com/en/fashion/interview -karl-lagerfeld-chanel-virgil-abloh-j-w-anderson-azzedine-alaia

O'Brian, N. A. 2020. "Before Reagan: The Development of Abortion's Partisan Divide." *Perspectives on Politics* 18(4): 1031–1047.

O'Connor, K. and Epstein, L. 1985. "Abortion Policy." In Yarbough (1985), pp. 204–229.

Oputu, E. 2014. "Majority of Top Editors Quit *Le Monde*." *Columbia Journalism Review*, May 6.

Osgood K. and White, D. E. eds. 2014. *Winning While Losing*. Gainesville, FL: University Press of Florida.

Osgood, K. and White, D. E. 2014a. "The Paradox of Success: Civil Rights and the Presidency in a New Era." In Osgood and White (2014), pp. 1–25.

Ostertag, S. 2013. "Communicating Right and Wrong: Morals, Emotions, and a Cultural Structure of Journalism." Manuscript. Tulane University, New Orleans, LA.

Ostertag, S. 2019. "Anti-Racism Movements and the U.S. Civil Sphere: The Case of Black Lives Matter." In Alexander et al. 2019c, pp. 70–91.

Ottawa, K. N. C. 2011. "Shirky Squares the Circle." *Economist*, January 5, 2011. www.economist.com/blogs/babbage/2011/01/politics_and_internet

Papacharissi, Z. and de Fatima Oliveira, M. 2012. "Affective News and Networked Publics: The Rhythms of News Storytelling on #Egypt." *Journal of Communication* 62: 266–282.

Parsons, T. 1954. *Essays in Sociological Theory*. New York: Free Press.

Parsons, T. 1954 [1939]. "Professions and the Social Structure." In Parsons (1954), pp. 34–49.

Pateman, C. 1988. "The Fraternal Social Contract." In Keane (1988), pp. 101–128.

Patterson, O. 1998. *Rituals of Blood: Consequences of Slavery in Two American Centuries*. Washington, DC: Basic Civitas.

Perez-Pena, R. 2007. "Times to Stop Charging for Parts of Its Website." *New York Times*, September 18. www.nytimes.com/2007/09/18/business/media/18 times.html?ex=1347768000&en=88011ab

Pettit, Philip, 1999. *Republicanism: A Theory of Freedom and Government*. Oxford, UK: Oxford University Press.

Pew Journalism Research Project. 2011. "The Wall Street Journal under Rupert Murdoch." July 20. www.journalism.org/2011/07/20/wall-street-journal-under-rupert-murdoch/

Pew Research Center. 2015. "Across Racial Lines, More Say Nation Needs to Make Changes to Achieve Racial Equality." August 5. www.people-press.org/2015/08/05/across-racial-lines-more-say-nation-needs-to-make-changes-to-achieve-racial-equality/

PEW Stateline Blog. July 31, 2018. "#MeToo Has Changed Our Culture. Now It's Changing Our Laws." Beitsch, R.

Pfohl, S. J. 1977. "The 'Discovery' of Child Abuse." *Social Problems*, 24(3): 310–323

Pickard, V. 2011. "Revisiting the Road Not Taken: A Social Democratic Vision of the Press." In McChesney and Pickard (2011), pp. 174–184.

Pillsbury Insights. October 8, 2018. "California Laws Change Legal Landscape on Sexual Harassment." Weber, P. and Adams, C. https://www.pillsburylaw.com/en/news-and-insights/california-laws-change-harassment-landscape.html

Piven, F. F. and Cloward, R. 1977. *Poor People's Movements*. New York: Pantheon Books.

Pocock, J. G. A. 1975. *The Machiavellian Moment: Florentine Political Thought and the Atlantic Republican Tradition*. Princeton: Princeton University Press.

Powell, W. W. and DiMaggio, P., eds. 1991. *The New Institutionalism in Organizational Analysis*. Chicago: University of Chicago Press.

PR News. October 23, 2017. "8 Days Later, #MeToo Movement Expands Well Beyond Entertainment Industry." Wood, S.

Putnam, R. D. 2000. *Bowling Alone: The Collapse and Revival of American Community*. New York: Simon and Schuster.

Rabinovitch, E. 2001. "Gender and the Public Sphere: Alternative Forms of Integration in Nineteenth Century America." *Sociological Theory* 19 (3): 344–370.

Ramirez, P. J. 2014. "In Spain, Fired for Speaking Out." *New York Times*, February 6: A23.

Rauer, V. 2006. "Symbols in Action: Willy Brandt's Kneefall at the Warsaw Memorial." In Alexander et al. (2006), pp. 257–282.

Real Estate In-Depth. September 2018. "The New NYS Sexual Harassment Law Requirements Take Effect on Oct. 9, 2018." Dolgetta, John. http://www.realestateindepth.com/legal-advocacy/the-new-nys-sexual-harassment-law-requirements-take-effect-on-oct-9/

RedState Blog. November 29, 2017. "NY Times Editorial Board Moves from Opinion Journalism into Straight-Up Political Activism." Lee, S.

RedState Blog. September 24, 2018. "Democrats Have Launched the Era of #MeToo McCarthyism." Slager, B.

Reed, I. 2013. "Charismatic Performance: A Study of Bacon's Rebellion." *American Journal of Cultural Sociology* 1(2): 254–587.

Reinisch, D. and Kane, A., eds. 2022. *The Irish Republican Counter-Public: Armed Struggle and the Construction of a Radical Nationalist Community in Northern Ireland, 1969–1998*. New York: Routledge.

Revers, M. 2013. "Journalistic Professionalism as Performance and Boundary Work: Source Relations at the State House." *Journalism* 15(1), 37–52.

Revers, M. 2014. "The Twitterization of News Making: Transparency and Journalistic Professionalism." *Journal of Communication* 64(5): 806–26. doi: 10.1111/jcom.12111

Revers, M. 2015. "The Augmented Newsbeat: Spatial Structuring in a Twitterized News Ecosystem." *Media, Culture & Society* 37(1): 3–18. doi: 10.1177/0163443714549085

Revers, M. 2016. "Digital Media and the Diversification of Professionalism: A U.S.–German Comparison of Journalism Cultures." In Alexander et al. (2016), pp. 228–246.

Revers, M. 2017. *Contemporary Journalism in the U.S. and Germany: Agents of Accountability*. New York: Palgrave Macmillan.

Roberts, S. 2017. "E. Clinton Bamberger, Defense Lawyer with a 'Fire for Justice,' Is Dead at 90." *New York Times*: B 13. February 17.

Rohlinger, D. A. and Claxton, E. 2017. "Mobilizing the Faithful: Conservative and Right-Wing Women's Movements in America." In McCammom et al. (2017), pp.150–171.

Rosen, R. 2000. *The World Split Open*. New York: Penguin.

Rucht, D. 1988. "Themes, Logics and Arenas of Social Movements: A Structural Approach." In Klandermans et al. (1988), pp. 305–328.

Ruffin, II, H. G. 2016. "Black Lives Matter: The Growth of a New Social Justice Movement." *Blackpast.org*. www.blackpast.org/perspectives/black-lives-matter-growth

Russell, C. E. 1933. *Bare Hands and Stone Walls: Some Recollections of a Sideline Reformer*. New York: Charles Scribner's Sons.

Ryan, M. P. 1992. "Gender and Public Access: Women's Politics in Nineteenth-Century America." In Calhoun (1992), pp. 259–288.

Ryfe, D. 2012. *Can Journalism Survive: An Inside Look at American Newsrooms*. Cambridge, UK: Polity.

Ryfe, D. 2013. "Journalism in American Regional Online News Systems." Paper presented at the Conference "Local Journalism around the World: Professional Practices, Economic Foundations, and Political Implications, Reuters Institute." Oxford University, February 26–28.

Said, E. 1978. *Orientalism*. New York: Random House.

Samuelsohn, D. 2017. *Politico*, June 6. https://www.politico.com/story/2017/06/06/mueller-russia-probe-trump-239163

Sanbonmatsu, K. 2002. *Democrats, Republicans, and the Politics of Women's Place*. Ann Arbor, MI: The University of Michigan Press.

Santa Barbara Independent, October 26, 2017. "Schools on #MeToo Track." Hamm, K.

Sanz, E. 2014. "Open Governments and their Cultural Transitions." *Public Administration and Information Technology* 4: 1–15.

Sapiro, V. 1986. "The Women's Movement, Politics, and Policy in the Reagan Era." In Dahlerup (1986), pp.122–139.

Sawyers, T. M. and Meyer, D. S. 1999. "Missed Opportunities: Social Movement Abeyance and Public Policy." *Social Problems* 46(2): 187–206.

Schlesinger, P. and Doyle, G. 2015. "From Organisational Crisis to Multiplatform Salvation: Creative Destruction and the Recomposition of News Media." *Journalism* 16(3): 305–323.

Schreiber, R. 2017. "Anti-Feminist, Pro-Life, and Anti-ERA Women." In McCammom et al. (2017), pp. 315–334.

Schudson, M. 1978. *Discovering the News: A Social History of American Newspapers*. New York: Basic Books.

Schudson, M 1982. "The Politics of Narrative Form: The Emergence of News Conventions in Print and Television." *Daedalus* 111(4): 97–112.

Schudson, M. 2010 "News in Crisis in the United States: Panic – And Beyond." In Levy and Nielsen (2010), pp. 95–106.

Schudson, M. 2016. "The Crisis in News: Can You Whistle a Happy Tune?" In Alexander et al. (2016), pp. 98–118.

Schumpeter, J. A. 1975 [1942]. *Capitalism, Socialism and Democracy*. New York: Harper and Row, 3rd edn.

Scott, A. O. 2015. "Review: In 'Spotlight,' the Boston Globe Digs Up the Catholic Church's Dirt." *New York Times*, November 5. https://www.ny times.com/2015/11/06/movies/review-in-spotlight-the-boston-globe-digs-up-the-catholic-churchs-dirt.html

Scott, J. W. 1990. "Deconstructing Equality-versus-Difference: Or, the Uses of Poststructuralist Theory for Feminism." In Hirsch and Keller (1990), pp. 134–149.

Scott, M. 2014. "Copyright Fees Lead Google News to Quit Spain." *International New York Times*. December 12: 15.

Seidman, S. 1991. *Romantic Longings: Love in America, 1830–1980*. New York and London: Routledge.

Seidman, S. 1992. *Embattled Eros: Sexual Politics and Ethics in Contemporary America*. London, UK: Routledge.

Seidman, S. 1999. "Contesting the Moral Boundaries of Eros: A Perspective on the Cultural Politics of Sexuality in the Late Twentieth Century U.S." In Smelser and Alexander (1999), pp. 167–190.

Seidman, S. 2001. "From Identity to Queer Politics: Shifts in Normative Heterosexuality." In Seidman and Alexander (2001), pp. 353–60.

Seidman, S. and Alexander, J. C., eds. 2001. *The New Social Theory Reader*. New York and London: Routledge.

Sewell, W. H., Jr. 1996. "Historical Events as Transformations of Structures: Inventing Revolution at the Bastille." *Theory and Society* 25: 841–81.

Shear, M. D. 2012 "Obama Speaks Out on Trayvon Martin Killing." *New York Times*, March 23. http://thecaucus.blogs.nytimes.com/2012/03/23/obama-ma kes-first-comments-on-trayvon-martin-shooting/

Shear, M. D. 2014. "White House Urges China to Act on Journalists' Visas." *New York Times*, January 31: A9.

Shelton, I. 1969. "Pat Nixon Irks 'Status' Women." *The Baltimore Sun*, May 18, p. FC4.

Shelton, I. 1970. "Women Demand Equal Rights." *The Baltimore Sun*, May 10, p. C3.

Shelton, I. 1971. "Women Gather for Unity." *The Baltimore Sun*, July 4, p. E15.

Shelton, I. 1972. "Strange Army Wins New ERA." *The Baltimore Sun*, March 26, p. C2.

Shelton, P. 1970. "NOW Broadens its Attack." *Christian Science Monitor*, September 18, p. 18.

Shils, E. 1975. *Center and Periphery and Other Essays in Macro-Sociology*. Chicago: University of Chicago Press.

Shils, E. 1975a. "Center and Periphery." In Shils (1975), pp. 3–15.

Shirky, C. 2008. *Here Comes Everybody: The Power of Organizing without Organizations*. New York: Penguin.

Shirky, C. 2010. "The Times' Paywall and Newsletter Economics." *Shirky.com*. www.shirky.com/weblog/2010/11/the-times-paywall-and-newsletter-economics/

Shirky, C. 2011. "Political Power and Social Media: Technology, the Public Sphere, and Political Change." *Foreign Affairs* 90: 28–41.

Sidner, S. and Simon, M. 2015. "The Rise of Black Lives Matter: Trying to Break the Cycle of Violence and Silence." *CNN.com*, December 28. http://edition .cnn.com/2015/12/28/us/black-lives-matter-evolution/

Siegel, R. B. 2003. "A Short History of Sexual Harassment." In MacKinnon and Siegel (2003), pp. 1–39.

Singer, J. B. 2005. "The Political J-Blogger: 'Normalizing' a New Media Form to Fit Old Norms and Practices." *Journalism* 6(2): 173–198.

Skinner, Q. 1978a. *The Foundations of Modern Political Thought: The Renaissance*. Cambridge, UK: Cambridge University Press.

Skinner, Q. 1978b. *The Foundations of Modern Political Thought: The Age of Reformation*. Cambridge University Press.

Skocpol, T. 1979. *States and Social Revolutions*. New York: Cambridge University Press.

Skocpol, T. 1992. *Protecting Soldiers and Mothers*. Cambridge, MA: Harvard University Press.

Skrentny, J. D. 2014. "Zigs and Zags: Richard Nixon and the New Politics of Race." In Osgood and White (2014), pp. 26–54.

Sleeper, J. 1990. *The Closest of Strangers: Liberals and the Politics of Race*. New York: Norton.

Smelser, N. J. and Alexander, J. C., eds. 1999. *Diversity and Its Discontents*. Princeton: Princeton University Press.

Smith, A. 1978. "The Long Road to Objectivity and Back Again: The Kinds of Truth We Get in Journalism." In Boyce, Curran, and Wingate (1978), pp. 153–171.

Smith, P. 1991. "Codes and Conflict: Towards a Theory of War as Ritual." *Theory and Society* 20: 103–138.

Smith, P. 2005. *Why War? The Cultural Logic of Iraq, the Gulf War, and Suez*. Chicago: University of Chicago Press.

Smith, P. and Howe, N. 2015. *Climate Change as Social Drama: Global Warming in the Public Sphere*. New York: Cambridge University Press.

Snow, D. A and Benford, R. D. 1988. "Ideology, Frame Resonance, and Participant Mobilization." *International Social Movements Research* 1: 197–217.

Snow, D. A., Soule, S. A., and Kriesi, H., eds. 2004. *The Blackwell Companion to Social Movements*. Malden, MA: Blackwell.

Sobral, A. 2011. "Performing a 'World Revolution'? Transnational Networks, Symbols and Scripts from Cairo to Madrid to …" Unpublished manuscript, University of Konstanz.

Somaiya, R. 2014. "Former Editor of The Times Leaving for News Nonprofit." *New York Times*, February 10: B1.

Somaiya, R., Isaac, M., and Goel, V. 2015. "Facebook May Host News Sites' Material." *New York Times*, B1. March 24.

Soule, S. A. and King, B. G. 2006. "The Stages of the Policy Process and the Equal Rights Amendment, 1972–1982." *American Journal of Sociology* 111(6): 1871–1909.

Spalter-Roth, R. and Schreiber, R. 1995. "Outsider Issues and Insider Tactics: Strategic Tensions in the Women's Policy Network During the 1980s." In Ferree and Martin (1995), pp. 105–127.

Spence, M. 1973. "Job Market Signaling." *Quarterly Journal of Economics* 87(3): 355–374.

Spruill, M. 2017. *Divided We Stand*. New York: Bloomsbury Publishing.

Spruill, M. 2018. "Feminism, Antifeminism, and the Rise of a New Southern Strategy in the 1970s." In Maxwell and Shields (2018), pp. 39–69.

Stack, T. 2019. "Wedging Open Established Civil Spheres: A Comparative Approach to Their Emancipatory Potential." In Alexander et al. (2019c), pp. 11–41.

Stamatov, P. 2013. *The Origins of Global Humanitarianism: Religion, Empires and Advocacy*. New York: Cambridge University Press.

Starkman, D. 2011. "Confidence Game: The Limited Vision of the News Gurus." *Columbia Journalism Review*, November 8. www.cjr.org/essay/confidence_game.php.

Starr, P. 2009. "Goodbye to the Age of Newspapers (Hello to a New Era of Corruption): Why American Politics and Society Are about to be Changed for the Worse." *New Republic*, March 4: 28–35.

Steen-Johnsen, K., Ihlebæk, K. A., and Enjolras, B. 2016. "News on New Platforms: Norwegian Journalists Face the Digital Age." In Alexander et al. (2016), pp. 190–210.

Stelter, Brian. 2011. "Camps Are Cleared, but '99 Percent' Still Occupies the Lexicon." *New York Times*, December 1: A1.

Stockman, F. 2016. "On Crime Bill and the Clintons, Young Blacks Clash With Parents." *New York Times*, April 18, A1.

Stone, I. F. 1963. "A Word about Myself." *Ifstone.org*. http://ifstone.org/biography.php.

Stout, L. J. 2012. *A Matter of Simple Justice*. University Park, PA: Pennsylvania State University Libraries.

Sullivan, J. 2014. "China's Weibo: Is Faster Different?" *New Media & Society* 16(1): 24–37.

Sullivan, J. et al. 2016. "In Fatal Shootings by Police, 1 in 5 Officers' Names go Undisclosed." *Washington Post*, April 1. www.washingtonpost.com/investigations/in-fatal-shootings-by-police-1-in-5-officers-names-go-undisclosed/2016/03/31/4bb08bc8-ea10-11e5-b0fd-073d5930a7b7_story.html

Tarrow, S. 1998. *Power in Movement*. New York: Cambridge University Press.

Tavernise, S. 2012. "Survey Finds Rising Strain between Rich and the Poor." *New York Times*, January 12, A15.

Tawney, R. H. 1920. *The Acquisitive Society*. London: Bell and Sons.

Taylor, V. 1989. "Social Movement Continuity: The Women's Movement in Abeyance." *American Sociological Review* 54(5): 761–775.

Taylor, V. et al. 2009. "Culture and Mobilization: Tactical Repertoires, Same-Sex Weddings, and the Impact on Gay Activism." *American Sociological Review* 74: 865–890.

teleSUR. 2014. "2014 Freedom Ride Arrives in Ferguson Today." August 29. www.telesurtv.net/english/news/2014-Freedom-Ride-Arrives-in-Ferguson-Today-20140829-0032.html

Thomas, J. 1971. "'We Mean Business, Mr. Nixon.'" *The Boston Globe*, July 15, p. 39.

Thorn, H. 2006. *Anti-Apartheid and the Emergence of a Global Civil Society.* London: Palgrave Macmillan.

Thumala Olave, M. A. 2018. "Civil Indignation in Chile: Recent Collusion Scandals in the Retail Industry." In Alexander and Tognato (2018), pp. 66–91.

Thurner, M. 1993. "'Better Citizens without the Ballot': American Anti-Suffrage Women and Their Rationale during the Progressive Era." *Journal of Women's History* 5: 33–56.

Tilly, C 1992. *Coercion, Capital, and European States, AD 990–1992.* Malden, MA: Blackwell.

Tilly, C. 1995. *Popular Contention in Great Britain, 1758–1834.* Cambridge, MA: Harvard University Press.

Tilly, C. 2002. *Stories, Identities, and Political Change.* Lanham, MD: Rowman & Littlefield.

Time. April 11, 2016. "A Brief History of Sexual Harassment in America Before Anita Hill." Cohen, S. http://time.com/4286575/sexual-harassment-before-ani ta-hill/

Time. February 21, 2017. "Uber Hires Former Attorney-General Eric Holder to Review Sexual-Harassment Claims." Patnaik, S.

Time. December 18, 2017. "The Silence Breakers." Zacharek, S., Dockterman, E., and Sweetland Edwards, H. http://time.com/time-person-of-the-year-2017 -silence-breakers/

Tognato, C. 2011. "Extending Trauma across Cultural Divides: On Kidnapping and Solidarity in Colombia." In Alexander et al. (2011), pp.191–212.

Trachtenberg, J. 1961. *The Devil and the Jews: The Medieval Conception of the Jew and Its Relation to Modern Anti-Semitism.* Cleveland, N.Y.: World Jewish Publication Society.

Tronto, J. C. 1987. "Beyond Gender Difference to a Theory of Care." *Signs* 12: 644–663.

Tronto, J. C. 1993. *Moral Boundaries: A Political Argument for an Ethic of Care.* New York and London: Routledge.

USA Today. October 8, 2018, B1. "#MeToo movement May Have Unintended Consequences." Ortiz, J. J.

Usher, N. 2011. "Professional Journalists, Hands Off! Citizen Journalism as Civic Responsibility." In McChesney and Pickard (2011), pp. 264–276.

Van Dijck, J. 2005. "From Shoebox to Performative Agent: The Computer as Personal Memory Machine." *New Media & Society* 7(3): 311–332.

Vanity Fair. September 12, 2018. "Tonight Show Axes Norm Macdonald Sit-Down After Controversial Interview." Bradley, L. https://www.vanityfair.com /hollywood/2018/09/norm-macdonald-metoo-louis-ck-roseanne-barr-tonight-show-canceled

Voss, K. 2009. "Vera Glaser: A Journalist's Ode to Offbeat Washingtonian Politics." *Hall Institute of Public Policy*, May 5.

Vox. May 7, 2018. "Republican Women Care about Sexual Harassment, but their Party isn't Listening." North, A. https://www.vox.com/2018/5/7/17272336/ sexual-harassment-metoo-me-too-movement-trump-republicans-roy-moore

Waghmore, S. 2013. *Civility Against Caste: Dalit Politics and Citizenship in Western India.* New Delhi: Sage

Wagner-Pacifici, R. 1986. *The Moro Morality Play: Terrorism as Social Drama.* Chicago: University of Chicago Press.

Wagner-Pacifici, R. 1994. *Discourse and Destruction: The City of Philadelphia versus MOVE.* Chicago: University of Chicago Press.

Wagner-Pacifici, R. 2000. *Theorizing the Standoff: Contingency in Action.* New York: Cambridge University Press.

Wagner-Pacifici, R. 2017. *What Is an Event?* Chicago: University of Chicago Press.

Walker, S. 2012. *Presidents and Civil Liberties from Wilson to Obama.* New York: Cambridge University Press.

Walzer, M. 1965. *The Revolution of the Saints.* Cambridge, MA: Harvard University Press.

Walzer, M. 1984. *Spheres of Justice.* New York: Basic Books.

Walzer, M. 1986. *Exodus and Revolution.* New York: Basic Books.

Wang, H. 2019. "Reconciliation through the Transnational Civil Sphere? Historical Dialogue and the Tri-National Joint History Project in East Asia." In Alexander (2019b), pp. 256–277.

Washington Post. August 2, 2016. "One Reporter Owns the Roger Ailes Story. Here's Why He Says It's Not Over." Sullivan, M.

Washington Post. October 13, 2017. "From Quentin Tarantino to Barack Obama, Big Names Are Speaking Out Against Harvey Weinstein." Butler, B. https://www.washingtonpost.com/news/arts-and-entertainment/wp/2017/10/09/more-big-names-are-speaking-out-against-harvey-weinstein-heres-what-theyre-saying/?utm_term=.793702a93ad3

Washington Post. October 16, 2017. "#MeToo Made the Scale of Sexual Abuse Go Viral. But is it Asking too much of Survivors?" Ohlheiser, A.

Washington Post. October 19, 2017. "The Woman Behind 'Me Too' Knew the Power of the Phrase When She Created It – 10 Years Ago." Ohlheiser. A.

Washington Post. December 7, 2017. "Al Franken's Resignation: He Followed in the Footsteps of Sen. Bob Packwood." Phillips, K. https://www.washingtonpost.com/news/retropolis/wp/2017/11/22/before-franken-and-moore-there-was-sen-bob-packwood-a-serial-sexual-harasser-reelected-anyway/?utm_term=.d1104e57c912

Washington Post. January 25, 2018. "The #MeToo Movement Will Be in Vain." Lenhoff, D.

Washington Post. September 26, 2018. "How #MeToo has Changed the DC Power Structure – So Far." Gerhart, A. and Rindler, D. https://www.washingtonpost.com/graphics/2018/politics/how-metoo-has-changed-the-dc-power-structure/?utm_term=.0e9a62345879

Washington Post. October 22, 2018. "How #MeToo Really Was Different, According to Data." Ohlheiser, A.

Weakliem, D. 2020. *Public Opinion.* Medford, MA: Polity.

Weber, M. 1927 [1904–05]. *The Protestant Ethic and the Spirit of Capitalism.* New York: Scribner and Son.

Weber, M. 1946. "Politics as a Vocation." In Gerth and Mills (1946), pp. 77–128.

Weber, M. 1978a. *Economy and Society.* Berkeley: University of California Press.

Weber, M. 1978b. "Appendix II: Parliament and Government in a Reconstructed Germany," *Economy and Society*, vol. 2: 1381–1469. Berkeley: University of California Press

Weintraub, J. 1997. "The Theory and Politics of the Public/Private Distinction." In Weintraub and Kumar (1997), pp. 1–42.

Weintraub, J. and Kumar, K, eds. 1997. *Public and Private in Thought and Practice*. Chicago: University of Chicago Press.

Weir, M., Orloff, A., and Skocpol, T. 1988. *The Politics of Social Policy in the United States*. Princeton: Princeton University Press.

Wenzel Fenton Cabassa, P.A. January 1, 2018. "A History of Sexual Harassment Laws in the United States." Fenton, M. K. https://www.wenzelfenton.com/blog /2018/01/01/history-sexual-harassment-laws-united-states/

Whittier, N. 1995. *Feminist Generations*. Philadelphia: Temple University Press.

Wilson, W. J. 1987. *The Truly Disadvantaged: The Inner City, the Underclass, and Public Policy*. Chicago: University of Chicago Press.

Winston & Strawn LLP. June 14, 2018. "Legislative Trends: 'Me Too' Movement and Sexual Harassment Disclosure Laws." Grumet-Morris, A. https://www. winston.com/en/thought-leadership/legislative-trends-me-too-movement-and-sex ual-harassment-disclosure-laws.html

Wolbrecht, C. 2000. *The Politics of Women's Rights*. Princeton: Princeton University Press.

Wong, E. 2015. "Suddenly Turning Strict, Beijing Slaps Its Mouthpiece." *New York Times*, February 14: A3.

Wood, G. W. 1969. The Creation of the American Republic, 1776–1787. Chapel Hill: University of North Carolina Press.

Workforce. April 3, 2018. "HR Responds to the #MeToo Movement." Rafter, M. V.

Yarbrough, T. E., ed. 1985. *The Reagan Administration and Human Rights*. New York: Praeger.

Young, I. M. 1990. *Justice and the Politics of Difference*. Princeton: Princeton University Press.

Young L. 2000. *Feminists and Party Politics*. Vancouver: UBC Press.

Yu, R. 2014. "Washington Post to Expand with more Spending under Bezos." *USA Today*, January 30. www.usatoday.com/story/money/business/2014/01 /30/washington-post-to-expand/5043415/

Zeyunep, T. and Wilson, C. 2012. "Social Media and the Decision to Participate in Political Protest: Observations from Tahrir Square." *Journal of Communication* 62: 363–379.

Zillgit, J. and Strauss, C. 2014. "Protests Greet Prince William and Kate at Cavaliers-Nets." *USA Today*. December 9. www.usatoday.com/story/sports /nba/2014/12/08/cavaliers-nets-protests-william-kate-lebron-james-i-cant-breathe- shirts/20122331/

INDEX